"To anyone who has taken out a mortgage, paid a hefty fee for the bank to appraise the house, and watched while lawyers pushed papers at one another across a table, *Funny Money* is nothing short of astounding."

—*Business Week*

"A real-life yarn. . . . A truly scary scenario of how a goodly portion of America's banking economy was threatened at its core."

—*Los Angeles Times*

FUNNY MONEY

MARK SINGER

"Admirable for its wit, wealth of anecdote, and lack of moral pretension. Mark Singer is a talented young writer with a gift for the apt phrase and the telling observation."

—*The Wall Street Journal*

"There are lots of delicious stories. . . . Oklahoma City in the late 1970s must have been quite a place; errands to the shopping center were run in baby-blue Cadillacs, trips to the golf course in helicopters . . . houses had private zoos. It must have made the television show *Dynasty* look positively restrained."

—*The New York Times Book Review*

FUNNY MONEY

FUNNY MONEY

MARK SINGER

LAUREL

A LAUREL TRADE PAPERBACK
Published by
Dell Publishing Co., Inc.
1 Dag Hammarskjold Plaza
New York, New York 10017

Portions of this work originally appeared in *The New Yorker*.

Laurel ® TM 674623, Dell Publishing Co., Inc.

ISBN: 0-440-52576-4

Reprinted by arrangement with Alfred A. Knopf, Inc.

Printed in the United States of America

May 1986

10 9 8 7 6 5 4 3 2 1

MV

For Rhonda

The gambling propensity is another subsidiary trait of the barbarian temperament.
—Thorstein Veblen, *The Belief in Luck*

May he not be knave, fool, and genius altogether?
—Herman Melville, *The Confidence Man*

Acknowledgments

The idea of writing a book about the strange life and demise of the Penn Square Bank was suggested to me by a cousin who lives in Oklahoma City. My cousin understands that whatever I have done here is not his fault. Nevertheless, he would just as soon not be identified. I have many other relatives in Oklahoma who probably feel the same way. Several members of my family were extremely helpful to me, and I am especially grateful for the encouragement that came from Alex and Marjorie Singer, George Singer, May Singer, and Joe L. and Janice Singer. Above all, I thank my wife, Rhonda, and my son, Jeb, who remained patient and a pleasure to be with during the two years that I spent more or less living in a cocoon.

I owe gratitude to many colleagues at *The New Yorker*—foremost to William Shawn, Charles Patrick Crow, and Dwight Allen.

At Knopf, my editor, Charles Elliott, nurtured this undertaking from beginning to end, and his assistant, Sharon Zimmerman, provided much support.

I benefited from the generosity of other journalists, among them Judy Fosset, of the *Daily Oklahoman,* and Mike Ward and Mary Hargrove, of the Tulsa *Tribune.*

Thank you also to Ian Frazier, William Zinsser, Robert Lantz, Joy Harris, and Doug and Jane Smith.

I could not have completed my task without the cooperation of dozens of people who took the time to teach me about certain aspects of banking and of oil-and-gas exploration. The Penn Square Bank was an unusual bank where unusual things hap-

FUNNY MONEY

pened during an unusual phase of history. There are many species of bankers and of independent oil-and-gas operators, and I would be disappointed if this book created a contrary impression.

February 1985   MARK SINGER

Characters in This Book

Bill P. Jennings: chairman of the board and principal owner of the Penn Square Bank, Oklahoma City, Oklahoma.

Robert A. Hefner III: Penn Square Bank borrower; geologist-as-artist-hero; prophet of the Anadarko Basin, a vast natural gas deposit.

William G. Patterson: head of oil-and-gas lending, major stockholder, and director of the Penn Square Bank.

J. D. Allen: Penn Square Bank borrower; owner of J. D. Allen Industries, Inc., and many other enterprises.

Carl Swan: oilman; Penn Square Bank stockholder, director, and borrower; business associate of J. D. Allen.

Eldon Beller: president of the Penn Square Bank.

Frank Murphy: vice-chairman and former president of the Penn Square Bank.

Roger Anderson: chairman of the Continental Illinois National Bank and Trust Company, Chicago.

John Lytle: vice-president, midcontinent oil-and-gas division, Continental Illinois National Bank and Trust Company.

Tomcat No. 1: a spectacular natural gas well in Caddo County, Oklahoma.

Buddy Appleby: oil-and-gas prospector, promoter of the Tomcat No. 1.

FUNNY MONEY

Clark Ellison: oil-and-gas prospector, partner of Buddy Appleby.

Cliff Culpepper: oilman; operator of the Tomcat No. 1; Penn Square Bank borrower.

Frank Mahan: oilman, Penn Square Bank borrower.

William E. Rowsey III: oilman, Penn Square Bank borrower, partner of Frank Mahan.

FUNNY MONEY

CHAPTER 1

The auctioneer had a full beard and a self-confident rat-a-tat palaver and he wore a three-piece powder-blue suit. At first the powder-blue suit threw me because I had expected a more somber style, something closer to the hues of a funeral director, but then I realized that, next to the dean of the bankruptcy bar, the auctioneer was probably the most light-spirited workingman in town. Once the prices of crude oil and natural gas broke, life began to settle down to where it belonged, and the auction business thrived: deep rigs, workover rigs, rig-up trucks, lowboy trailers, derrick trailers, forklifts, heater treaters, separators, compressors, cranes, welders, graders, mixers, dumpers, crushers, chains, boomers, blocks, floats, frac tanks, pickups, jets, choppers, quarter horses, polo ponies, lithographs—they were all for sale.

This one was an automobile auction and these were not just anybody's cars. "Everyone except the members of the news media behind the ropes," the auctioneer commanded. He introduced himself as Donovan Arterburn, Jr. No need to spend a lot of time on a formal introduction of the merchandise. I did not intend to bid on any of it, nor did most of the three or four thousand other people who had turned out, but we knew why we were there. Most of us intended to elbow as close as possible to the rope barricades and gawk at what used to be the corporate fleet of the Penn Square Bank, Oklahoma City, Oklahoma. Two long rows of vehicles— forty-six late-model passenger cars and one three-wheeled utility truck—faced each other, ten yards apart. Hours earlier, the hoods had been raised for anyone who wanted to view the innards, but now they were closed and the bid spotters and security guards had

3

ushered us away. I was reminded of news photos of captured war prisoners and matériel.

The Office of the Comptroller of the Currency, which is a branch of the Department of the Treasury, determines when a national bank has failed. On July 5, 1982, the Comptroller declared the Penn Square Bank insolvent, and the Federal Deposit Insurance Corporation (FDIC) moved in immediately to settle the bank's affairs. According to the Comptroller, the Penn Square Bank owned a portfolio of uncollectible loans whose face value exceeded the bank's capital; too many of the bank's customers had borrowed more money than they could ever repay; liabilities considerably surpassed assets; the bank was bankrupt. Two months into the liquidation, the automobile auction took place. The bank building stood about three hundred yards due east, tucked into a corner of the Penn Square shopping center, and the FDIC auditors toiled there right now, sifting for clues. The auditors believed that the bank had designed its own demise. The bank's owners, employees, customers, and admirers were convinced that liquidating the bank was a mistake. Whatever the case, Donovan Arterburn, Jr., had come to sell the cars.

Holding the auction in the Penn Square parking lot made good sense. It was not a puny parking lot. One of the newer shopping malls, further north into the suburbs, had a larger lot, but the one at Penn Square could handle a sizable crowd. And, after all, these had been the bank's cars. Announcements in the newspapers had said that the auction would get underway at seven o'clock in the evening. Ever since the previous morning, when the cars had begun arriving, pensioners in knit shirts and straw fedoras—men with some time to kill while their wives canvassed the mall—had been dropping by, irritating the armed guards with the same questions, questions that the guards did not have answers to and would not have answered even if they had known the facts.

"Which of these cars did Jennings drive?" the men in the summer fedoras wanted to know. "Which one was Patterson's?" Bill P. Jennings had been the chairman of the board and the largest stockholder of the Penn Square Bank, and Bill Patterson, his protégé, had been the head of the bank's oil-and-gas lending department. It had taken Jennings, Patterson, and the bank's employees less than three years to book almost two and a half billion dollars in oil-and-gas loans—three exhilarating years which had brought to Oklahoma more out-of-towners in quest of fun and profit than anything since the land rush of '89. If not for Bill Jennings and Bill Patterson, there would not have been an auction. All of us rubberneckers out for a free show appreciated that.

Frequently, the Oklahoma City cognoscenti described the scuttlebutt they fed one another as "just street talk." That phrase always aroused my skepticism because I knew that in Oklahoma City a pedestrian was a person in transit to or from his automobile. I had picked up some street talk to the effect that Patterson drove a sea-green Porsche and Jennings was chauffeured in an oyster-white Rolls-Royce Silver Shadow. Or perhaps I had heard something completely different. Keeping rumors straight was a task. In any event, I could look over the parking lot and see that there were no Porsches or Rollses for sale. There were some decent Lincoln Town Cars, a Continental, a Cadillac, plenty of smooth-riding Ford and GM sedans—loaded with options like cruise control, tilted steering wheels, FM with the AM, a few tape decks and CBs—but nothing truly ostentatious.

As big little cities go, Oklahoma City has some imperfections. During the 1960s, for instance, the downtown business center was subjected to an urban-renewal blitz that eliminated whatever looked uncontemporary. After the bulldozers had finished their work it became evident that no one had given much thought to what might replace the old structures that had just been destroyed. Ever since, no-there-there architecture has flourished. You do not see many human beings at street level because most of the buildings are connected by a network of air-conditioned pedestrian tunnels. Summer usually lasts five punitive months. On hazy days all of downtown threatens to disappear. A six-lane piece of east-west interstate forms a southern perimeter that can deposit you in the business district unless you prefer to keep driving until you hit Fort Smith or Amarillo. Fighting the brain-fogging heat, you pass the oilfield supply yards, heavy-metal industrial sprawl, idle pumping units, stacked rigs, gizmoid billboards. When the wind comes in from the south it carries the aroma of stockyards beyond the North Canadian River. The road surface elevates as downtown presents itself—a canned silhouette of undifferentiated boxes, many of them covered by aluminum foil or whatever that material is that buildings are wrapped with to divert attention from their missing details. The glare deprives the senses, and the whole place seems to evaporate. You look into the foil and try to reassure yourself that you can see where you are and that it is someplace.

The shopping center where the Penn Square Bank lived and died is about twenty minutes northwest of downtown and it sits a literal stone's throw from Route 66, very centrally situated on the North American continent. It opened in 1960, the first satellite shopping center of its kind in Oklahoma City. Twenty-one years later, after a major renovation, it became an enclosed air-conditioned mall. When you cruise through one of those places you can easily fancy that you are comfortably outdoors, although climate-controlled shopping malls are not mentioned in the Bible and therefore, in the eyes of God, you are perhaps nowhere at all—just like downtown. This, for the sake of history, happens to matter. The Penn Square Bank did not vanish without a trace. Its fall resonated, with grotesque consequences. The largest bank in the Pacific Northwest, Seattle-First National Bank, turned to ash, courtesy of Penn Square. Then the Continental Illinois National Bank & Trust Company, of Chicago—an institution that had lent more money to American business and industry than any other bank in the country—found itself so deep in the turbid backwash of Penn Square that only a multibillion-dollar government-sponsored rescue was able to prevent its failure. Defending this extreme intervention, federal banking regulators argued that neglecting to save Continental Illinois would lead to the demise of dozens and perhaps hundreds of other banks.

Not since the Depression had there occurred a banking event so bizarre or so unsettling. Bad fantasies loomed within easy traveling distance. What if first the Penn Square Bank folded, followed closely by the largest banks in the Pacific Northwest and the Midwest, and what if those failures were followed by the failures of the industrial economies of, say, Mexico and Argentina? What if Western capitalism took a dive? What if a global economic apocalypse started in an enclosed air-conditioned mall in Oklahoma City—out there in the company of the Stout Shoppe and the Peanut Shack and the video arcade and the gift store where for $12.95 you got a room freshener disguised as a porcelain duck? Exercising your imagination with that bad fantasy, you could be excused for thinking that the Penn Square Bank seemed like a peculiar first domino.

"Folks, we're gonna have fun tonight, but you've got to realize this is a business proposition and this is no circus," Donovan Arterburn, Jr., announced over the public-address system, which was loud enough to be heard in Arkansas. He explained the most important rules: To buy a car you had to pay with cash, a cashier's check, or a certified check. Any buyer who was carrying less than the full purchase price could make a two-hundred-dollar deposit with cash, MasterCard, or Visa, but he had to show up with the balance before five o'clock the next day. And the balance, naturally, had to be in cash, cashier's check, or certified check. That meant American dollars, no pesos, no personal checks, no promissory notes, no letters of credit, no IOUs. Donovan Arterburn, Jr., repeated the ground rules and then he repeated them about ten more times.

Arterburn stood now in the rear of an overpopulated yellow Toyota pickup truck that was idling between the two rows of cars. A policeman hugged the tailgate, another sat behind the steering wheel, a pretty young woman with dark hair and sunglasses rode shotgun, and three older women whose job would be to collect money sat around a folding table in the cargo space.

At last the bidding started. The serious spectators were poised with their used-car-buying reference books, and—*bam bam bam*—item number one took about ninety seconds to sell. It was a 1982 Lincoln Town Car with low mileage and it went for seventeen thousand dollars to a middle-aged man who transgressed the rope barrier and headed unsteadily for the yellow Toyota pickup. There was applause and busy whispering while the resident experts tried to figure out whether he had paid too dear a price—that depending, of course, upon the intangible value that the car would have if it had been driven previously by someone notorious.

The bidding on the second car got underway. Arterburn said, "This next car has an appraised value of thirteen thousand five hundred dollars. Who'll give me fifteen thousand for it?" Arterburn's bid spotters had spread themselves out and they surveyed the crowd with the beady circumspection of Secret Service agents.

Whenever one of them saw a hand go up he gave a startled yell, like someone slamming a thumb in a drawer. When the bidding had reached half the appraised value, Arterburn interrupted.

"Hold everything," he said. "The gentleman who bought the first car did not buy the first car after all. He did not have cash. He did not have a cashier's check. He did not have a certified check. He did not have two hundred dollars. He did not pass Go. We're going to have to resell the car. All right, let's finish the bidding on this car and we'll go back and resell the first one. Wait, no, excuse me, it seems he's found someone in the crowd who's going to lend him the money. He now has the two hundred dollars."

There was laughter and more applause, and I contributed to it. As a gawker, I felt rewarded. On a late-summer evening I had gone to Penn Square to watch some used cars being liquidated. In no time at all I had witnessed an easy-money unsecured loan to someone who simply had not understood the rules.

The first productive oil well in Oklahoma was drilled by accident and stirred no enthusiasm. In the northeast corner of Indian Territory, in 1859, a Cherokee salt prospector named Lewis Ross used a spring pole—a percussion drilling device fashioned from a green sapling—to make a seven-hundred-foot hole. Instead of the brine he was hoping to find, Ross turned up some black gooey stuff that appeared to have useful applications only if you were suffering from rheumatism or a flesh wound. This happened the same year that Colonel Edwin Drake (who was infinitely less a real colonel than Lewis Ross was a real Indian) drilled his famous well in Titusville, Pennsylvania. For a few months, Ross's well produced ten barrels of crude a day, and then it died. Almost four decades passed before a commercially successful well materialized in Oklahoma. This was the Nellie Johnstone No. 1, completed in 1897 in Bartlesville, along the Caney River.

Ten years after the Nellie Johnstone No. 1 came in, Oklahoma joined the United States. Oklahoma Territory—roughly speaking, the western half of what became the state, comprising a mixture of rankled Native American plains roamers, pious European immigrant soil-scrapers, and Dixie interlopers who had shown up for the land rush of 1889—merged with Indian Territory, which was populated by civilized Native Americans who had been forced to abandon their homes in the Deep South and by more Dixie interlopers and their spiritual kinfolk from other neighborhoods—creatures who resented having to work for a living but were nevertheless willing to put in a few hours a day devising ways to rook the Indians out of some more land. The new state needed a capital, and a town called Guthrie, which had been the capital of Oklahoma Territory, was chosen. In 1910, however, the site was changed to Oklahoma City, which was selected though it had no natural physical beauty and very little water. Worse than that, it gave the impression as the years passed of having no oil. It did happen to be smack-dab in the center of the state, but that mainly gave rise to unflattering comparisons, as whopper oil and gas discoveries erupted everywhere else—near Tulsa and in the Osage and along the Cimarron River at Drumright and Cushing, all to the northeast; in Garfield County, due north; in Seminole, to the east; in Healdton, to the south. Vindication finally arrived in 1928. The discovery well of the Oklahoma City Field, the Oklahoma City No. 1, produced oil from dolomite sediments six thousand four hundred feet beneath the surface, and in the first twenty-four hours it flowed almost five thousand barrels. Shortly thereafter the well was deepened, and it began to gush more than sixty-five hundred barrels a day.

The Oklahoma City No. 1, was a perfectly accurate harbinger. One historian has written that the Oklahoma City Field "was characterized by wild wells, floods of crude, and almost uncontrollable flows of natural gas." Overproduction got so far out of hand that within four years the price per barrel had fallen from a dollar and a half to fifteen cents. On three occasions during the nineteen-thirties, the governor dispatched the Oklahoma National Guard to enforce orders to curtail production. Five years after the discovery well was drilled, the Oklahoma City Field's annual output peaked; within the first ten years, more oil was produced than has been produced in the succeeding four and a half decades. There has been one estimate that during those first ten years one trillion two hundred billion cubic feet of natural gas escaped into the atmosphere: three and a half billion dollars at today's somewhat depressed prices. In its lifetime, it has yielded more than seven hundred thirty-five million barrels of oil and more than two trillion cubic feet of gas. The entire Oklahoma City Field—comprising about two hundred active wells—currently produces less than twenty-five hundred barrels a day. Surveying the landscape now, you would hardly assume that production had been declining for such a long stretch and had reached such a low level. In the Oklahoma City suburbs, where there are two taco joints for every tree, you see wellheads surrounded by high fences in undeveloped residential zones, you see pumping units in strip-shopping-center parking lots. Four-story derricks straddle the wells on the grounds of the state capitol and the governor's mansion, and it matters very little that so many of the wells are just barely oozing crude—that the derricks' main function is to provide a remembrance of things past. Appearances count. Mythology counts.

There is a fact not of regional character but of geography and geology that makes Oklahoma City a place where a Penn Square Bank could happen. Forty minutes south and west of town by car (fifteen by helicopter), lies an imaginary rectangle 125 miles by 250 miles. On a map, the rectangle runs on a southeast-to-northwest axis, covers roughly equal portions of the southwest and northwest quadrants of Oklahoma, extends into the Texas panhandle, and thus bounds the surface above what geologists know as the Anadarko Basin—a rising arid plain of red-orange Oklahoma dirt, mostly clay, but high in iron oxide, passable for growing wheat and peanuts and cotton if you can figure out a way to water it. What makes the arid plain worthwhile is that beneath its surface is an almost inconceivably large volume of methane. As an Oklahoman might put it, there is a whole bunch of natural gas down there. The usual Ordovician and Pennsylvanian remains are concentrated in an unusual way. Perhaps one hundred fifty thousand cubic miles of hydrocarbon-bearing limestone, sandstone, dolomite, chert, gravel, and shale make up the sub-strata, an accumulation that stretches back five hundred million years. Liberating the Anadarko's deep reserves, in the view of a prominent school of current thinking, could render trivial the wastage of gas that occurred in the Oklahoma City Field.

Widespread oil production in the Anadarko Basin began during the 1920s—shallow wells, in the two- to three-thousand-foot range—and along with the oil there was methane that is referred to as "casinghead gas" or "associated gas." For decades, geologists and petroleum engineers with the least imagination, viewing oil production histories and knowing how far the remaining reserves had descended the slope of the bell curve, would look at the Anadarko and conclude that the gas was running out along with the oil. And they were correct: the gas that was associated with the oil *was* running out. Relatively shallow formations where oil was not plentiful also produced commercial quantities of gas. This could be found generally in the eastern part of the basin, at depths ranging from seven thousand to twelve thousand feet. The shallow gas and casinghead gas, however, were not what made the Anadarko Basin fascinating. Its most ardent partisans believed that to reach the most gratifying zones you had to go to great depths— fifteen thousand or twenty-five thousand or thirty-five thousand feet. A more prevalent belief, one that was current well into the 1970s, held that the geological "overburden" made the deep-gas hypothesis unlikely because the very deep sediments could not possibly be porous or permeable enough to contain hydrocarbons or to permit their flow. The cumulative weight of a three- or five- or seven-mile-thick crust, it was presumed, would slam shut the pores in the rocks—just as depressing a damp kitchen sponge with a one-ton marble pillar would squeeze out all the moisture.

Someone was going to have to drill and produce from a deep-gas well before the skeptics would accept the idea that the gas was there. And even if it was there technological limitations would mean coping with erratic pressures and extremely high temperatures that could make the available tools about as effective as Lewis Ross's spring pole. Not that anyone gave a lot of thought to testing the equipment. In the absence of serious complications, a fifteen-thousand-foot well would cost three to four million dollars. As long as the price of gas that traveled through interstate pipelines remained regulated by the federal government, which kept it very low in relation to the price of crude oil, no gambler with an inclination to see his money again cared to roll the dice.

During the late seventies and early eighties, however, the value of fossil fuels changed, the odds changed, and a new mythology emerged. Oil and gas assumed an urgent aura of manifest destiny. It was not like high technology or any other growth industry that seemed headed toward a blindingly bright horizon. It involved mining a finite resource. The thought of *running out of oil* promised that an enormous amount of money could be made between now and when the last economical drop came out of the ground, and to enjoy the benefits an opportunist did not necessarily have to take heroic chances. An acquaintance of mine, a bankruptcy lawyer, once pointed out, "You've got thirteen thousand oil and gas companies in Oklahoma. Maybe fifteen hundred of them are looking for oil and gas. The rest are looking for investors." Another friend once endeavored to explain to me how Oklahoma City is distinctive—how it differs from, say, Tulsa, which is regarded as sleek and "Eastern" by Oklahomans who have never tasted the delights of a St. Louis or an Indianapolis. "Three years ago I bought a new Mercedes," my friend said. "I asked the salesman to deliver it to my house. He drives it out on a Friday afternoon and I meet him in the driveway. He parks the new car and gives me the keys, and then I give him the keys to my old car because I'm trading it in. Then he hands me a business card and says, 'Well, that's the last car I'll ever have to sell. I'm going into a new business Monday morning.' I look at the card and it says 'Fraley Oil & Gas.' That was his name—Wyman Fraley. He said that before he sold cars he'd been a preacher. The last thing I heard about him was he owed the bank a million dollars and he'd been accused of torching his office to collect on the insurance and he was telling people the Atlanta mob was looking for him. A guy like that could never get banked in Tulsa." Oklahoma City was blessed with a novel strain of cosmopolitanism. If you pursued a dollar there and persevered in a special way, you might be able to get yourself tailed by gangsters. But, inevitably, they would be gangsters from Atlanta—in other words, too small to make the varsity. Wyman Fraley banked at Penn Square. So did my friend who bought the new Mercedes-Benz from him. An institution such as the Penn Square Bank could have dared to be great only in Oklahoma City.

CHAPTER 2

Great Oklahoma institutions helped to make Bill P. Jennings, the chairman and chief executive officer of the Penn Square Bank, a great man: Oklahoma Military Academy, the University of Oklahoma (Class of '48), the University of Oklahoma chapter of Sigma Chi, the University of Oklahoma School of Law, the Oklahoma Air National Guard. He interrupted his college career to spend a year with the Army Air Forces. After law school, he did a tour with the United States Air Force. As a teenager he had developed an interest in flying, and as an undergraduate he had been the only Sigma Chi who owned a Cessna 140. (The plane perished one spring in a tornado. It was on the ground and Jennings was not aboard.) In adulthood, Jennings continued to add to his record of achievement and community service: member of the finance committee of the United Appeal, corporate director of the Oklahoma City Chamber of Commerce, member of the boards of the Salvation Army and the Young Men's Christian Association, active in the Mummer's Theatre, chairman of the Oklahoma Symphony fund-raising campaign, chairman of the Oklahoma Industrial Finance Authority, chairman of the Oklahoma Medical Research Foundation. He was infected with the spirit of philanthropy. He was married and had five handsome daughters. His late father-in-law, a dedicated collector of poetry about Abraham Lincoln and a distinguished citizen of Enid, Oklahoma, had been chairman of the board of a bank in that city. His mother, well into her eighties, was chairman of the board of the Bank of Healdton, in the southern Oklahoma town where Jennings had grown up. In 1973, when Jennings was elected president of the state Chamber of

13

Commerce, he declared, "Our primary objective is to make Oklahoma a better place to earn a living and raise a family."

No one who had shaken Bill Jennings' hand could insist that he was less than a nice guy. To be introduced to Jennings and not be taken with his affability, his earnest good nature, you would have to be a misanthrope. Knowing that he was a banker sealed the favorable impression. Gamblers, salesmen, roving promoters—wisdom taught that when those people smiled and looked you in the eye you maintained skepticism. An excessively warm and friendly banker was a peculiar proposition, more difficult to figure. From a banker who wanted to convey that he was tough when it came to credit and even tougher when it came to collecting, you would normally expect cool solicitude. Bill Jennings fancied himself that way: tough when he needed to be. In practice, however, he could never come across as tough as he might wish. He looked you in the eye and smiled and all that natural affability got in his way.

No doubt Jennings' charm had something to do with his having grown up a small-town banker's son and an only child. He knew that he was special, but he understood the rules that his neighbors lived by—one being that, whatever you do, you do not want to alienate the banker—and he learned never to condescend. His given name was Billy Paul, and some of his pals—mainly the old Sigma Chis who had stayed close across the years—still called him that. Otherwise he was "Beep"—Beep Jennings—a nickname that seemed to mesh with his style: pinstripes and bold cigars. He could easily have applied his charm to politics, but he seemed to have made an early career decision to become professionally avuncular. His hair was all white by the time he was fifty-five, his eyes were blue and crinkly, and when he got rolling in Beeperese—gusty, vibrant speechifying, the flowing cadences of a Dale Carnegie *summa cum laude*—he would often grimace and squint into the distance above your head, toward the low clouds. His hairline had receded considerably, and what hair remained he parted about an inch above the top of his left ear and swept east. In a few more years, his cheeks, which were pink and jowly, would begin to resemble dewlaps. He was six feet tall and leaner than his face suggested. Seeing him in charcoal-gray pinstripes, you might look for a pocket watch chain, thinking that one would fit in, but Bill Jennings was swifter than that. The total package had equal measures of Lionel Barrymore and game-show host. Seated, he held his cigar between the tips of his thumb and forefinger and he kept it poised like a horn player anticipating a cue. Each short puff had delicacy.

The oil boom arrived in Healdton, in Carter County, Oklahoma, in 1913, ten years before Billy Paul was born. His father, O. T. Jennings—the initials stood for Owen Thomas, but everyone called him Al—had started out at the Bank of Healdton as a teller and, in the late nineteen-twenties, had bought the place. One of his goals was to cultivate an unbankerlike reputation. A newspaper reporter who was fond of Al Jennings once wrote, "He's liable to have his hat turned up like Joe College and he may okay a deal by yelling across the street." After enumerating some other appealing traits, the reporter concluded, "He's quite a guy." Al Jennings died in 1965, and the newspaperman wrote of him: "He built a good bank, mostly by his own rules, some of which would have given a serious-type examiner apoplexy—until he found the books were in order." There was a period of time, around 1920, when the oilfield of Carter County was one of the most productive in the world, but Al Jennings was not a venture capitalist. He did what was expected of a small-town banker—conformed his ambitions to reality, lent money to the feed-store owner and the car dealer and any oilfield roughnecks who were reasonably likely to pay it back, and endured some marginal moments. The Bank of Healdton survived the Depression, but barely. In 1932, the deposits were eighty-three thousand dollars, loans were twenty thousand, and the capital and surplus totaled sixteen thousand five hundred. In grander times, when the bank actually had funds to lend, Al Jennings regularly received requests for credit information about customers. When several of these query letters arrived in the mail one day, Bill Jennings, who had gone to work for the bank full-time in 1953, showed them to his father and asked what procedure he should follow. Al Jennings laughed and said, "If they don't put anything in the letter, we just throw it away. If they put in two bits, we answer it. And if they stick in fifty cents, son, we tell them the *truth*."

One spring day in 1976, during a regular 8 a.m. loan committee meeting at the Penn Square Bank, Bill Jennings said, "I want to start an oil-and-gas department at this bank." Not many specifics accompanied this proposal, but it was evident that Jennings meant exactly what he said. Penn Square's assets totaled less than forty million dollars, and there was only one oil-and-gas loan among them. No one else in the room knew anything about oil-and-gas lending, but everyone knew that Jennings had not tossed the idea out idly. He owned the bank and he intended to make it grow.

When the Penn Square Bank opened, in 1960, Jennings had moved from Healdton to Oklahoma City to run it. The new bank was organized by a developer named Ben Wileman, who had built the shopping center in which the bank was situated, and by the families of Senator Robert S. Kerr and his associate Dean McGee—two men whose opinions of how commerce ought to proceed in Oklahoma mattered no more than rainfall, sunlight, fertilizer, and pest-killer do to a garden. Kerr and McGee were interested in banks but not in operating a bank. Most of the time, Kerr kept busy running the United States Senate, and McGee looked after Kerr-McGee Oil Industries. Wileman was the bank's chairman, and Jennings was hired to manage it day to day. In 1964 Jennings left Penn Square to become executive vice-president and chief lending officer of the Fidelity Bank, an established downtown institution that was also controlled by the Kerrs and the McGees. Ten years later, someone other than Bill P. Jennings was named president of Fidelity.

Chances are that Jennings would have become president of Fidelity had he not been the loan officer primarily responsible for the Four Seasons Nursing Centers account. In 1972, a federal grand jury in New York indicted eight men on charges that they had conspired to falsify information about Four Seasons and to defraud the investing public. It was alleged that, in the process, the defendants had cost investors two hundred million dollars. Over a period of several months, the price of Four Seasons stock had gone from eleven dollars a share to more than a hundred dollars and then had become nearly worthless. When the indictments were returned, Four Seasons was described as the largest criminal securities fraud in United States history. Four of the eight indictees were convicted, and two went to prison. The government attorneys described Jennings' role in Four Seasons as that of "unindicted co-conspirator." Officially, Jennings was guilty of nothing. At the Fidelity Bank, however, his star would rise no further.

Jennings was fifty-one years old. It was not too late to start over, provided that he could start at the top, so he decided to return to Penn Square, this time as owner. The bank cost Jennings and two partners three million dollars. Each of the new owners had held modest amounts of Penn Square stock before the sale, and each ended up with a quarter of the bank. The remaining quarter was divided among several stockholders. As a result of subsequent trades and new stock offerings, Jennings and his family controlled the largest proportion—about 30 percent. For a time, when he listed the asset on his financial statement, he assigned to it a value of between eight and nine million dollars.

There were half a dozen Penn Square officers present when Jennings said, "I want to start an oil-and-gas department." One of them was a thirty-five-year-old former national bank examiner named Bill Lakey. After the loan committee meeting adjourned, Lakey approached Jennings and said, "I'd like to try some of that." Later he recalled, "Nobody else knew anything about oil-and-gas lending. I didn't either, but at least I was interested."

Lakey's formal training as an energy lender began immediately. He took a one-day trip to Dallas for a tutorial with an officer at the RepublicBank, one of the largest banks in the Southwest. Back in Oklahoma City, he sought advice from a couple of people at the Fidelity Bank on how to collateralize and secure an oil-and-gas production loan. A lawyer who represented Fidelity drafted deed-of-trust forms that were virtually identical to the forms used by RepublicBank, and oil-and-gas mortgage forms that were similar to Fidelity's. "That was it," Lakey said. "We were in business." Except for the one oil-and-gas loan that was then on the books— Lakey remembers that it had not yet been designated a nonperforming loan, although the customer happened to have financial problems—virtually everything else in Penn Square's loan portfolio was committed to small-business loans, real-estate and construction loans, and consumer loans for automobiles, boats, and new patios. The bank's capital was four million dollars, and this meant, according to banking regulations, that the most the bank could lend to a single customer was four hundred thousand. If Jennings wanted to involve Penn Square in energy lending, he was going to have to entice customers somewhat smaller than Gulf and Mobil and Texaco.

Eighteen months later, Lakey decided to quit his job at Penn Square. Jennings wished him well and suggested that he lacked aggressiveness and should give thought to becoming a school-teacher—an opinion that disturbed Lakey because he more or less agreed. Although Lakey naturally liked Jennings, working for him had been frustrating. "Beep was a can't-say-no guy," Lakey recalls. "His attitude toward everyone was always 'Come in, we'll talk to you.' The way it worked was, he'd give a verbal commitment to someone and if I didn't want to make the loan I was supposed to turn it down. He didn't want to be the one to do that. Beep would call me and say, 'We want to lend So-and-So four hundred thousand.' I'd ask him, 'By when?' He'd say, 'Today.' He'd say, 'Just lend it and get the information later.' Well, hell, I might need to spend a little more time than that. If you work that way and find out six months later you've got a problem but you're still trying to get the documents and the collateral together—if you haven't got everything filed and recorded and secured but meanwhile the guys you banked already have the money, they aren't necessarily going to be interested in cooperating with you. Beep would take on people that a lot of other bankers wouldn't touch. He's never been one of those my-chair's-up-here-and-you're-sitting-down-there type of bankers. His attitude was more like 'I'm gonna show you what a man can do.' Beep liked to make a guy feel like he was helping him out. In effect, he'd be saying, 'I'm doing things for you that nobody else'll do for anybody else.' And I always had a feeling that people would pay Beep back before they'd pay anyone else."

Al Jennings once told his son, "Only about twenty percent of the people will pay you when they say they will." Ample measures of trust and optimism blended in Beep Jennings' personality. In Healdton, where his father knew not only the customer but also the customer's parents, in-laws, grandparents, pediatrician, and undertaker, it made some sense to base a lending decision on an evaluation of character as much as upon collateral and credit history. The banking habits that dispirited a sane man like Lakey were regarded as strengths by Jennings' champions. Jennings, it was said, *believed* in people. Jennings gave you the benefit of the doubt. Certain businessmen would testify that Jennings was their only banker-friend. Jennings had lent them money when nobody else would, Jennings would "bank some risk," Jennings would "do the unusual deal." The unusual deal that turned out all right fortified the original optimism. It was a banking philosophy that depended upon scruples and conscience. At Penn Square, Beep Jennings would demonstrate to the local marketplace: "*Here's* how you can bank, and it can *work*.

Much later, trying to explain what had happened, Jennings said, "I had a concept." Simply stated, the concept held that a bank did not have to lend its own deposits, because it could lend other banks' deposits. Penn Square could earn interest lending its own funds but could generate far greater earnings, with very little risk, by arranging loans and collecting fees as a middleman. Thus could a modest suburban bank in Oklahoma City become a loan-brokering merchant bank in the style of the great, loosely regulated financial institutions of Central and Western Europe.

The details were somewhat complicated, but Jennings' concept involved no chicanery; nor was it even a brave new idea. Small banks have always relied upon bigger banks—or, as the terms have evolved, "community" and "regional" banks have relied upon "money center" banks. Penn Square was, of course, a community bank that grew into a regional bank. In the United States, "money center" means New York, Chicago, Boston, Los Angeles, San Francisco, Houston, Dallas, Miami. There is a range of special services that the small banks cannot economically provide for themselves. Performing these services is often barely profitable for the big banks, but they do it because of the unavoidable interdependency of banks. Furthermore, in the course of things a big bank gets a chance to do profitable favors for a small bank without having to do much work, such as buying "overlines"—that is, lending money to customers of the small bank. The bank that buys the overline is said to "participate" in the loan. By law, a national bank can lend no more than one-tenth of its capital to a single customer. At its zenith Penn Square could legally lend up to three and a half million dollars at one time. A customer who wished to borrow four and a half million would place the bank in the situation of needing to sell a one-million-dollar overline. Banks also sell loan participations because they do not have sufficient funds on hand to make a loan (they lack "liquidity") or because they wish to diversify their portfolio (they have filled their quota of, say, commerical real estate loans and now along comes another real estate loan request, so they direct it to another bank) or because they lack expertise in a loan applicant's line of business (in other words, because they do not wish to diversify their portfolio). A bank can sell loan participations to banks either larger or smaller than itself. Fluid metaphors characterize these transactions. A larger correspondent bank is an "upstream" bank, a loan sold to a smaller bank goes "downstream." Transitive verbs blossom like waterlilies: "We upstreamed that loan to Chase Manhattan," or "We downstreamed a hundred thousand to First National of Tishomingo." Liquidity is paramount. Trust flows freely.

There was such a creature as a 100-percent loan participation. In this instance the loan-originating bank had in effect ceased being a bank. It found the borrower and delivered him into the hands of the big lender, collecting a fee but not retaining any investment in the loan. For its fee, the originating bank—Penn Square, say—would "service" the loan. The bank that had bought the loan wanted tangible evidence that the borrower was worth the risk, and Penn Square had a duty to provide this. Penn Square agreed to perfect any secured interest in collateral and to forward interest payments to the lender. From Penn Square's point of view the numbers looked irresistible. Life would be wonderful indeed if, all in a day's work, you could sell a 99-percent participation in a ten-million-dollar loan, retaining only one hundred thousand dollars of risk, with the rest of the deal belonging to one other or many other banks. Penn Square's loan origination fee—usually one percent—would come to one hundred thousand dollars, and so the bank would earn overnight a 100-percent return on its portion of the credit. Life would be even more wonderful if you could collect fees while selling 100-percent participations, thus earning an infinite return.

A potentially limitless cycle of growth could result from all this. Through aggressive salesmanship, a bank with, say, fifty million dollars in loans on its own books could originate two hundred fifty million dollars' worth of loans. More often than not, because the borrowers would live or conduct business near the bank that arranged the loan, the bank would enjoy the benefit of increased deposits in the operating accounts of the borrowers. Greater deposits plus the income collected in the loan origination fees would mean greater profits, and greater profits would add to a bank's capital and permit it to make larger loans and also to increase its credibility and stature as a loan broker. Growth begets growth. Upon assuming control of Penn Square, Jennings announced that within ten years its assets would grow from thirty-five million dollars to one hundred million. The man underestimated himself. The goal was reached within four years, and within six years Penn Square's assets totaled almost a half-billion dollars. Along the way, the bank sold two billion dollars' worth of additional loans.

Why do other small banks not attempt what Jennings set out to do at Penn Square? Above all, most small banks do not enjoy access to a large pool of eager borrowers willing to assume huge liabilities at exorbitant interest rates. The Penn Square Bank, however, *was* so endowed. When Beep Jennings began to envision himself as a merchant banker, oil-and-gas lending was not yet part of his concept. He was actually thinking real estate. During the mid-seventies, however, real estate began to lose its allure and petroleum developed an allure that it had never quite demonstrated before. Automobile bumpers in Texas and Oklahoma and Louisiana started bearing stickers that said, "Let the Yankee bastards freeze in the dark" and "If you don't have an oil well, get one." Jennings was a registered Democrat who voted for Republican presidential candidates. He could bridge a gap and he could easily recognize an unpragmatic sentiment. As a patriotic Oklahoman, he instinctively understood the chauvinism of the oil-and-gas-producing heart of the country, but the truth was that the decent, right-thinking people who had gone to the trouble of owning or leasing mineral rights throughout Oklahoma, Texas, and Louisiana did not have the capital that they needed to get the oil and gas out of the ground. The Yankee bastards, among others, had the capital. That was what could make Jennings' concept work: an understanding that if the Yankee bastards had the dollars, what good did it do if you froze them? His role as merchant banker was to bring the two parties together for some common profit. "The government gave us a mandate, didn't they?" Jennings liked to say, referring to the exigencies of the energy crisis.

A mandate meant that somebody had better get out there and do something. And if you left the job to people who took six weeks to look at a deal that could be sized up and shaken on by the time the waitress brought the tab, then New England would shiver and Oklahoma would still be no better than a dust bowl.

CHAPTER 3

At times, trying to understand what the Penn Square Bank had been all about strained my capacities, made me feel that my grasp of the big picture was slipping, and I would consult an attorney whom I will call Murray. I valued Murray's ability to focus. We would meet for breakfast occasionally at a molded-plastic bistro called Denny's. I liked Murray, although he talked a bit too much, and I liked him *because* he talked a bit too much. You could stay as long as you pleased at Denny's; the waitresses just kept pouring the coffee. Murray started out in the Bronx or someplace like it, but he had been in Oklahoma enough years so that his monologues contained frequent pauses which were followed by the statement "Now, mister, I'm gonna tell ya somethin'," whereupon he would launch into a parable full of local color and universal implications. When I called him on the telephone to make a date I would always ask how he was and he would always say, "Well, sir, I'm still short and I'm still chubby." Murray was in his late forties, he had a graying dark beard, and he chain-smoked unfiltered Camels. Diamonds encircled the face of his gold Rolex wristwatch. He wore a big diamond ring and a gold bracelet, and I think there may have been a gold chain around his neck. A friend told me that Murray had had a coronary attack at a tender age but this had not curbed his appetite for high-risk cuisine. He would instruct the waitress, "Bring me a Number Four—the eggs Benedict—and make sure you put a lot of that fattening sauce that's real bad for you all over it. Get plenty of sauce on the bacon, too." Then he would light a Camel and explain once again how the cosmos worked.

One morning, Murray's lecture began, "In the past, we have

had irresponsible borrowers, and in the past we have had irresponsible lenders, but what we had here, and are having to witness the consequences of in profusion, is the meeting, for the first time, of the irresponsible lender and the irresponsible borrower. Any bank that lends money to Poland is nuts. Any bank that lends to Yugoslavia is nuts. Anybody who lends a billion dollars to Mexico is out of his ever-lovin' gourd. And you know what is at the bottom of this? An irresponsible government. The guys who ran Penn Square weren't born mad killers. They were a symptom." Oklahoma's oilies, in other words, were just a bunch of semi-domesticated third-world borrowers.

When the waitress delivered the eggs Benedict, Murray had a chance to regroup his thoughts. Lots of pepper atop the hollandaise, lots of salt atop the pepper. Then he held forth on Aramco, King Khalid, Colonel Qaddafi, OPEC, Exxon, and the culpability of David Rockefeller and Walter Wriston and their ilk; returned to Mexico, Poland, and Yugoslavia, with side trips to Chile and Morocco; and went on to the stupidity of experts, the timidity of bureaucrats, rampant inflation, worldwide recession, Dwight Eisenhower, Jimmy Carter, the corruption inherent in the tax codes, the indecent motives of the typical oil-and-gas drilling fund investor, and simple everyday greed—in other words, the vast matrix at the center of which, or in there somewhere, was an ambitious bank in Oklahoma City that had been run by promoters whose only sin was believing their own hype.

I had done some thinking along these lines myself, but Murray had a poetic manner of expression and I did not want to insult him by accusing him of unoriginality. The big picture *did* look like that. The fact was that for the better part of a decade there had existed a virtually global belief: the price of petroleum and everything that depended on it would go no way but up. Pessimists accepted the inevitability, optimists saw an opportunity, and cynics winked. You could take this belief to the bank and declare it as collateral. Or, if you looked like an O.K. person, the bank might even come to you. This was a magical phase of history, and while it lasted the Penn Square Bank radiated enormous charm. The Penn Square Bank was operated by freedom-loving patriots for the benefit of themselves and their kindred spirits and for the higher goals of the United States, a civilized democracy that sought to liberate itself from economic blackmail by dubious foreign oligarchs—hypo-

crites who persisted in chopping off the hands of petty thieves
even as they engorged themselves with trillions of dollars from the
export of petroleum that they'd never deserved to own in the first
place—men with unsightly beards who hung out in the desert and
worshipped the wrong god and dressed funny and had swarthy
skin, unpronounceable names, and more wives than any law
should permit. The whole weird situation was simple, but it was
complicated too.

By the last cup of coffee that morning the conversation had
shifted to a client of Murray's—a likable oilman whose assets
Murray was trying to protect from litigious investors in twenty-two
states who kept mentioning the word "fraud." I eased into the
subject by dropping such phrases as "blue-skyed" and "due dili-
gence" and "full disclosure." Before I got far, Murray became
overwrought.

"You want to know what's really fraudulent?" he said. "I'll tell
you what is. It's when you run a movie studio and you take a lousy
script and make a grade-B picture from it and all it shows is some
twenty-two-year-old actress who's never been in front of a camera
before but when you shake her up and down you get people
excited. Maybe you splash some water on her to make her look
better. Then you take that and call it art and sell it to the public for
five dollars a ticket. And the public, because all they've done is
watch TV, want to pay the five dollars, so you've got no risk when
you decide to make one of those lousy movies. In California they're
cranking them out as fast as they can and when they've made
enough money they say, 'Uh-oh, I'm gonna have to pay taxes, I
better go drill me an oil well or something.' So they go invest in a
drilling fund and it says right on the front cover of the prospectus
that there's a risk involved. But these people aren't accustomed to
taking risks—they want a one hundred percent tax deduction
without having to put up any money. Then, if they end up losing
any of that money, they scream 'Fraud!' Well, in the oil business at
least we were punching holes in the ground."

As a defense of the oil-and-gas industry this seemed rather
oblique, but I had no quarrel with Murray's basic thesis. I cannot
report anything else he said that morning, however, because my
attention lapsed when he said "punching holes in the ground."
The most nouveau oilies were always referring to drilling wells as
"punching holes in the ground." Hearing that and similar locu-

tions invariably launched me into daydreams about how the mental-health profession might regard the oil business. The etiology of the boom and the Penn Square Bank could be traced to the sources that Murray had mentioned, but he had omitted the substance that gave all these elements force and dynamism. The substance was Okiesmo.

Believing that yahooism was perverse did not make you unwelcome at Penn Square, but it meant that you had to wait your turn in line behind the guys who had superior Okiesmo. At the head of the line were open-minded independent oilmen whose meritocratic intuitions told them that anyone who could afford to own, say, a few houses that came equipped with private zoos and climate-control regulators in all the bathrooms that would make it either rain or snow or feel like the Mojave indoors—being able to pay for that meant that you had collected a reasonable return on your investment. The rewards were Providence's gifts to anyone who labored diligently, the sowers were reaping for a change. Because of Okiesmo, men did not merely set out to find hydrocarbons, they punched holes in the ground. Okiesmo (accent on the second syllable) emanated from the rig floor up. All the roughnecks had Okiesmo because they handled heavy pipe and got dirty every day—they toted some iron. The bosses in the office paid for the iron and imputed Okiesmo to themselves. When something went wrong out on a rig, men with mucho Okiesmo knew how to jam their hands in their pockets and utter four-letter words polysyllabically. Naturally, the more you owed the bank the higher your Okiesmo Quotient. It grew even more complicated: the more you borrowed to pay the interest on your previous debt, the higher your O.Q. Ironic self-pity was permitted, whining was not.

Okiesmo dialogue went:

"Only time I found oil last year was when I checked my dipstick."

"Butch, you cain't *find* oil if you're looking for it over at the Petroleum Club."

You could begin life as a runt, but if you worked out with weights and swallowed plenty of starch, got square-faced and jowly, you could develop your Okiesmo potential. Okiesmo was a sort of acquired nucleoplasm.

It manifested itself in drilling rigs, aircraft, hand-tooled boots.

Rigs that could drill to twenty-five thousand feet flowed more Okiesmo than rigs that could go to only twelve thousand. Okiesmo traveled well to Acapulco and Vegas. A jet got you there faster than a turboprop, two jets were better than one, every jet deserved a helicopter as a hangar mate, jet-propelled helicopters beat everything. Slaved-over cowhide boots had plenty of Okiesmo, but lizardskin had even more and eelskin topped that. If you ran across something with more Okiesmo than anteater, you were supposed to buy it. Upwardly mobile Okiesmo was a white Lincoln Continental with one hubcap missing. The bumper sticker said, "Don't tell my folks I'm working in the oil patch. They think I play piano in a whorehouse." A good Okiesmo way to travel to the golf course was by helicopter. If you made a habit of driving ten miles in one direction, parking your Continental, choppering fifteen miles back in the direction you had just come from, and landing next to the first tee two minutes before your starting time, you would not be unique, but no one would ever question your Okiesmo. Having too much Okiesmo aged you. It encouraged the illusion that life could imitate a previous lifetime. No matter how old you were, you were always seven or seventeen—ageless. Ex-linebacker turned fried okra connoisseur was standard equipment—very few ectomorphs. Excessive Okiesmo got dissipated during forty-eight-hour saturnalias in hotel suites, complete with flaming hundred-dollar bills, plenty of company, and room service charges that ran to four figures. ("Hey, stud, you wanna send us up the left side of the menu real quick?") No women had Okiesmo. Men with Okiesmo coupled with women who admired men with Okiesmo.

Okiesmo gave wings to myth.

And what gave Okiesmo wings? Money, of course.

Any quest for oil and gas must yield to the preliminary quest for capital, and a cooperative banker can be a rewarding acquaintance. Classic, conservative petroleum banking theory rests upon two easy-to-grasp principles: the Catch-22 and the pyramid scheme. A classic, conservative banker will not lend money for oil or natural gas exploration to anyone who cannot pledge as security already-existing oil-and-gas production: you cannot enter the game—here is the Catch-22—unless you have previously played and won. The pyramid metaphor looms once you have borrowed money to drill for oil and gas and have explored successfully. It becomes very difficult to stop borrowing, unless you choose to assume the tax burdens that come with success. Because the oil business is as much about avoiding paying taxes as it is about selling a product, that option is, practically speaking, irrelevant. As long as an operator can manage to discover new oil-and-gas reserves, his most sensible approach will be to continue borrowing and exploring, exploring and borrowing. One credit device that permits the borrowing pyramid to grow is the "evergreen revolver." True believers believe that in an inflationary cycle the evergreen revolver costs nothing. It operates according to the idea that a banker, once he has lent money to, say, a rancher who pledges as security a hundred head of cattle, can keep lending him more as long as he adds sixty calves every year. The new calves pay the interest on the original loan, create security for a bigger, spring-time-fresh new loan, and keep the credit revolving—i.e., "ever-green." If, instead of cattle, the banker lends against oil-and-gas reserves, the borrower has an annual obligation to explore and thereby increase the value of his reserves. The evergreen revolver is no-tomorrow credit—money that never has to be paid back as long as you keep drilling, adding reserves, snowballing. During the oil-and-gas boom, it was a license that permitted the borrower and the lender to have a mitt deep inside each other's pocket.

When it comes to avoiding paying taxes, Exxon and Mobil ask themselves different questions from those asked by the so-called independent oilmen whose lives are ruled by the Catch-22 and the borrowing pyramid. Broadly speaking, an independent oil operator is an entity—an individual or a company—that finds oil and gas and depends upon other entities to transport the raw material, refine it, and market it. Independents tend not to be vertically integrated. Independents do not drill exploratory wells in the North Sea or in Prudhoe Bay, Alaska, but they drill more domestic oil wells and gas wells and discover more hydrocarbons each year than the twenty largest integrated oil companies combined. There are, among others, large independents, small independents, and Oklahoma-type independents. The Oklahoma-type independent—

who exists not only in Oklahoma but also in Texas, Louisiana, California, Kansas, Arkansas, Colorado, Wyoming, Ohio, Pennsylvania, Michigan, Illinois, New York, West Virginia, and other venues—has a balance sheet that looks dire. An active Oklahoma-type independent is a theoretically wealthy man with no money who borrows and spends dollars this year in quest of oil-and-gas production that will pay off last year's trade creditors as well as the interest owed on this year's bank debt.

I spent my youth up the turnpike from Penn Square, in Tulsa, which the Chamber of Commerce somehow felt entitled to call "The Oil Capital of the World." I recall strange and wonderful tales of Oklahoma-bred independent oilmen, wildcatters who combatted the Saturday-night fidgets by going to the Philtower Building downtown, tossing fifty- and hundred-dollar bills from the rooftop, and, as the bills fluttered to earth, shooting at them with .38-caliber revolvers. These interesting people owned private airplanes, and when they went out for dinner they remembered to bring along their own dance bands. Mini-fleets of limos double-parked for them in front of the Waldorf. When asked, they explained that their riches came from "th' awl bidness." Usually, of course, they went broke; the most legendary among them went broke several times. Perhaps apocryphal, although probably not, these independent oilmen should not be mistaken as representative of an entire industry. There are, in reality, as many breeds of independent oilmen as there are ways to screw up and lose a promising well. The lending standards of the Penn Square Bank were conceived with goodwill toward all Oklahoma-type independent oilmen, although among the subspecies who found their way to the bank were an inordinate number of arrivistes. These "new oilies"—as they were derisively called by the older oilies—did not seem to be interested in geology for geology's sake, did not carefully discriminate among theories of continental drift and collision, basin-and-range formation, plate tectonics, compaction of sediments, magma flows, and all of that. What attracted this fresh blood to the oil business in general and to the Penn Square Bank in particular did not really have much to do with concepts or blueprints for the twenty-first century. As a group, the new oilies tended to be either too young or too little concerned with history to realize that the oil business ran in cycles, subject to the law of gravity. Many of these customers did not know for sure what a balance sheet was, much less what one was supposed to look like. This did not prevent them from developing Exxonish fantasies which starred themselves.

To illustrate a couple of other principles of petroleum finance, I will use the small-potato sums one million and two million, because they're easy to work with. Now, one of the fundamental rules of oil-and-gas banking says that you can borrow more or less half the future value of the oil-and-gas production that you can prove you own. Two million dollars in the ground will get you a million dollars at the bank. To borrow a million dollars, you have to pledge as security "proven reserves"—an inventory of fossil fuel in the ground—with a future worth (discounted for inflation) of two million dollars. Bankers who do oil-and-gas lending are not meant to be artists. The banker's role is supposed to be functional rather than inspirational. The banker tells himself that as long as he sticks to the guidelines set by his bank he has done his job. He is supposed to say "no" until the cushions against risk justify a "yes." The petroleum engineer interprets the reservoir and suggests a range of recoverable hydrocarbons. The banker is supposed to take the engineer's most conservative figures and ask, "Is this oil or gas production? From how many wells does it flow? What are the prices of oil and gas and money today? What will happen to those prices during the term of the loan and beyond?" The banker is supposed to remember to divide by two. The classic, conservative petroleum banker's job is to secure the exits.

There are also what bankers call "negative oil-and-gas lending parameters." Undeveloped leases have no collateral value; drilling rigs and other equipment have virtually no collateral value; even wells that have been drilled and that show oil and gas but do not yet have a history of significant, consistent production—all of these potentially valuable assets were, for collateral purposes, once considered worthless. As the boom of the late 1970s intensified, some banks would refuse to lend to anyone who had been in the oil business less than a decade. Penn Square happened not to be such a bank. Beep Jennings believed that "character" could compensate for missing collateral. Where the asset banker saw only one approach ("You propose the collateral and I decide what it's

worth"), the character banker could conceive of other justifica-
tions for making a loan ("Here's the money. I trust you. I think
you'll pay it back"). Beep Jennings once said, "There are a limited
number of banks in Oklahoma that are willing to aggressively
pursue the oil-and-gas business." The key adverb—aggressively—
implied that the old lending standards, the mandatory as well as
the negative, need not apply in every case. A character banker
could overlook the rules if they didn't fit the situation.

Having a friend like Beep Jennings offered one possible breach of
the common barriers to independent oil-and-gas entrepreneur-
ship. Otherwise, there was a more generally accessible path—an
arrangement known as "third-for-a-quarter." (The term can be
used as a noun, a verb, or an adjective.) Third-for-a-quarter is the
garden variety of syndication that prevails throughout the Oklahoma-type independent oil-and-gas business and beyond. When
you third-for-a-quarter a deal you try to barter your labor for oil-
and-gas production. In the lowest-common-denominator version,
three passive investors share equally the cost of drilling a well.
Each passive investor pays a third of the initial cost, in the hope of
getting back a quarter of the ultimate payoff, and the promoter
hopes to earn the fourth quarter as a reward for his legwork and
prospecting ability. The promoter's share in a third-for-a-quarter is
usually referred to as "a carried interest" or "a free carry." Only the
rare third-for-a-quarter, however, contains these basic ingredients
and no other wrinkles. The specifics of any prospect will dictate its
terms—mineral owners' royalties, back-in arrangements, over-
rides, discounted working-interest shares awarded to drilling contractors, many strains of mumbo jumbo. Most third-for-a-quarters
are said to go only as far as the "casing point"—the point at which
steel pipe is placed in the hole to prepare for a "well completion,"
which enables oil and/or gas to flow from the reservoir to the
surface. An operator or a promoter who has been carried to the
casing point must share the costs of completing the well unless he
has negotiated the right to be "carried all the way" or "carried to
the tanks," which permits an expense-free ride clear to the bank.
    I once heard a successful and candid oilman describe third-for-
a-quarter as "a license to steal," but I told myself that this was a
subjective observation and a fine specimen of cynical hyperbole. I

told the candid oilman what I thought third-for-a-quarter meant: on a well that costs a million dollars, I put up nothing while three other guys each put up a third of a million and— The oilman cut me off, saying, "Yeah, well, that's what it says in the third-grade books, but when you get up in the sixth-grade books it's different." To illustrate his point, he walked me through a rigmarole whose rudiments were that to be successful in the oil exploration business you did not have to turn up live hydrocarbons when you went exploring. You could third-for-a-quarter by raising a million three-three-three and drilling up only a million, and it didn't matter whether you found oil and gas because, with material mark-ups, inflated overhead, and creative cost overruns, you would still make out fine. "A guy who drills third-for-a-quarter figures that if he doesn't get lucky he at least wants to get rich. A lot of these guys lately were excellent promoters but they weren't very good at finding oil and gas. But so what? Completing a well and getting production is nice. But getting rich up front is what this is all about."

When the candid oilman said "these guys lately," I knew that he meant the new oilies. The million-dollar wells that sold for a million three-three-three often had a former recreational vehicle salesman working on the promotional side. In certain heavily explored areas of Oklahoma, the geology was so predictable that you had to go out of your way to get into trouble or to fail to "hit oil." These oilfields were new-oilie magnets. You just needed the right group of investors. Whoever was human and frail and willing and had five thousand dollars to spare would do. Finding a deal was no problem. You could sell it to your friends. You'd just get some money and go drill the damn well. Jerry knew Jim, who knew Larry from church, who used to sell real estate with Ken, who played golf every Sunday with Gary—Ken and Gary didn't go to church, but Gary knew three guys who got together a couple of months back and leased two hundred acres of minerals up in Kingfisher County, and there was an operator there who'd been doing fine drilling some shallow wells and he'd have a rig free in two months. Many new oilies were sincere. It did not matter that the wells they drilled started out looking flashy but six months later dripped like a faucet with a worn-out washer. For a while, it did not matter that the price of oil would probably have to reach seventy dollars a barrel before their deals could make sense. They tended to complete 100 percent of the wells they drilled, never mind what the economics said. They were the gift of the boom, the new oilies. After turning a couple of deals, regardless how much oil and gas materialized, an optimistic new oilie could begin to assume that he was creditworthy. And if he could befriend an uncharacteristically optimistic banker, he would be.

CHAPTER 4

Early believers in the deep potential of the Anadarko Basin—the zones below fifteen thousand feet—grew accustomed to seeing their enthusiasm translated into actual drilling only about once every four or five years. In 1946, in Caddo County, which is one of eleven Oklahoma counties situated above the Basin, Superior Oil drilled a well to 17,823 feet, a world-record depth. Wireline tests revealed the presence of hydrocarbons in a dozen different zones, or strata, but temperature problems made it impossible to complete the well and bring gas to the surface. Throughout the fifties and sixties, several major oil companies were persuaded to participate in deep wells in the region—Conoco in 1953, Gulf in 1957, Conoco again in 1961, Phillips in 1965. The Gulf venture, the Anadarko Basin No. 1, reached a total depth of 21,021 feet, another world record. Before the well could be completed, however, the crew blundered and cemented the drill pipe in the hole. Attempts to salvage the situation led to expensive misery and to repercussions. Major oil companies had supplied good portions of the money to drill these wells, but independents had done the work of identifying the prospects, assembling the acreage, trading the acreage to come up with whatever it took to participate in the wells themselves. Drilling the deepest hole in the world and coming up empty-handed did not make it easier to sell the next deal. Yet, doggedly, the next deal always emerged. In retrospect, every early deep well in the Anadarko seems a necessary precursor of the ones that followed.

In Beckham County, near the heart of the Basin, a well called the No. 1 Green was begun, or "spudded," in late 1967 and was completed a year and a half later. It had distinctions: at 24,454 feet, it was the second-deepest well ever drilled, and it was the first "ultra-deep" producer, four thousand feet deeper than any previous Anadarko producer. If left to flow unchoked, it would yield methane in auspicious quantities—twenty-four million cubic feet a day. Ultimately, the reserves would total at least fifteen billion cubic feet, the equivalent of two and a half million barrels of oil. The only ungratifying thing about the No. 1 Green, really, was that it was an economic calamity. Leasing, surveying, drilling, and completing it had cost six and a half million dollars and its harvest sold for twenty-two cents per thousand cubic feet, which gave it a chance to recover only slightly more than half its cost. The well had been financed in large part by Sun Oil and Amerada Petroleum but it was operated by the GHK Company, a small independent whose managing partner was a thirty-four-year-old geologist named Robert Alexander Hefner III. On the strength, if you could call it that, of the No. 1 Green, Hefner—the H of GHK—emerged as the foremost propagandist for the deep Anadarko. The deep Anadarko Basin had not demonstrated any facility for making friends, nor did its few friends have many friends, nor did its best friend, Robert A. Hefner III, give a damn. Hefner believed in the superior power of his own beliefs. And, in an alarmingly quixotic way, he believed that if you wanted to drill lots of holes five miles deep and deeper you ran the risk of self-destruction, but that self-destruction was perhaps not such a terrible thing if you could manage it with style.

The G and the K of GHK were, respectively, Laurence Glover and David O'D. Kennedy, both of whom lived in New York. Hefner and Glover had met in 1961, in a waiting room outside an office on Park Avenue, where each happened to show up because the gentleman whose office it was had substantial funds and neither of them did. Like Hefner, Glover had substantial personal appeal. He was tall, lean, ruddy, and handsome. Although he was born in Massachusetts, he had lived for several years in England and, as a result, was more often taken for a retired Royal Navy officer than for an oil-and-gas promoter. Glover and an earlier, monied partner, a White Russian émigré named Vadim Makaroff, had participated in the fruitless Anadarko Basin No. 1 in 1957. Five years later—by which time Glover had introduced Hefner to Makaroff, and Makaroff in turn had become friendly with Kennedy, who was the principal owner of Kentile Floors—the four men created a partnership that invested in another Anadarko wildcat well, the Weatherly. The Weatherly was deep and dry. Its investors, however, earned shares in a large block of undeveloped Anadarko leases. Before long, Makaroff died and Kennedy bought the Anadarko mineral interests in his estate. With what now amounted to an inventory of about a hundred thousand acres, GHK was born— a partnership that would levitate for years on Kennedy's sound credit, Glover's impeccable manners and deadly skill as a pigeon-stalker, and, above all, Hefner's evangelism in the name of the deep Anadarko Basin.

Robert A. Hefner III was a splendid study in self-study, a fully realized persona. In Oklahoma, if you were going to attempt certain stunts it helped enormously to be a Hefner—a genus that, locally, passed for royalty. Hefner's grandfather, the original Robert A. Hefner, consistently delivered himself to the right place at the right time: to Beaumont, Texas, in 1903, on the heels of the blowout of the Spindletop well, which ignited the East Texas oil bonanza; to Ardmore, Oklahoma, soon after statehood, where he established an oil-and-gas law practice that benefited from the opening of the great Healdton Field; to Oklahoma City in the late twenties, just a year before the Oklahoma City No. 1 came in.

A biography of the family founder, titled *The Judge*—he served a term as a justice of the Oklahoma Supreme Court, though his friends had called him "Judge" long before he became one—was issued some years ago by the Oklahoma Heritage Association, which is housed today in the Hefner family manse, in Oklahoma City. According to this book, Judge Hefner narrowly escaped penury early in his legal career when, in reckless self-sacrifice, he undertook a contingent-fee case on behalf of four Choctaw families who felt that they had been deprived of their tribal land allotments; although the Judge won the case, his clients turned out to be ingrates. He bounced back and went on to write the seminal state property laws pertaining to the sale of minerals.

Reading *The Judge*, one learns that by the time the protagonist began his Supreme Court term, in 1927, he owned almost fifty thousand acres of surface and minerals, mainly in southern Oklahoma. After retiring from the court, he served two terms as mayor of Oklahoma City and more than dabbled in the law, the oil business, and real estate. Along the way, he made only one dumb mistake. That happened in 1934, when he sold to an oil operator from New York City the "deep" rights to all his minerals in Carter County. Everything below four thousand feet he gave up for ten dollars an acre. Drilling below four thousand feet in southern Oklahoma was unthinkable because the Judge had not yet lived long enough to know better. His biographer notes that the Hefner Company, which he founded, never went outside its own treasury to come up with operating capital. When the eldest of the Judge's children, Robert Jr., semi-retired a few years ago, he gave a newspaper interview that included this quotation: "There is one thing I'm proud of. I have never borrowed one cent and never had a promoted dollar in my business. I have always dealt on what I have. But things are different in the oilfield now."

After Judge Hefner, no one had trouble remembering the family name. In Oklahoma City it was attached to a water reservoir, a park, a junior high school, a nursing home, a baseball field, street signs. Judge Hefner died in 1971, at the age of ninety-six. He lived long enough to witness his grandson's effort to take the family legend a lot deeper than four thousand feet. The grandson, to get there, was willing to borrow or promote whatever dollars happened to be available.

When Robert A. Hefner III was born, in 1935, his parents lived in Washington, D.C. Still *in utero*, he attended a dinner party at the White House the evening of his birth. As a child he was called Bobby, and he has never quite outgrown the name: business associates call him Bob or Robert; his detractors complain about Bobby Hefner this and Bobby Hefner that. His monogram— stitched in blue on his French cuffs, stitched in gold on the insteps of his velvet formal pumps, embossed in silver on the matchbooks in his home—contains no initials, just a III. When Bobby Hefner was very young, his parents divorced and his mother settled in California. He did his growing up in Beverly Hills and did not arrive in Oklahoma to stay until he was a freshman at the University of Oklahoma. He earned a bachelor's degree in geology and in the process took a course in stratigraphy that influenced all his future thinking.

The professor who taught stratigraphy enabled Hefner later to understand continental drift and plate tectonics, the crustal shifts that might in theory have deposited thick layers of hydrocarbon-saturated sediments deep in the Anadarko Basin. This theory appealed to Hefner even more as he became convinced that methane would soon sell for sixty cents per thousand cubic feet. Sixty cents was four or five multiples of its price at the time. Years later, when a journalist printed and others repeated that while at the university Hefner had written a "thesis" on the potential of the deep Anadarko, he made no effort to correct this statement. Hefner's "thesis" did not exist on paper. It was a portable postulatum that went wherever he went, a proposition that he unspooled for any willing audience, exposing it, refining it, believing it more and more intensely.

If deep gas exploration had made economic sense as early as the 1960s, Hefner's devotion to the Basin would have been unremarkable; he would have been forced to line up behind the major oil companies, along with all the other independent promoters. Nature had behaved capriciously where deep Anadarko zones had been tested, but the *existence* of deep gas in western Oklahoma should have been neither debatable nor mysterious. Unreconstructed oilmen and government bureaucrats had the most difficulty accepting the idea that the gas was there. One easy way to offend Hefner was to refer to him as an oilman; crude-oil production shared a future with whaling. Natural gas—methane, a carbon atom bound to four hydrogen atoms—was the ticket. Hefner preached energy self-sufficiency through the divine gift of methane. He would pound the tabletop and say, "I learned early on that I couldn't talk to my father and my grandfather, because I had knowledge that they didn't have, that they couldn't see. They were *oil*men. Oil and gas are distinct in every way—geologically, technologically, politically." Nurturing the Anadarko Basin's full mythical potential was to become his greatest accomplishment. Manipulation could make real its economic potential. The myth that deep gas did not exist Hefner combatted with the myth that the Anadarko Basin held the key to the salvation of the planet.

Hefner was hard to resist. He had Apollonian good looks. His suits and shirts came from Savile Row, his neckties from Hermès. His coloring was Nordic and his facial features seemed a cross between Native American and Leading Man. Part of him was a grim, drawn, clench-mouthed philosopher and part was a voluble, exuberant salesman. He had a straight nose that flattened across the bridge, a broad, strong jaw, thin lips, and a vast number of teeth, which made his turn-on smile—high-wattage, complete with dimples and often a hollow laugh—startling. Hefner's gray-blue eyes, full of intelligence, could widen and sparkle and obtrude and then quickly retract and focus upon something inward or distant. When windblown, his long, fine, finger-combed blond hair looked just right. His skin looked as if he never needed to shave. To burnish the myth, he perfected his social skills. He sailed in the Caribbean and off Newport in his yacht, the *Anadarko*, summered and wintered in Aspen, went to the races at Churchill Downs and Ascot, hunted grouse with the Duke and Duchess of Marlborough, squired actresses and heiresses, collected ink in the New York society columns, and graciously assumed the burdens of being Oklahoma's contribution to the fast track. He was acquainted with everyone everywhere. Frequently, after a digression, the floor was littered with names.

To get at the reality of Hefner—to sort out the distractions and understand that *your* money was needed to underwrite *his* ambition, because, appearances notwithstanding, he was usually, you see, *broke*—you first had to penetrate the verbal agility and the luminous persona. Geologist-as-artist-hero was the identity that he had selected. After college, he spent a year in Phillips Petroleum's training program. He learned more geology and he learned about seismic contouring and well-site economics. Some time spent in Phillips' economic analysis section convinced him that "no one there cared about gas; their economic analyses were entirely based upon the wellhead price of oil." He left Phillips. For six months he was employed by the Hefner Company, the firm that his grandfather founded. When he left there, in 1959, he was twenty-four, a divorced father with custody of a girl and two boys (including a Robert A. Hefner IV). His stated intention was to become a consulting geologist. His father gave him a microscope and lent him thirty thousand dollars. The money went to buy leases in the Anadarko Basin.

During the sixties and early seventies, Hefner was able to lease mineral rights by paying bonuses of between ten and twenty-five dollars an acre, the object being to farm them out—to persuade capable exploration companies to drill on those leases and to carry GHK for a free ride. The world around Hefner had trouble figuring out whether he was ahead of his time or just pathological in a diverting way. He seemed free of self-doubt. He remarried, his second wife being a wealthy woman whose father warned her against exposing her inheritance to Hefner's majestic vision. (The marriage lasted twelve years.) Once, he sold a car to pay a grocery bill. Other bills he managed to ignore. But if his faith waned, he failed to show it. A banker who chose not to do business with Hefner remembers visits from him when he was trying to raise money to drill the No. 1 Green. "His eyes were on fire," the banker said. "He always struck me as one of those guys just on the line between insane and brilliant. I didn't lend him money because of his reputation. He'd never *made* any money. He was always drilling with *other* people's money. He was talking about producing deep gas when gas was selling for fifteen cents. I didn't care how many trillion feet of gas there were in the deep Anadarko, you weren't going to make money at that price. Everyone thought he was a fool. He was delinquent in paying his dues at the country club. I don't know how he got away with it as long as he did. Maybe he knew that you had to have some deep gas first, to prove it was there. So he drilled the No. 1 Green. It was *uneconomical*, period. It was other people's money. He was trying to prove the gas was there and he was dead right. But *then* what?"

The Penn Square Bank first lent money to Hefner in 1977. Beep Jennings remembers the amount as three hundred thousand dollars. When he was asked not long ago to describe the state of Hefner's financial affairs at the time of the loan, he said, "They were strained." Tact is one of Jennings' many virtues: the loan officer to whom Jennings delegated Hefner's account recalls looking at a financial statement and concluding that "the guy's company was broke to the tune of twelve million dollars." Jennings had enough banking experience to be broad-minded. Insolvency was just one of those things that could befall a busy man. When Jennings had been an officer of the Fidelity Bank, the Kerr-McGee bank downtown, the president was a friendly man named Grady Harris. Speaking of Hefner, Harris once said to Jennings, "He'll be the wealthiest oil-and-gas producer in Oklahoma or he'll be broke."

Around that time, Harris lent Hefner money. Somewhat later, Harris was forced to dislodge Hefner from his office in the Fidelity Bank building. (The matter concerned nonpayment of several months' rent, and Harris did not do the actual dislodging. He gave that job to Jennings.) By the time Hefner went to Jennings at Penn Square and asked for a loan, he had forgiven and forgotten. Evidently, he did not hold the dislodging against Jennings any more than he held it against him that Jennings had a mere money-making concept while he, Hefner, had a blueprint for saving the universe. Hefner ascendant was exactly the sort of risk that Jennings loved to bank.

Encouraged by Hefner, Jennings expanded and clarified his thoughts about energy lending and merchant banking. Intelligent opinion had it that fifteen trillion cubic feet of natural gas was trapped within the Anadarko Basin. And what if the true figure was two hundred trillion? Hefner could imagine that as well. Deftly, Hefner coaxed Jennings, delivering in installments a message that added up to this: Penn Square, as merchant bank, was in a position to do more than simply lend money and sell loans. Trillions of cubic feet of gas meant billions of dollars. Jennings should push his concept as far as possible. He should go to London, Paris—get to know the right people at Barclays, Westminster, Paribas. The American banking and energy exploration businesses were on the brink of deregulation, the world economy was in need of regeneration. With methane, a plentiful source of clean, safe energy, the world would sail into the twenty-first century. Hefner told Jennings to think of Oklahoma City as Athens. A dazzling opportunity—and a vacuum—existed. Once the architecture of the dream had been drafted, the billions of dollars would rush into the vacuum.

You would need real architecture, of course, a real edifice, and they discussed that, too. According to the Jennings–Hefner view of reality, the PennBank Tower would become the locus of methane financing in this solar system until at least the mid-twenty-first century. Eventually, along with some other partners, they started building it—a twenty-two-story box the color of fired red clay, sheathed in amber glass, with a crown of angled trapezoids, planted in a V-shaped gap between Route 66 and a suburban expressway, a stone's throw and a half from the Penn Square shopping center. GHK and the Penn Square Bank would become the main tenants. (GHK intended to occupy eight floors, and would presumably never be threatened with eviction.) What Jennings and Hefner could not foresee was that the PennBank Tower would near completion just as the bank failed. The tower was destined to become more memorable as artifact than as architecture. Only after I had driven past it several times a week for several months did I notice that there was a McDonald's next door. The McDonald's forced me to regard the tower more sympathetically; at least they had tried. It might have worked in another context. In that part of Oklahoma City, regrettably, it had a stranded look, like a temporarily grounded interplanetary vehicle, an expensive metaphor. It was out of place, the way the Penn Square Bank began to be out of place when Jennings decided that it no longer had to be just a little shopping-center bank. While the blueprints were still being drafted, however, only bright hopes seemed called for. The Penn Square Bank, steeped in expertise, more knowledgeable about the geology of the Anadarko Basin than any other financial institution, would funnel the capital that would make dreams real. Getting the gas out of the ground presented some logistical challenges, but if you could do that Oklahoma City could become, if not Athens, perhaps a dry-land Strait of Hormuz, a conduit through which things of great value must flow.

Jennings and Hefner, grandiloquent optimist and Olympian believer—did Jennings believe two hundred trillion cubic feet? "I heard numbers," Jennings has recalled. "I believed that if they were one-quarter what Bob Hefner said, once the economics were in place the possibilities were tremendous. I accepted his concept of the Anadarko Basin. I thought he was the most visionary oilman I'd ever met, and I've met a lot. I liked his style. Bob Hefner discussed with me more than anybody else the potential of the Anadarko Basin, and I considered him the foremost developer of the Anadarko Basin. And I sat through presentations by him and his personnel during which they outlined their estimates of the potential of the Basin. Let's say that I was highly motivated by Bob Hefner's opinion." That sufficed. Hefner needed Jennings to be motivated. Whether Jennings had great depth, whether he truly believed what Hefner told him, did not matter. Jennings was the first banker who had ever paid sustained attention. That mattered. Already, Hefner had leased a hundred and seventy thousand acres in the Basin, and now that the price of energy was moving up there was every reason to lease as much as possible. "You furnish the ship, I'll furnish the ocean" was the promise of the proverbial promoter. If Jennings could find the money, Hefner could find the gas. The gas, after all, was there.

CHAPTER 5

ellhead, a magazine that would be easier to find on a newsstand if publication had not ceased a few years ago, published an article in the October 1981 issue that began this way:

> Most often a man is measured by his achievements. Occasionally a man is measured by his achievements and his intrinsic nature. That part of a man that cannot be found in a biographical sketch, résumé or bank account, but which is more the man than any or all of his accomplishments. When a man measures up in both categories, he is unique. He is what America is about.

When I first read that, my thought was that it was not quite as strong a beginning as, say, "Stately, plump Buck Mulligan..." but that it might nevertheless grow up to be a contender. I read on and on—and in the process learned about J. D. Allen, "one of those special men who are the foundation on which this great country thrives." J. D. Allen was "more than words on a page that list his many accomplishments; more than the sum total of the worth of the companies he operates; more than the balance at the bank. He is unique." J. D. Allen was "a successful businessman, measured by his achievements over the last twenty years . . . a man that will listen to the new idea that presents a unique opportunity in the world of business . . . will always recognize the imminent importance of people." J. D. Allen was "the core of humanity, the crux of the American way of life."

In measuring J. D. Allen's achievements over the last twenty years, the editors of *Wellhead* had totted up everything he had accomplished since age fourteen. That was no minor accomplishment in itself, for Allen was a person who frequently came up with the new angle, the bold innovation. Allen grew up in Ringling, the only town in southern Oklahoma named after a circus. Ringling was only seven miles from Healdton, where the Jennings family owned the bank. Allen's father had taught at Ringling High School, where he supervised the Future Farmers of America chapter, and had later acquired an interest in a feed store and an automobile dealership. And he knew Beep Jennings—not well, but well enough.

There was a time in Allen's life when he decided that he wanted to become J. D.—that he no longer cared to answer to his given name, which was Jerry Dale. Years later, when certain people who had known him in Ringling or at the University of Oklahoma heard about J. D. Allen or read in the newspapers about J. D. Allen, they would not immediately grasp that J. D. Allen and Jerry Dale Allen were the same person. Not until he became J. D. did he grow a Clark Gable mustache and start wearing his dark hair in a wavy pouf. When he became J. D., his dimpled face grew rounder and his physique filled out to light-heavyweight dimensions. Many of the brothers in Sigma Alpha Epsilon, Jerry Dale's college fraternity, had called him "Ringling." A Sig Alph once told me, "Ringling was his main nickname. In pledge class, they'd call him terrible names and it wouldn't even faze him. You know how they do it to everybody. After about a minute of it, Jerry Dale would have this silly grin on his face. Like it wasn't happening to him. Either it didn't bother him or he didn't understand what was going on."

Allen's fraternity brothers underestimated him. Very few saw that he had the natural ability to become the core of humanity, co-chairman of the finance committee of the Republican National Committee, and a friend of Wayne Newton, a couple of Presidents of the United States, and other significant public figures. Allen himself had no serious doubts about his talents. He once reflected, "Success and money just come naturally to me." A former business associate of his has said, "Numbers never intimidated him. You know how a lot of smart people are intimidated by their own capabilities? Well, J. D. never had that problem." Anyone who neglected to predict that big things would happen to Jerry Dale

Allen had simply not been paying attention. During college Jerry Dale and a partner sold industrial-strength floor wax, wax stripper, and all-purpose cleaner along fraternity row; ran a business called Party Pics, which specialized in taking candid photographs of happy couples at fraternity and sorority parties; and maintained a franchise of several vending and pinball machines. "Pinball," Allen once said to me, puffing cigar smoke in a pensive way. "That's where the money was."

The autobiography that J. D. Allen enjoyed reciting had an early chapter in Burkburnett, Texas, in 1961, when he was fourteen years old. He had roughnecked and hauled hay in southern Oklahoma and northern Texas. Not far from Burkburnett he noticed a ridge where several oil wells had been drilled. In the gully below the ridge there were no wells. Talking to the old-timers at the coffee shop in town, he learned that the existing wells had been drilled by steam-driven rigs and that the gully had been dammed to create a water reservoir for the boilers. So Allen leased the gully, found some partners who had money, and drilled three shallow wells, all productive. By the time he finished high school, according to the autobiography, he was making more money than his parents.

Not that Allen's career became a series of unalloyed successes. There was the low moment, for example, when he was eighteen years old and the Old Red River flooded. Water seeped into and ruined a couple of wells that had already been completed. Allen was forced to sell the lease, and he still did not have enough to pay his bills. He went to see a banker in Ryan, Oklahoma, and was told that, as a minor, he was not legally responsible for his debts and therefore had nothing to worry about. "He told me I could just forget about it," Allen said. "I told him, 'I don't live that way.' He says, 'I guess if you'll pay them other guys back you'll pay me.'" Whereupon the banker lent Allen the money he needed. To quote *Wellhead*, "J. D.'s credo for doing business: 'A man's word is his honor and without that you don't have anything.'"

During his senior year of college, Allen signed up for on-campus job interviews with recruiters from several oil companies. "At the end of the interview they'd always ask you how high you wanted to go with them," Allen has recalled. "One time, a guy asked me, 'How high do you think you want to go with this company?' and I said, 'I plan to own it.' Matter of fact, I told the guy from Mobil I planned to be chairman of the board. He said, 'Do you think there's a chance you could ever become president of Mobil?' I said, 'Nope. Chairman of the board.' "

For four years, Allen worked for Mobil, in the land management, exploration, and production departments, based in the company's offices in Houston and Corpus Christi, Texas. In 1974, by which time he had not quite completed his ascent to the boardroom, he went into business for himself. He had been married and divorced, he owned a new Oldsmobile Cutlass (burgundy with a white interior), and he was about to become chairman and chief executive officer of a company called L-X Exploration. "I remembered how Exxon said they chose that name for themselves because they found out 'x' was the most remembered letter in the alphabet," Allen told me, describing the strategic planning that preceded the founding of L-X Exploration. "So I started with the 'x' and just went through the alphabet—A, B, C, D, E—till I hit a letter that sounded good with 'x'. That was it. L-X."

The trunk of the burgundy Cutlass became the L-X Exploration main office and the white interior became Jerry Dale Allen's home. L-X specialized in lease and royalty trading in several southern and western Texas counties. Exploration companies always lease more acreage than they can drill themselves, so they "farm it out." For a negotiated price or some future consideration—it all depends on the attractiveness of the prospect—they assign a "farmout," or leasehold, to a broker or another operator. The broker or operator who obtains the farmout is thereby making a commitment that a well will be drilled within a prescribed period of time. Buying and trading farmouts, which was to become one of Allen's subspecialties, is a form of betting on the come, and if you cannot unload the merchandise it becomes risky. A busy lease broker might end up doing a lot of sleeping in cars, although one does not necessarily have to end up domiciled in a car. Sleeping in the Cutlass did not damage Allen's Okiesmo but it did give him backaches. He traded for a baby-blue Cadillac, which was roomier and more comfortable. His address was "Box JDA, Ringling, Oklahoma." Sometimes he slept in Midland or Dallas. "I was just doing deals," he said. "I've always liked women. I really like women. If you're in the oil business, who do you date? Oil company secretaries. I'd get them to do my typing when I needed it."

FUNNY MONEY

One day during the summer of 1976, Allen and Beep Jennings both happened to attend a wedding in Dallas. They chatted about business, and Jennings came away impressed by Allen's account of how much he had been hustling and how well he was doing. Jennings said, more or less, "I own the Penn Square Bank in Oklahoma City now. Next time you're up there, come on by." The fact was that Allen had already dropped by the Penn Square Bank and had arranged a modest loan—less than thirty thousand dollars—secured by some leases and oil-and-gas production. Encouraged by Jennings, he returned a few weeks later, intending to borrow more. This time, he made the mistake of subjecting himself to the scrutiny of a loan officer who did not realize that Ringling was only seven miles from Healdton. Allen wanted sixty thousand dollars to buy some leases. When the loan officer took a look at the collateral that he had to offer—leases, oil-and-gas, and accounts receivable—his response was that securing the collateral might take some time. Because Allen felt that he had no time to spare, and because he had been led to assume that borrowing money at Penn Square would not lead to an invasion of his privacy, he went directly to the chairman of the board. Very soon thereafter, Jennings extended to Allen a hundred-thousand-dollar line of credit for lease purchases.

Within a few months, Jerry Dale had paid back the hundred thousand. Next he borrowed two hundred thousand dollars to pick up some acreage in southern Texas. Unexpectedly, he encountered obstacles when he tried to resell the leases. What another banker might have regarded as a potential problem loan, Jennings regarded as an opportunity. In Allen, he saw someone who, as he later described him, had "unique instant conceptual abilities"—a mover who, you might say, could transport himself from A to C without passing through B. It occurred to Jennings that with a more stable home address, a telephone, an office unencumbered by a spare tire, adequate financing, and a bit of guidance, Allen could cover great distances in effortless leaps. It occurred to Beep Jennings to introduce his new friend Jerry Dale Allen to his old friend Carl Swan.

Carl Swan was more beloved than Beep Jennings. Nice as Jennings was, compared to Carl Swan he came off tougher than beef jerky. Simply by being associated with Jennings, Swan did him a big favor: he made Jennings seem almost coldly ruthless, and thus enhanced his reputation as a banker. What a thoughtful way to give a pal a boost! Everybody in the oil business knew Carl Swan and everybody like him. A drilling contractor who was a friend of both Swan and Jennings said, "You could play poker over the telephone with either one of those guys." Swan loved horses and fermented grains, he was nice to ladies, and he was honest—as in "Carl Swan's basically an honest person, you know," or "Carl's reasonably honest," encomiums that happen to be the two most exalting character references in the Kingdom of Okiesmo. There were all those young honchos Carl Swan boosted when they were just getting started. There were cocktail waitresses and account-ants, lounge hounds and you-name-its out there, and Swan had gone to bat for a bunch of them. He had guaranteed their loans, he had invested in their enterprises, he *believed* in people. His reward was a world of loyal affection. A chronic cosigner is what Swan was. If you asked all the people who admired Swan whether he had any bad habits, they would mention one: he was too easy a touch.

Carl Swan had made some money. In 1964, after spending almost two decades working for other people—as field hand, floorman, roughneck, derrick man, mud engineer, and mud sales-man—Swan set out on his own. Along with two partners, he formed a company called Basin Drilling. The principal asset was a ten-thousand-foot-capacity drilling rig, which Swan had bought for $35,000 after mortgaging his house. A couple of years later, assisted by some established oilmen from Tulsa and Odessa, Texas, Swan and his partners merged with a small shell company and created a new enterprise, called Basin Petroleum. During the next several years, Basin focused much of its activity on an area of north-central Oklahoma known as the Sooner Trend. "Anyone who drilled in the Sooner Trend and used a little judgment did pretty well," Swan later said. "We did well." In the process, Swan was becoming asset-rich. He owned 30 percent of Basin Petrole-um's stock, and, in 1976, when Basin was bought by Reserve Oil & Gas, a large California independent oil company, his in-the-ground assets became liquid assets. Swan's share of the sale proceeds was ten million dollars. Reserve Oil & Gas was itself subsequently taken over by Getty Oil, which in turn got bought by Texaco, in

1984, for ten billion one hundred million dollars. In retrospect, Swan's ten million dollars does not stack up as a bottomless fortune, but it happened to be ten million dollars more than he had in the bank when Basin Drilling was born. A story went round that one of the other Basin partners, when asked what Swan intended to do with his new money, replied, "Well, Carl might like to make a billion dollars."

A good friend of Swan's has said, "Carl's the most likable guy in the world. If you like cigars." By chance or by design, photographs of Swan rarely showed him without a cigar—a long one. A cigar nicely complemented the rest of him. He had a sturdy member-of-the-posse physique, dark-reddish-brown hair, a walrus mustache, long sideburns, corn-fed cheeks—stolidity and no pretense. Ostentation was foreign to Swan. What you saw was what there was—except for the money. You did not see that on the surface because Swan lived true to the heartland etiquette which ordained that, watching two men walk down the street, you should not be able to tell whose pockets were deeper. When Swan and his friends spent long evenings at Junior's—an Oklahoma City restaurant that during Penn Square's happiest hours became the sanctum sanctorum of new-oilie-ism—they did not debate at length who among them had the most piercing intellect. A perfect conversation starter or stopper was "He's a great oil finder." Swan's admirers knew that he had gravitated from the source of all Okiesmo—the side of the oil business where you physically got dirty. His years of toil as roughneck and mudman conferred dignity on his fresh wealth. Although he had been born in Missouri and had lived in Kansas and New Mexico, the Oklahoma oilies saw him as a hometown hero. Drilling all those fine Sooner Trend producers in the 1960s and 1970s had ennobled him. The backing that Swan had received from his friends in Tulsa and Odessa when he formed Basin Petroleum made a permanent impression, made him ripe for the easy touch.

One of the first people to join the board of the Penn Square Bank after Jennings bought it was Swan. That was in 1976, a year in which Swan's financial statement began to make him resemble a one-man conglomerate. A new independent oil-and-gas exploration company, Swan Petroleum, was formed that year, as were several other ventures that could not help making money once they had, say, a Carl Swan cosigning in the background. Swan demonstrated his optimism by investing in real estate, restaurants, coal, cattle, silver, gypsum, office buildings, electronics, a travel agency, a commuter airline, a nightclub. He owned a big horse farm south of Oklahoma City, and his horses raced at tracks all around the Southwest. "Carl's philosophy was: If I have enough going on, something's going to work out," a friend said. "He'll give people the benefit of the doubt every single time. I don't think Carl ever purposely got into a deal that he knew was rotten."

When Beep Jennings brought together Carl Swan and J. D. Allen, J. D. had a hundred thousand acres of leases in southern Texas and no money to drill them up. Swan had some underutilized space in his office. Jennings did not need to propose anything specific; Carl and J. D. could figure out a way to fill in the blanks.

"Why J. D. Allen?" Jennings was asked later.

"I thought he was one hell of an oil finder," Jennings replied. "I was not thinking of what J. D. could do for Carl; it was what Carl could do for J. D."

Old oilies would ask, "Who the hell is J. D. Allen?" The answer was: J. D. Allen is a friend of Carl Swan. Jennings could see that Allen was not a stopper and pauser and weigher of relative equities. Allen had just enough Ringling in him to say, "Now, Carl 'n' me is gonna *drill* these wells, see. So you wan' in or you wan' out?" The significant phrase was "Carl 'n' me." Allen was ready to roll; he just needed a Carl Swan on his letterhead. With a nudge in the proper direction, J. D. Allen stood a chance of becoming highly bankable.

CHAPTER 6

To hatch and execute a successful disaster demands a sustained level of competence and dependability that is, by definition, unavailable to an average group of would-be conspirators. That is why calculated calamities are rare achievements and why, no matter what many of us often insist on believing, thieving conspiracies can almost never be built to last. Coincidence, meanwhile—four vehicles without headlights, all traveling at different speeds, converging on an unmarked intersection at dusk—gets less credit than it deserves. Entropy, random natural chaos, innate stupidity—all are important sources and forces of destruction, and all are quite underrated.

Monstrously funny consequences grew out of the fear of OPEC. By the standards of American antitrust law, which happened not to apply in this case, the OPEC cartel fitted the description of an open-and-shut price-fixing conspiracy. The fixers did not even have the decency to operate in secrecy, and look what they could get away with. The cartel's brazenness became one of its most threatening weapons. *Morality* was offended; in the spring of 1977, the President of the United States said so, in a memorable speech. Jimmy Carter raised the specter of "national catastrophe." He said that the sacrifices demanded by the "energy crisis" called for "the moral equivalent of war." A barrel of OPEC oil then cost thirteen dollars, ten dollars more than it had before 1973 but only about a third of the level it would reach in 1981. The boldest visionaries believed that forty-dollar-a-barrel crude was not the potential problem. Eighty- or ninety-dollar oil by 1990, or whatever the cartel desired—that was the problem. In 1977, the

United States spent forty-five billion dollars to import oil. It seemed at the time that if inertia ruled and consumption and prices kept escalating, by 1985 the figure would be five hundred fifty billion. (As things have turned out, of course, the volume of imports has come to far less than that—at least five hundred billion dollars less.)

The President made more speeches. He spoke, on the one hand, of the imperative to conserve, to plan ahead, to reduce. Then, to mitigate his heresy against the godliness of bigness, the President declared, on the other hand, that Americans had to discover more oil. When the oil-and-gas producers heard this, they said that more exploration demanded greater incentives. You would need, first, to eliminate the price regulations that allowed American producers to receive only two thirds of what OPEC received for a barrel of oil. To achieve this patriotic payoff you needed virtually endless lines of credit. You needed bankers.

I once heard a bankruptcy lawyer declaim, "See, bankers got into the oil business late. Bankers are always several years behind the rest of the planet." I regarded this as misinformed class bigotry because it implied that bankers are universally naïve and vulnerable when in fact many have the potential to be as imaginative and exploitative as any bankruptcy lawyer. After 1973, alert bankers sensed that the standards for oil-and-gas lending could use some modification. Radical changes in the system were not called for, but as oil prices evolved, bankers, to be competitive, had to permit lending standards to evolve as well. Simultaneously, other new banking strategies were evolving, including one that called for a colossal quantity of money to be shipped abroad. By the end of 1982, the Chase Manhattan Bank had lent one billion seven hundred million dollars to Mexico; almost two and a half billion to Brazil; a billion to Venezuela; another billion to Argentina, Yugoslavia, and Chile combined. Those loans represented 220 percent of Chase's equity. Chase was hardly alone. The ten largest banks in the United States had risked more than one-and-a-half times the value of their equity in loans to less-developed countries; if two thirds of the loans became losses, all the banks would break. Familiar headlines seemed interchangeable: "Poland, Banks to Resume Talks on Debt Accord," "Volcker Meets with Creditors on Brazil Debt," "Argentina Nears Showdown with Bankers," "Peru Refinancing Pact Signed," "Bankers to Meet on Management of

Morocco Debt." Whether or not the leaders of Poland, Brazil, Argentina, Peru, Morocco, and many other countries regarded those debts seriously, the bankers certainly did. Several years before the problem of foreign loans became dinner-table conversation, bankers knew that they had overcommitted themselves.

But the banks, because they were overloaded with deposits, had to lend the money to *someone*. Where did the deposits come from? From the very people who had jacked up the price of oil. You could think of it as a vicious circle or as a grotesque global joke. The money that the biggest banks lent to developing countries was the same money that the world was paying to the OPEC countries. With the exception of a few borrowers, such as Mexico and Venezuela, who happened to be oil producers, the borrowers needed the loans to cover deficits that existed because they were spending so much to import oil. The excessive bank deposits were the fabled "petrodollars," and bankers knew that they had to keep them in motion, they had to keep pushing the stuff out the door. A prime crime in banking is idle money. (Losing it is the ultimate crime, but stuffing it inside a mattress comes next.)

By the early 1980s, when it began to dawn upon the banks that they had overlent to developing countries, they were well aware that other lending markets were no longer as available as they had once been. Large corporations that had once depended heavily on banks for financing had begun during the late 1970s to raise operating funds by issuing their own commercial paper. In frustration, the bankers watched as their best customers learned self-sufficiency. The pressure on the banks was made greater by the need to recover losses they had suffered as a result of the recession of the mid-1970s—a recession that could be attributed, in part, to the cost of energy. American bankers' problems worsened when they were forced to compete with European banks, which were relatively free of regulation and were now pursuing the traditional customers of the American banks. After these foreign lenders found borrowers at the *Fortune* 500 level, they explored the next level down. The competition for new business continued until some big American banks were forced to discover the independent oil-and-gas business. Here were thousands of companies that had a terrific appetite for investment capital but lacked the heft and the credit rating to sell a debt issue or commercial paper to the general public. Oklahoma was just another underdeveloped country. The independent oil-and-gas business was said to be "interest-rate inelastic." Whatever the freight might cost, the oilies would pay it, because as long as energy prices kept rising, who could lose?

So the "energy crisis," with its mixed consequences, offered at least one complex element of an incipient coincidence. Here's another:

Just as OPEC was becoming the scourge of America, as the pool of petrodollars deepened, the management of the Continental Illinois National Bank & Trust Company, of Chicago, decided that becoming America's supreme commercial lender was a worthwhile idea. Roger Anderson, a career employee who had been named chairman of Continental Illinois in 1973, announced in 1976 his wish that within five years the bank would lend enough money to rank it in the uppermost tier, along with Citibank and the Bank of America. Anderson's bank was, as they say in the boardroom, nicely positioned to pursue this ambition. Continental Illinois enjoyed a reputation as one of the most efficiently managed, prudent, and secure banks in the world. The archetypal Continental banker was a midwestern Catholic who rode the commuter train home each night to one of the leafy northern or western Chicago suburbs—wonderful places to raise families. The bank was a sound, trustworthy institution that reasonably rewarded diligent labor.

In 1976, Continental was the eighth-largest bank holding company in the country, with more than twenty billion dollars in assets. Although it was hardly starting from scratch, aggressiveness would be needed to execute the chairman's plan. Aggressive commercial lending had not always been the Continental Illinois style. Walter Cummings, who ran the bank for a quarter of a century, from the Depression through the fifties, believed that the only good loan was one that had been repaid. During his rule, a high proportion of Continental's funds was invested in government bonds. Growth then held a lower priority than sober hegemony. The Roger Anderson manifesto seemed at once tantalizing and puzzling, like an epidemic of concupiscence in a retirement community; it was plausible, but what would it prove and what would it cost?

Continental Illinois's headquarters occupies a square block at the base of La Salle Street, in the Loop, opposite the Federal Reserve Bank branch and catercorner to the Chicago Board of Trade. Immense fluted Ionic pillars flank the entrance to the main building, a twenty-three-story granite-and-limestone structure that went up in 1924. Next door, accessible by an aerial walkway, is the Rookery Building, a much older, weathered, soot-covered structure, where certain of Continental's retail banking functions are performed. One of the Rookery Building's architects, Daniel Burnham, once uttered this credo: "Make big plans. . . . A noble logical diagram once recorded will never die." The banking floor inside the main building is among the grandest in the world. It contains dozens more immense pillars, of Italian marble. The ceiling, fifty feet high, has an apron of brightly illuminated frescoes, offset by apothegms dedicated to the theme of international commerce. The architecture successfully conveys the desired impression. Between 1977 and 1981, when Continental's assets were, according to plan, swelling—from twenty-three billion to forty-five billion dollars—a consensus existed among bankers, particularly among bankers who operated west of the coastline of New Jersey: whatever Continental Illinois does, it won't be messy and it will probably make money. In the Midwest, Continental's preeminence was a given. If Continental is involved, other bankers could assure themselves, it must be right.

Of the thirteen thousand people who worked for the bank, some twelve hundred had lending authority. Continental Illinois lent money to International Harvester and Standard Oil of Indiana, and it lent to Sears, Roebuck and Company, Marshall Field & Company, and the Quaker Oats Company. The bureaucracy of lending divided potential customers among six major departments, each of which was organized into smaller domains— groups, divisions, sections, teams, and so forth. An oil-and-gas account officer assigned to Oklahoma would, in theory, report to a vice-president in the midcontinent energy lending section who would himself answer to a senior vice-president in the oil-and-gas and mining group, which was part of the special industries department, the executive vice-president in charge of which reported to the executive vice-president in charge of all commercial lending, who, presumably, had access to the president and the chairman of the board. And vice versa. The employees of Continental Illinois understood that the bold new strategy—"Book loans, sell money"—flowed explicitly from the top.

Distinction as an energy lender was something that Continental had enjoyed since the mid-1950s, when it had begun to emerge as *the* coal bank in America. An effort to lend to the independent oil-and-gas industry got underway at that time, but it was conducted mainly by long distance, which meant that to be bankable you had to be more or less visible from Chicago. The operator who needed a few hundred thousand dollars to participate in some shallow gas wells in southwestern Louisiana did not fit the borrower profile that Continental then had in mind. In 1975, the bank opened a loan production office in Houston, and four years later it opened another, in Denver. The Continental Illinois money salesman who was assigned to Oklahoma at that time was expected to call on Phillips Petroleum, Cities Service, Kerr-McGee—giant Oklahoma-based oil companies—and to look for independents to whom he might be able to lend a million dollars or more. Everything west of the Mississippi except Texas, Colorado, and California belonged to this single loan officer's territory. Only Oklahoma showed growth potential, but even that seemed uncertain. As late as the spring of 1980, only three Continental Illinois representatives traveled regularly to Oklahoma looking for assets.

Two years later, Continental Illinois had on its books more than a billion dollars' worth of loans that had originated at Penn Square. Something had happened. In a world governed by tidy conspiracies, it might appear that Beep Jennings, skillfully preying upon the institutional cupidity of Continental Illinois, had suckered Chicago's biggest bank into a neatly plotted trap. The chairman of the House Banking Committee said as much at hearings held late in the summer of 1982, when the Congress launched a brief crusade to find out precisely what had happened at Penn Square. "These fellows conned . . . Continental Illinois," the chairman said. "They conned the best." The flaw in this analysis was that the world is not tidy. Penn Square Bank was not a neatly plotted phenomenon. Something else had happened.

CHAPTER 7

There was a point in the life of the Penn Square Bank at which it became, in effect, two banks: the dull-sweet little shopping center bank and the ambitious oil-and-gas merchant bank that Jennings grafted onto it, like a Formula One racing engine on a roller skate. The bank that Jennings bought in 1975 had thirty-five employees and assets of thirty-five million dollars, including a loan portfolio valued at less than twenty million dollars. It had taken fifteen years to get that far, and during the last ten the bank's president was Frank Murphy. Penn Square was then a modest, sensible, cordial bank and Frank Murphy was a modest, sensible, cordial banker. He was a slender man with light blue eyes, gray hair that he brushed straight back, a small mouth, a prominent forehead, and a cast of self-willed invisibility. He had arrived at Penn Square as an assistant vice-president four years before becoming president. Most of his training had taken place with a commercial credit company, where he had made loans on business equipment and consumer products. Asked to describe his style of banking, he would say, "Very conservative." He was an installment lender at heart and a dedicated Kiwanian. He liked to fish and play golf.

Jennings took the view that he wanted things done "right" but above all he wanted the loan *made*, the deal *done*. Murphy's approach had been, in effect, "Here are ten reasons why you can't have the money. Now, let's see whether you can overcome them. Get the documents in order. Bring me the collateral. Then we'll consider a loan." Penn Square's profits, as well as its rate of loan delinquency, were directly proportional to Frank Murphy's ambition. Among Oklahoma City banks it ranked seventeenth in total deposits; statewide it ranked thirty-ninth. Once Jennings moved in, Murphy's ambition was to hold his ground for seven years, until he turned sixty-two, and then retire. "With my pension, my dividends, and some consulting work, I'd be in good shape for a country boy from Chelsea, Oklahoma," he said.

New employees were recruited, a stream of fresh arrivals that grew along with the bank. One of the recruits was William George Patterson. The most concise theory of Bill Patterson that I ever heard came from a woman who did not really know him but had attended the University of Oklahoma while he was there. She said, "I never met a Sigma Chi who wasn't crazy."

I gathered that that was supposed to explain the end of the oil boom and the deep-gas mania in the same way that Archduke Franz Ferdinand's rotten luck was supposed to explain several million other people's rotten luck. Originally, Patterson intended to become a physician, and he often wore hospital greens around the fraternity house. One of the Sigma Chis had a slow-healing surgical wound that required a fresh dressing every day for months, and Patterson volunteered for the job. He enrolled in the Reserve Officers' Training Corps, risking a long visit to Vietnam, because he thought a kind word from the Pentagon would help him stop at medical school along the way. If Patterson had managed better than a 2.5 grade average—and if the war in Southeast Asia had not wound down, which made the Army less eager for doctors—he might have had a chance to fulfill his goal. Late in the game, he considered studying Spanish and applying to the medical school at the University of Guadalajara. By that time, however, overlooked details had caught up with him.

When Patterson was a freshman, an upperclassman had the inspiration to call him "Monkeybrains." It immediately stuck. Someone who grew up with Patterson in Bartlesville, Oklahoma, and attended high school with him there said, "In high school we didn't call him Monkeybrains, but there wasn't any reason we didn't." Patterson had blue eyes, brown hair, a fleshy face, a round-tipped straight nose, a lopsided grin, and large front teeth. His dimensions were size 40. Dressed up, he looked all right. He looked as if he could be expected to go to the office in the morning and make it home for dinner that night. Well into college, he often wore his high school letterman's jacket—he had been a decent varsity wrestler—knowing that this was not a cool thing to do. More than once the Sigma Chi brothers expressed their appreciation of Patterson by unclothing him and tying him to a tree. Once he pushed a practical joke far enough to get himself locked inside a garbage dumpster for an hour and a half. If there was a beer-chugging contest or if six guys were going to moon the Thetas, you could count Patterson in. He worked hard at getting people to laugh at him, and if someone else in the room knew how to be funny he was a good audience. Someone told me that Patterson once let in some fresh air by throwing a lamp through a window, but another Sigma Chi swore that it couldn't have happened. "Hanging nude from the light post, yeah, that's Monkeybrains. But throwing a lamp—no, no. Bill wasn't destructive."

Patterson's first job in banking did not require him to make any credit decisions. He was a janitor. This was one of several part-time jobs that he held while still in college. After graduation, in 1973, he went to work for the First National Bank & Trust Company of Oklahoma City as a management trainee. His annual salary was in the mid-teens. Comfortable survival was possible because during his senior year in college he had married Eve Edwards, the only daughter of one of the wealthiest families in the Texas panhandle. Bartlesville, where Patterson had grown up—the home of Phillips Petroleum, a company town if one has ever existed—had a population of thirty thousand, three Republicans for every two Democrats, and one of the highest per capita incomes in the nation. It also had a rigidly stratified social system that no one complained about loudly. Bill Patterson's father, Pat, was a museum curator and an artist. He had enough Apache blood to sign his Indian name, Kemoha, to his oil and watercolor landscapes. Around Bartlesville, Pat (Kemoha) Patterson was as close to bohemian as you could get.

Marrying Eve Edwards exposed Bill Patterson for the first time to people who meant business when they talked about estate planning. Eve's father, Gene, had grown up in Oklahoma City and had attended law school at the University of Oklahoma but had spent his working life in Amarillo. He was the chairman and chief executive officer of the First National Bank of Amarillo. Gene Edwards' father-in-law, Edward Johnson, had built a fortune in oil and cattle and real estate. Even by Texas standards, these were wealthy people. Two brothers of Eve's had attended OU and they knew Bill Patterson. When Eve and Bill announced that they were getting married, the family's joy was restrained. Eve was intelligent, even-tempered, and uncommonly well mannered. The closest she ever came to rebelliousness was when she married Bill Patterson.

One day not long after Patterson began working at the First National Bank, he went to lunch with an old friend. The friend asked him how he had spent his morning.

"Counting quarters," Patterson said.

The friend said, "No, seriously."

Patterson said, "*Counting quarters*. Counting them, putting them in paper rolls, folding the ends of the rolls."

The Sigma Chis would bump into Patterson downtown and say, "Hi, Monkey," and he would smile and say something funny. He toiled in the metropolitan accounts department. There were nonborrowing First National customers who had savings accounts with robust balances. For a time Patterson's job was to call upon these depositors and try to sell them other banking services. If a customer said yes, he might like to borrow money, Patterson would refer the account to someone in the loan department. Patterson stayed at the bank three and a half years—long enough to persuade his superiors that he was not "loan officer material." The president of the First National Bank & Trust Company—unable to sense Patterson's special skills and gifts—had unambivalent feelings. Years after Patterson had departed, he said, "There was no way we were going to let Bill Patterson lend a dime of the bank's money."

As a favor to Patterson's father-in-law, who was a friend of long standing, Beep Jennings asked Frank Murphy late in 1977 to talk to Patterson. "I thought he seemed like an intelligent young man," Murphy said later. "I hired him and put him to work in the credit department."

Before Patterson could lend a dime—or, for that matter, several hundred million dollars—of Penn Square's and other banks' funds, there would be a necessary apprenticeship. In Patterson's view, working with Frank Murphy and reviewing loan documents and learning the paperwork side of credit transactions only slightly surpassed counting quarters. Unfortunately, to get to the fun stuff you had to wade through that phase. The fun stuff, of course, was selling money. Within six months, Jennings instructed Murphy that he himself, and he alone, would supervise and train Patterson. Jennings said later that Patterson was "willing to work harder than any young man I've ever met. And he developed what I interpreted as a tremendous grasp of oil-and-gas economics with a limited background." Patterson had been at Penn Square only about a year and a half when Jennings put him in charge of oil-and-gas lending. Within a few more months, Jennings was telling him that he looked forward to the day when Patterson would preside over the bank. And there would come a day when Patterson would tell friends that *he* was looking forward to the time when he would buy out Jennings.

When Patterson began to manage the oil-and-gas division in the middle of 1979, Penn Square's officer corps was still small—fewer than twenty. The bank was growing, but not in a manner that seemed unmanageable. A barrel of oil cost twenty-two dollars. The price had risen steadily, but the "second price shock"—a single leap of eight dollars, which was a consequence of the fall of the Shah of Iran—still lay a few months ahead. With encouragement from Jennings, Patterson proceeded conscientiously. He had wanted to become a lender, and now that he had a chance he seemed eager to do it properly. Even the skeptics at the Penn Square Bank paused and scratched their heads. There were oilies, it was said, who could not be bombed out of the downtown banks and Patterson, at Jennings' bidding, was prepared to romance them. If landing an oil-and-gas customer meant offering a home mortgage at well-below-market rates, no problem. If it meant offering a ten-year term on a loan that another bank would expect to be repaid in seven or five years, that could be arranged as well.

The ascension of Patterson made it evident that Murphy had outlived his usefulness. Although Murphy had hired Patterson, it took him only a few months to develop an antipathy toward the young man. "Did I think Patterson was funny? Hell, no," Murphy has said. "I take attending meetings and being prompt seriously. I think appearances matter. I don't care who you are. I disapproved of his lateness, his insubordination."

One morning Patterson arrived at a loan committee meeting late but still in time to present a six-figure proposal. In Murphy's estimation, there were no grounds for making a loan, no documents upon which to base a judgment. To Murphy, a credit of, say, three hundred thousand dollars that went sour would be like thirty bad loans on midsize family automobiles.

Patterson listened to Murphy's objections and said, "Your old-style way of banking is a thing of the past."

Murphy told Patterson, "As long as you're making loans here, you're going to do them the way I think they should be done."

Murphy was wrong on that point. That was the day that Penn Square, in a practical sense, divided into two banks under one roof. Because Murphy wanted to hang around long enough to collect his retirement benefits, he did not resign. Because it was in Jennings' nature to massage as many constituents as possible, he did not invite Murphy to leave. Jennings' taste was nothing if not eclectic. He believed in Bobby Hefner's cosmic vision. He looked at Jerry Dale Allen and saw great potential. When it came to Carl Swan, there was nothing he would not do. And Bill Patterson, it seemed, he loved.

CHAPTER 8

When the traditional oil-and-gas lending standards were being formulated, decades ago, Bill Patterson was not yet born. It is possible, therefore, that he never did grasp the vital distinctions between the old rules and the new ones. Perhaps, during his career, he stayed too busy having fun to pay attention to vital distinctions. Any banker will acknowledge that money lent at 22 percent fits the definition of "fun." From a bank customer's point of view, fun is a loan that on its surface appears to cost 22 percent per annum but in a practical sense costs nothing. Beep Jennings, who had a generous and warm feeling toward the Continental Illinois National Bank & Trust Company of Chicago, often remarked that he had learned a great deal about oil-and-gas lending by observing that institution. "Penn Square, to the extent that it was able to do so, adopted the mineral lending philosophy of Continental Illinois," Jennings said. "If Continental escalated oil prices, we escalated oil. If they held the price level, *we* held it level." Continental, after all, had invented the "evergreen revolver"—the free-money loan.

His hat in his hand (and his merchant-banking concept between his ears), Jennings wooed Continental Illinois and other potential upstream banks. Besides Chicago, he tested markets in Houston, Dallas, New York, New Orleans, Los Angeles, and Seattle. Jennings' earliest encounter with Continental Illinois was not encouraging. An Oklahoma City oilman whose company had run into obstacles while trying to arrange a line of credit at Continental sought Jennings' help. This was in the autumn of 1977. The loan officer who at that time covered Oklahoma for

Continental Illinois was Dennis Winget. Jennings called Winget and offered to assume part of the loan. Because Penn Square had done nothing to originate the loan request, Winget responded with an unfriendly counterproposal. "How about if you tell me where *you* come into this deal?" Winget said. In the end, Jennings escorted his oilman friend to Dallas, and the company borrowed from a bank there.

A few months later, the tables turned. In Tulsa, Winget made one of his periodic calls on the Utica National Bank. Continental had always had a solid foothold in Tulsa, where the average oil company was older than in Oklahoma City and so was the money. An out-of-town banker just had to devote some time to the challenge. The chief lending officer at Utica National had attended high school and college with Bill Patterson. When Winget said that he was interested in buying overlines, the young banker said, "You ought to get acquainted with Bill Patterson, down at Penn Square, in Oklahoma City. They're going to be aggressive." Following this lead, Continental Illinois within the next few months bought from Penn Square three loan participations—a one-million-dollar credit to a small refinery and two production loans for roughly a million and a half each. One of the production loans went to a colorfully egotistical oilman who had become annoyed with a downtown Oklahoma City bank, and the other went to Carl Swan. Although Swan was not short of cash, having recently collected ten million dollars from the sale of Basin Petroleum, he recognized the economic wisdom of leverage and the evergreen revolver.

Each of these deals was, according to Winget's recollection, "done to perfection." Petroleum engineering reports were scrutinized well in advance of the loan closings. Financial statements were current. Mortgages were duly filed with county clerks. The borrowing was secured. This was still the early phase of an uncertain courtship. The relationship between a bank the size of Continental Illinois and its smaller correspondent banks is delicate and tricky. The larger bank can steal the smaller bank's business just as easily as it can extend assistance. Even Jennings, a man equipped with a loan-merchandising concept, was wary of that possibility. When Swan went to Chicago to be wined and dined by Continental Illinois, Jennings went with him, like a watchful father chauffeuring his son on a first date.

Continental had an admirable policy of shooing its young banking associates out into the field quickly, giving them considerable responsibility at a tender age. Opportunities abounded—opportunities for individual bank officers as well as for the institution as a whole. Movement up through the ranks would come to those who returned to Chicago bearing quality assets. Winget had the services of a series of fresh graduates from the bank's credit training program. Like an encyclopedia salesman, the graduate would make cold calls upon prospects: walk into an office, introduce oneself as a representative of the Continental Illinois Bank, and explain that Chicago had come to Oklahoma to lend money to the right people. Sometimes the rookie got invited out to the country club for martinis and lunch, and sometimes the brusque response was "I'm too busy to talk to anyone now. I'm on my way out to a rig."

Continental's representatives in Oklahoma noticed, perhaps a year and a half into the Penn Square era, a shift in the ground rules. No longer could a banker approach a prospect with the attitude: "Look, chances are you're not really worthy of credit, but let's talk anyway." Now the oilies were saying, "What can you do for *me*? I have a *right* to borrow." Cold-calling was becoming a harder sell. This is where Jennings and Patterson came in handy. Because they knew so many people who could use some money, they eliminated the need for the hard sell. Beating the bushes for new business began to seem inefficient. Why bother with that routine when you had Patterson doing your legwork? The word went out that Penn Square was becoming "Continental Illinois' Oklahoma loan production office."

During the first four years that Jennings controlled Penn Square, the bank's loan portfolio nearly quintupled. At the end of 1979 it stood at ninety-two million dollars. During that same period, the volume of loan participations sold to out-of-town banks went from a negligible figure to seventy-seven million dollars. More than half of the participations were bought by Continental Illinois. Two other significant banks, meanwhile, had become upstream lenders—the Northern Trust Company, of Chicago, and Seattle-First National Bank. The Northern Trust link grew, in part, out of the old Sigma Chi tie; one of Northern's petroleum engineers had been a fraternity brother of Patterson. Seattle-First—the largest bank in the Pacific Northwest, usually referred to as Seafirst—entered the Penn Square orbit when Patterson put in a call to it with a question about a customer who did business with both banks. By late 1979, Seafirst's loan purchases totaled only four million dollars. Northern, which had more energy lending experience, had picked up almost thirty million dollars in business. Both banks saw in the close friendship between Continental Illinois and Penn Square proof that the Oklahoma oil patch was a good place to put money to work. Continental Illinois was an imposing competitor but it was, above all, a legitimizer. The waiting area outside Patterson's office was becoming cluttered with importuning bankers, all of whom regarded Continental Illinois with envy and respect.

The freedom that Continental's lenders enjoyed in the field had to be balanced with accountability to the home office. Even when a Dennis Winget found a loan that he was eager to make, he could not do it alone. Winget had the authority to commit to lend a million dollars but the approval of a second lending officer was required to put a loan on the books. Winget reported to Alvin J. (Jerry) Pearson, the head of Continental Illinois' oil-and-gas lending division, and Pearson was exacting. Roughly fifty people worked in Jerry Pearson's division—from administrative assistants to loan officers—and that number included three petroleum engineers. A petroleum engineer and banker both, with thirty years of combined experience, Pearson had a sterling reputation. Officially, the limit of his lending authority was five million dollars. In practice, however, it was ten million dollars because the officer above Pearson almost never vetoed his decisions. Former Continental Illinois employees, waxing nostalgic, now describe the Pearson era as "the glory days."

Pearson left Continental in the late summer of 1980 to go to work for one of his customers, Nucorp Energy. The initial Continental loan to Nucorp—which, in 1982, went into bankruptcy, owing the bank a hundred seventy-three million dollars—was booked in 1979. The loan officer on the account at that time was a vice-president named John Lytle. Lytle was a "section head" in charge of "independent oil and gas lending worldwide." When he moved into that job, in 1977, he inherited a four-hundred-million-dollar loan portfolio. After Pearson left, the organization chart at Continental took on a different look, and Lytle ruled a new bailiwick called the "midcontinent oil-and-gas division"—meaning America east of Denver, except Texas. As a result of the across-the-board growth in loan volume at Continental, Lytle, despite having lost much geographical territory, emerged with responsibility for eight hundred million dollars' worth of credits.

Lytle had lived all his life in Chicago, had graduated from the University of Illinois with a degree in economics and finance, and had given the United States Navy two years and Continental Illinois the rest. The son of a banker who had worked forty years for one institution—the Harris Trust Company, of Chicago—Lytle had been at Continental Illinois eighteen years when he began to learn oil-and-gas lending. That year, 1977, he earned a salary of forty thousand dollars and a profit-sharing bonus of about four thousand dollars. With his wife and three children (a fourth came along later), he lived in a house in Northfield, a thirty-minute train ride from the Loop. The house had cost him sixty thousand dollars in 1967; some years later he spent forty-five thousand dollars for property that brought the size of his plot to slightly less than two acres. Lytle was not hard to like. He had no abrasive edges, no starchiness. He was conventionally handsome, mid-forties graying, with dark eyebrows and a vaguely wistful presence. Meeting Lytle in a bar, you could easily engage him in relaxed, enlightened conversation. While not compulsive about work, he could, under pressure, function as if he were. He grasped that he was better at marketing bank products than he was at running a bank. He could evaluate his own strengths and shortcomings. "In terms of temperament, I'm a sales manager, not a general manager," he said. "I rate myself a hundred on new business, a ninety on credit. I was tremendous with customers, I made friends all over. I was a real oilie—with only three or four years' experience, but I don't think that showed. The home office—I didn't have that much interest in it."

The self-aware organization man whom Lytle described turned out to be just the sort of banker with whom Jennings and Patterson enjoyed doing business. With Lytle they could communicate easily—often virtually by code. Upon becoming head of the midcontinent oil-and-gas division, Lytle at last qualified for Continental Illinois's special incentive bonuses for upper middle managers. The limit of his lending authority had doubled, from two and a half million dollars to five million. Subsequently, it would double again. During 1980 Penn Square's size doubled and the volume of loan participations quintupled. Continental now owned two hundred and fifty million dollars' worth of Penn Square-originated loans— approximately two thirds of all the loans sold by the smaller bank. Continental Illinois was programmed for growth, Lytle wanted to grow, and Penn Square meshed neatly with those corporate and personal ambitions. Everywhere the push was on. It was one of those coincidences. Lytle pushed.

Corporate citizens learn the advantages of maintaining a distance from bright new ideas; new ideas usually cost money. When the need for heavy cogitating arises, the politic manager subcontracts the job. In 1976, the Chase Manhattan Bank asked McKinsey & Company, the management consultants, to advise how Chase's correspondent banking division could make more money. Traditional correspondent banking has roughly as much appeal as trusts-and-estates work in a large law firm. I have heard it described as "basic blocking and tackling"—selling non-loan services such as cash letters, coupon collection, foreign collection, security safekeeping, international remittances and transfers. Competition is high and profit margins tend to be low. McKinsey & Company produced a document titled "Chase Institutional Banking Strategy." It came to two hundred pages, of which ten discussed the wisdom, tactics, and mechanics of loan participation purchases. Until McKinsey suggested making an effort to buy loan participations, Chase had provided this service only for its very closest correspondent banks. McKinsey's advice was that Chase should become more bold, but within necessary limits. Chase should buy no overlines greater than five million dollars, and no more than ten million in total purchases from any single bank. And Chase should restrict its dealings to well-established banks with historically low rates of loan losses. Correspondent banking was part of the domestic institutional banking department, which in Chase Manhattan's scheme of operations was far away from corporate lending and energy lending. Nowhere in the report did McKinsey & Company mention energy lending.

In the fall of 1980, a Chase correspondent banker named Richard Pinney attended a banking convention in Chicago and saw an old friend, Mike Tighe, who worked for the Northern Trust Company. At Chase, Pinney covered the "West," which meant everything beyond the western shore of the Mississippi, plus Illinois and Wisconsin. Tighe, during most of his career, had been a corporate lender. He had also worked as a correspondent banker and he had regularly encountered Pinney on the road. The two bankers had not crossed paths for almost two years, however, because during that time Tighe had been in charge of oil-and-gas lending at Northern Trust. Pinney respected Tighe, who was a matriculant in the work hard-play hard school. "I thought he was a helluva guy," Pinney said. "Everyone I knew thought he was smart, able, and one of the best producers Northern Trust ever had. He knew how to have fun, but at eight o'clock the next morning he was up and ready to work."

The principals at Northern Trust liked to think of their bank as a Chicago version of the Morgan Guaranty Trust Company. While there is but one House of Morgan, Northern Trust could claim to be at least as conservative. Its assets were five billion six hundred million dollars, which made it the fourth largest commercial bank in Chicago, thirty-first in the nation. When Northern's strategic planners decided, in 1977, to pursue energy loan business, they consulted with some of Chase's oil-and-gas lending officers. In the Midwest, Northern was one of Chase Manhattan's closest correspondent banks. Upon hearing that Pinney was eager to buy overlines, Tighe said, "You ought to call on Penn Square, in Oklahoma City. They have an uncanny ability to generate loans."

Pinney knew—as Tighe knew, as the bankers from Continental Illinois and Seafirst knew, as, indeed, all the bank representatives who were then knocking on Bill Patterson's door knew—that the real estate business was in a slump, New England was on its keister, the commercial fishing and lumber industries of the Pacific Northwest were dying, the upper Midwest had already been scrubbed down by the embalmers, and there was not a soothsayer in the country who did not believe that an acute energy shortage would descend before the end of the century. "Sunbelt" was the word of the day. Chase Manhattan's own economists predicted sixty-five-dollar-a-barrel oil not far down the road—a rather conservative prognostication, some would have said. Although Pinney did not board the next plane to Oklahoma City, this useful information mattered to him. What also mattered was his confidence in Tighe and Northern Trust.

That week in Chicago, Lytle had met with Paul Souder, who was the vice-chairman of the Michigan National Bank—the main subsidiary of a bank holding company with combined assets that made it comparable in size to Northern Trust. Souder had an interesting way of expressing how difficult it was to sell money at home. He said to Lytle, "The only thing we have in Michigan is unemployed blacks and empty automobile factories." What Souder hopefully envisioned was an arrangement whereby Continental Illinois would share with Michigan National portions of its oil-and-gas loans. Logical reciprocity would be for Michigan National to offer to Continental some participations in loans that it had originated. Within a few weeks of this first conversation, Lytle and members of his staff held a number of meetings with bankers from Michigan National. By November, the Michigan bankers had met Bill Patterson and had bought twelve million dollars' worth of Penn Square loan participations. Several months later, the president of the flagship branch of the Michigan National Bank contacted a friend at Chase Manhattan to confirm that Penn Square was a credible, satisfactory source of loans. The Chase friend was Richard Pinney.

The first Chase Manhattan emissary to Penn Square arrived in February of 1981. The banker whom Pinney dispatched was Margaret Sipperly, a poised and outgoing woman in her mid-twenties. She had worked at Chase since 1976, had passed through Chase's "credit development" program—the indoctrination that every lending trainee in the bank undergoes—and had been a correspondent banker for slightly more than three years. A few months earlier, she had been promoted from assistant treasurer to assistant vice-president. Her annual salary was in the mid-thirties. The first Penn Square officer she met was Frank Murphy, the lame-duck president. Not long into their conversation, Meg Sipperly realized that her credit training had taught her no specifics of oil-and-gas lending. When Murphy mentioned a customer with a "fishing operation" who needed a six-million-dollar loan, an unsettling feeling descended upon her. She tried to imagine which town in a state where the wind comes sweeping down the plain might be the home of an oyster breeder who needed six million dollars. Perhaps Murphy knew an extraordinarily ambitious catfish farmer. Before long, Sipperly figured out that fishing meant retrieving drilling equipment that had been inadvertently left in a well bore.

Within two days, Sipperly called at Penn Square three times, meeting Bill Patterson along the way. As a result, Chase bought six loan participations, totaling two and a half million dollars. Relatively speaking, this was not a great deal of business, not something that Chase's corporate lenders would have deigned to pursue. It was, nevertheless, an important beginning. Within a month, Chase had agreed to buy a three-million-dollar-plus participation in a loan to a Florida marina project called Maximo Moorings. (The principal developer of the marina had also received oil-and-gas loans from Penn Square.) Jennings later recalled a meeting in the summer of that year—a meeting held in the office of Thomas Labrecque, the president of Chase Manhattan. This was the first time the two men had met, although three years earlier Jennings had gone to Chase—to the correspondent banking division, of all places—looking for a loan buyer. Politely, he had been rebuffed. The meeting with Labrecque went differently. Jennings has recalled, "Labrecque said that he was well aware of the treatment I'd received a few years earlier. But he said that he was impressed by our activity with Continental Illinois and that his bank looked forward to being part of that relationship. He said that they intended to become our major correspondent bank."

The alliances that bound Penn Square and its various correspondent banks would, if rendered in a diagram, defy easy comprehensibility. A school friend of Patterson's mentions Penn Square to a banker from Continental Illinois. Before long, Continental believes in Penn Square and Penn Square believes in Continental. A college fraternity pal of Patterson's works for Northern Trust and soon that bank is involved. Penn Square finds its way to Seattle-First by apparent happenstance. Everywhere you look in America, industries are dying. Oil-and-gas is not dying. Michigan National calls upon Continental Illinois. Chase Manhattan bumps into Northern Trust. Michigan National consults Chase Manhattan. A foamy egalitarian spirit—the spirit of opportunity—suffuses these relationships. None of the bankers who came to Oklahoma to deal with Penn Square were handcuffed and blindfolded. They were all looking, as they say in banking, "to put out assets." And they were looking at one another. A pyramid was at work—not a pyramid scheme, but a pyramid of belief: I believe in you and you believe in me and we are all in this together.

Yet for all the talking that the money-center bankers did among themselves, they did not discuss their Oklahoma bonanza with the Office of the Comptroller of the Currency, where there were officials who cared plenty about the Penn Square Bank. Therefore the bankers did not know that federal bank examiners had spent a month in early 1980 looking closely at Penn Square and had found "a combination of financial, operational or compliance weaknesses ranging from moderately severe to unsatisfactory." In the wary eyes of the Comptroller, Penn Square was burdened by excessively rapid growth, inadequate capital, and strained liquidity. Its employees were overworked, its loan portfolio was out of balance, its lending policies were insufficiently defined, its committee structure and credit-review apparatus were inadequate, insiders had overborrowed. Technical violation of banking laws abounded. The directors of Penn Square were required to sign a formal agreement to clean up the bank's act. Penn Square was, in sum, a bank that required "special supervisory attention." The upstream bankers knew none of this because no one told them. They knew only what they could learn by reading Penn Square's financial statement each quarter, and they saw a bank that was growing and thriving. Patterson and Jennings were rapturous salesmen. Everyone was having an enchanting time.

CHAPTER 9

Better even than Bob Hefner comprehended the confounding geology of the Anadarko Basin, he comprehended the value of "debtor's leverage"— the notion that someone who owes a banker a hundred thousand dollars he can't pay back has more reason to lie awake nights than someone who owes ten million. Owe a hundred thousand, the reasoning goes, and the bank controls you; owe ten million and you control the bank. Bankers prefer to avoid either of these circumstances. Most of the bankers whom Hefner approached avoided them by declining to lend him anything, and this led him to cultivate surrogate bankers.

By 1977, the year that Hefner first borrowed from the Penn Square Bank, he and an ostensibly monied partner, David O'D. Kennedy, had run up a debt to the Northern Illinois Gas Company, or NIGAS, of more than fifteen million dollars. NIGAS, which was a public utility company, had become a commercial lender inadvertently when, in the mid-1960s, it lent three million dollars to the primary Hefner-Kennedy partnership, the GHK Company. Kennedy also owed Manufacturers Hanover Trust three and a half million dollars, an obligation that was the oldest classified, or substandard, loan on that bank's books. GHK had annual oil-and-gas income in 1977 of roughly seven hundred thousand dollars. This amount did not suffice to meet interest payments, much less retire any of the principal or defray the company's expenses, such as overhead, salaries, and mineral lease renewals. Nor could it easily sustain Hefner's personal habits, which included polo in Palm Beach and Palm Springs, sailing off Antigua, grouse-shooting in the Cotswolds, and wintering in Cancún.

The Hefner methodology was audacious, maddening, and irre-pressible. When Hefner first set out to buy the Anadarko, leases ran ten years and lease-signing bonuses cost between ten and twenty-five dollars an acre. You could not hold the acreage forever unless you drilled wells. To do that, capitalists with tangible capital were required. Hefner farmed out acreage and negotiated fancy third-for-a-quarter partnerships. He manipulated most of the nat-ural human virtues and vices, paying special attention to goodwill and cupidity. No one who ever sat through a Hefner sales presen-tation—which was less a pitch than a multimedia adaptation of the Book of Revelation—doubted his abilities as a promoter. The man believed in his product. Meeting a prospective buyer, he would trot out seismic charts, structural maps, wire-line logs, magnetic and gravimetric surveys, satellite photos. When he was done, he would exit stage-whispering, "This is too good to sell. We've got to keep it all!"

Working with mirrors, Hefner was running a glorified lease brokerage enterprise that appeared to be one of the most daring exploration companies on earth. Survival hinged on his ability to buy leases cheap with borrowed money; to sell part of the acreage to exploration companies that had the resources to drill expensive deep wells; to use lease-trading profits to participate in the wells; and, above all, to become the operator—in effect, the general contractor—during the drilling and afterward. As an operator, GHK would bill its partners each month for their share of drilling and other costs. Dollars are dollars are dollars. Before redistribut-ing his partners' money to subcontractors, Hefner would do with it whatever he could. He paid annual mineral rentals, he paid for seismic surveys on new prospects, he paid leftover debts from his previous deals. Masterfully, he stalled his most recent creditors and he tested his partners' patience.

In extending credit to the GHK Company, NIGAS unintention-ally stumbled into a variation of an evergreen revolver. When NIGAS agreed to finance GHK's effort to acquire Anadarko leases, it did so because the company's executive subscribed to Hefner's basic geological theories and because, if the methane could be produced in the quantities that Hefner predicted, NIGAS would have an inside track on the supply. Indeed, some elements of the plan worked out. Methane from the No. 1 Green, GHK's seminal deep Anadarko producer, warmed hearths in Chicago. The hitch was that a winter in Chicago could get insufferably cold and, no matter, the No. 1 Green, flowing methane at twenty-two cents per thousand cubic feet, would always be a fiscal fiasco. The next challenge was to come up with a project that, even more than the No. 1 Green, could make a banker blanch. Hefner succeeded in 1971 with a deep well called the Farrar. He did not achieve this all by himself; David Kennedy also participated—but that was it, just the two of them. At 22,408 feet, the Farrar was the deepest well ever drilled "straight up"—that is, with a single party assuming the entire risk. It cost three and a half million dollars, in return for which GHK discovered reserves in the range of eight to ten billion cubic feet. This enterprise was as economically disappointing as the No. 1 Green.

NIGAS was left with little practical choice but to roll over the GHK debt. It did this not with the blithe optimism that later made Bill Patterson and Bill Jennings so popular but with the cynicism of an unwitting venture capitalist. Most of the mushrooming wad that GHK owed NIGAS was interest that had accumulated on the original debt. In the beginning, Hefner's bargaining strengths had been his pervasive knowledge of the Anadarko Basin and his foresight in having amassed large blocks of acreage. As time went on, those became secondary to his debtor's leverage. But the lender had some leverage as well. NIGAS believed in the moral correctness of quid pro quo. Each time the utility company renewed a note, its overseers grabbed another piece of GHK's title to the Anadarko, usually in the form of overriding royalty interests. Little things like paying bills might not have concerned Hefner, but losing acreage made him feel as if someone were slicing up his heart. The urge to get out there in the Basin and reclaim his stake forced Hefner into perpetual motion. It also forced him to refine his promotional skills.

In 1970, 1971, and 1977, Hefner negotiated significant deals with the Lone Star Gas Company, the El Paso Natural Gas Company, and the Apache Corporation, respectively. At the peak, his leaseholdings amounted to roughly two hundred thousand acres. Most of this existed within a hundred-square-mile area around Elk City, a town that was destined to become the unofficial capital of the Anadarko Basin, and the major lease parcels were known collectively as the Elk City Project Area. Each time Hefner traded a portion of his interest in the Elk City Project, he received a commitment from a larger company to spend a certain amount of money drilling a certain number of wells. Although Hefner's motives never changed, the results varied. Almost immediately, the El Paso transaction began to work out nicely for both sides. The Apache exploration program produced certain disappointments—things like dry holes—but it might, in the long run, prove worthwhile to Apache. Then, there was Lone Star.

Some people who have observed Hefner closely across the years regard the Lone Star deal as a paradigm of his modus operandi—his relentless effort to pay past dues by taking another deep plunge. In this instance, GHK received from Lone Star seven million dollars in cash plus a pledge to spend at least ten million dollars drilling two ultra-deep wells. GHK was expected to pay a quarter of the drilling costs and it would be carried free by Lone Star for an additional quarter. Lone Star did not anticipate, however, that Hefner would be using the brand-new seven million dollars to pay some stale old debts, after which GHK would have very little left to pay its share of the drilling costs. When this complication became apparent, it disturbed the Lone Star Gas Company more than it disturbed Bob Hefner.

The first Lone Star well, the No. 1 Baden, was completed in 1972. It was the deepest hole in the world drilled for hydrocarbons. When the second well, the Bertha Rogers, was completed, in 1974, *it* became the deepest hole in the world drilled for hydrocarbons. Together they ultimately cost not ten million dollars but fifteen. Each well pierced zones below thirty thousand feet, and each ended up producing uneconomical amounts of gas from zones much shallower than the target depths. By the time the Bertha Rogers was drilled, Hefner had been forced to trade additional acreage to Lone Star. Rather than owning half of that well, he wound up with a negligible interest. Nevertheless, he was willing to exploit the "success" of the Bertha Rogers, which had revealed traces of methane and ethane at 31,441 feet; he later would cite this as evidence that natural gas pervaded the greatest depths of the Anadarko Basin. The Bertha Rogers literally discovered Ordovician hellfire and brimstone—satanic vapors and molten sulfur. The pressure at the bottom of the hole was twenty-seven thousand pounds per square inch and the temperature was almost five hundred degrees. Brine in the well's drilling fluid reacted with hydrogen-sulfide gas to produce sulfuric acid that corroded the drilling pipe, rendering it uselessly brittle. Rock cuttings impregnated with sulfur crystals circulated to the surface along with the drilling fluid. Hefner retrieved some of this material and placed it in a small linen bag which he inscribed "Man's deepest penetration of inner space." Then he donated the bag to the "21" Club, in New York, on the theory, presumably, that it couldn't hurt.

At this rate, God was not going to permit Bob Hefner to drill his way to glory. The experiences of the Farrar and the Baden and the Bertha Rogers had a depressing effect not only upon GHK and the Lone Star Gas Company but upon the Anadarko Basin as a whole. The self-generating Hefner mythology increasingly bore an odd resemblance to a fairy tale: white knight versus fire-breathing dragon. Metaphor and reality had begun to overlap and the dragon had built a huge lead.

Hefner needed fresh credibility. He needed a much bigger accomplice than he had ever promoted before—a world-power government, say. Thoughts similar to this had occurred to him in the past. In 1969, he had campaigned for 1,440-acre well spacing units in the western Anadarko region. (The typical spacing unit for gas wells in Oklahoma, set by the Oklahoma Corporation Commission, is one square mile—640 acres—although, depending upon the field, the units can run as small as 40 acres.) Hefner's argument to the Corporation Commission was that, with deep wells costing so much to drill and interstate gas selling at such a low price, a producer needed to drain more acreage per well to make a profit, Many mineral owners initially opposed 1,440-acre spacing, but Hefner prevailed. The *federales* were whom Hefner really needed to agree with him, and they were not as easily impressed as the Oklahoma Corporation Commissioners. In 1970, Hefner had testified before the Federal Power Commission (FPC), declaring that "there is a national shortage of natural gas" and that to increase reserves you had to drill deeper. Across the next few years, he turned up in Washington whenever the FPC held rate-setting hearings. A routine evolved. Hefner would deliver the most recent edition of his basic sermon, and the FPC would respond, in effect, "Yeah, we think the deep gas is probably there. We know it's expensive to drill the wells. We know you're in a bind. But we're not completely convinced. Go drill some more."

Democracy in action was not cheap, but it cost less than drilling deep, dragonlike dry holes. It was cheaper to petition, pray, dilate, and expostulate. Hefner organized a little club called the Independent Gas Producers Committee and introduced himself on Capitol Hill as its delegate. The Independent Gas Producers Committee hired lawyers and lobbyists. Hefner testified before the Senate Interior Committee, the Senate Commerce Committee, the Senate Committee on Energy and Natural Resources—any congressional committee or subcommittee that would have him. He launched position papers written in a hybrid of Washingtonese and Hefnerese, he issued reports, sent Mailgrams, dictated his thoughts, made statements, called press conferences, dispatched press releases and Q&As and outlines and Alternatives to Administration Policies and open letters to congressmen and governors. *He italicized crucially important passages of these declamations.* He riddled them with exclamation points! Sometimes multiple exclamation points!!! He tended toward prolixity. He feared not redundancy. He came off like an obsessive-compulsive, somewhere between a bore and a madman. And, indeed, he could not help himself. During the 1976 presidential campaign, he was chairman of Oil and Gas Men for Carter. In the spring of 1977, a reporter from the Los Angeles *Times* interviewed him. Self-restraint eluded Hefner. "If it works," he told the reporter, "maybe I'll get rich."

Not quite two years after Jimmy Carter took office, by which time Hefner had lost affection for him, the President signed the Natural Gas Policy Act of 1978 (NGPA)—at a stroke changing all the rules. One section of the new law exempted from federal price controls any newly discovered natural gas produced from below fifteen thousand feet. Free-market forces would now determine the value of the deep Anadarko. Suddenly, gas from wells such as the No. 1 Green, rather than selling for twenty-two cents per thousand cubic feet, could go for two and a half dollars, perhaps much higher. More than any other artifact, the new law gilded the mythology of Robert A. Hefner III. Independent oil and gas producers, including many who were not fond of Hefner, believed that he had single-handedly drafted the provision for deep-gas deregulation. The truth was that he had feared becoming too closely identified with deep gas and had deliberately spent the last year or so of the legislative battle away from Washington. Hired lobbyists had done the legwork. Whatever Hefner's influence on the passage of the act, he could easily grasp its significance: it was as if Congress, with the acquiescence of the White House, had pointed a finger at western Oklahoma and said, "O.K. Those people right there—we'll make them rich."

Life was about to become even more peculiar. In the past, in the role of romantic and elegant deadbeat, Hefner had successfully maintained the illusion of wealth. Now that great wealth seemed plausible, and even imminent, he was still strapped for cash. Early in 1978, he had gone to the Continental Illinois Bank with a high-dollar request. To bolster his case, he took along a bottom-hole rock sample from a productive deep well called the No. 1 Gregory. With the rock, he intended to prove that it was possible to drill a five-mile hole and encounter sediments with porosity and permeability sufficient to contain methane that would pay back any loan. By now Hefner owned interests in about fifty producing wells. Prudent energy bankers prefer diversified collateral. Unfortunately, four-fifths of GHK's gas production flowed from three wells. Continental's petroleum engineers looked at the rock. Jerry Pearson, the vice-president in charge of Continental Illinois's oil-and-gas lending division, who had been a practicing engineer before he became a banker, looked at the rock. "The rock's too tight," Pearson said, meaning that hydrocarbons could not flow through it. Continental Illinois refused Hefner's loan request.

Farming out small pieces of acreage, making deals on a well-by-well basis, Hefner spent two more years maneuvering for liquidity, seeking a lender capable of major financing. At work in his favor was the rising price of deep gas—from two and a half dollars per thousand cubic feet to five dollars and then to seven-fifty. Any banker who worried that a customer's collateral might be shaky could watch the natural gas market and breathe a sigh. Finally, in the summer of 1980, NIGAS was able to relinquish its role as Hefner's surrogate banker. With a major assist from Penn Square, Hefner closed on his first big bank loan—fifty-five million dollars from the First National Bank of Dallas. He used thirty-five million to extinguish most of his debt to NIGAS, spread the leftover twenty million around in the customary manner, and realized that he needed much more money.

Within six months, Hefner was invited back to Continental Illinois, and Bill Patterson accompanied him. Jerry Pearson had resigned from the bank and John Lytle now managed the midcontinent oil-and-gas lending division. Suddenly, Continental was more than eager to do business with Hefner. The timing was not accidental. In what looked like the farmout to end all farmouts, Hefner had just promoted the Mobil Oil Corporation. Back in 1963, Hefner had tried to sell Mobil a half-interest in a hundred and twenty thousand Anadarko Basin acres for nine million dollars—and had been turned down. Seventeen years later, to earn a half-interest in a hundred thirty-five thousand acres of the Elk City Project Area, Mobil agreed to spend two hundred million dollars drilling for deep gas. Up front, Mobil threw in thirty-two million dollars for the GHK treasury.

As discombobulating as the numbers might sound, the Mobil agreement was just an inflated version of what Hefner had been doing all along—turning leases, latching on to big partners. Now, for the first time in Hefner's experience, Wall Street beckoned. If GHK were to sell shares to the public, Hefner and Kennedy could get out of debt forever and into, say, a hundred million, maybe two hundred million, in cash. With that Hefner could buy tax-free municipal bonds or groceries or whatever he pleased. Unaccustomed as he was to solvency, he decided instead to borrow whatever the Continental Illinois National Bank & Trust Company would let him have. Between January and April 1981, this premier energy bank—the bank that desired to become the leading commercial lender in America—negotiated with Hefner a hundred-million-dollar line of credit. There were formal discussions and informal ones. The Penn Square Bank, in the person of Bill Patterson, tagged along, with Patterson assuming the role of shuttle diplomat. He wanted to help his friend and fellow banker John Lytle confect loan terms that would fly past his superiors. And he wanted his friend and customer Bob Hefner—the godfather of Patterson's youngest child—to be able to borrow a hundred million dollars without having to promise to restrict his future borrowing from other sources.

The bankers and Hefner agreed that he had no choice but to borrow this money. To abandon the Anadarko Basin just as its true promise was about to be revealed would have made no sense.

Because Hefner had always thought of himself as rich, becoming a millionaire—merely Oklahoma-rich—did not impress him. He intended to become a billionaire—world-class rich. Banking with Continental Illinois made that a possibility. If the gas that Hefner had been saying all along was there was indeed there, and if it was finally worth something, why not try to own the whole thing?

CHAPTER 10

"Father of the Anadarko Basin" was a title that others conferred upon Bob Hefner after he cut his quarter-of-a-billion-dollar deal with Mobil. It sounded grand, yet even Hefner knew better. He knew that his own ideas and schemes flowed from many sources and that, if he had to single out a progenitor, the credit belonged to Kenneth Ellison. To validate his sincerity, Hefner would tell how he had stood at Kenneth Ellison's grave and had vowed to conquer the Anadarko's nethermost regions.

Half a generation ahead of Hefner, Ellison, an independent geologist, extolled the deep potential of the Basin. The only photograph of Ellison that I have seen is a copy of a newspaper clipping, with a caption that reads, "Kenneth Ellison spots deep wildcat location." It shows a sturdy, well-tailored gentleman—dark suit, white shirt, narrow striped tie, breast-pocket handkerchief—as he stands before a large-scale oil-and-gas acreage map and uses a wooden pointer to designate a prospective drilling site. There is Kenneth Ellison's noble profile, his strong nose and chin, large ears, dark eyebrows, his silver hair brushed straight back. Ellison's eyes, half closed, make him look as if he could use a nice long rest.

The accompanying article, which was published in the *Daily Oklahoman* in the summer of 1963, gives an account of Ellison's plans to redrill a deep Anadarko well called the No. 1 North Corn Unit. Two years earlier, the Continental Oil Company had abandoned the hole at 17,323 feet, in a zone of Mississippian limestone approximately three hundred million years old. It was Kenneth Ellison's desire to go four thousand feet deeper and a hundred fifty million years further back into geologic time—into Ordovician sediments known in Oklahoma as the Bromide sands. Four months after this story appeared, Kenneth Ellison was dead. While duck-hunting one morning with his son, Clark, he had a heart attack, and it was all over. So was the plan to redrill the No. 1 North Corn Unit, which had proceeded far enough to run up nearly half a million dollars in expenses. Ellison had wanted to drill this well for the usual reason: he believed that the North Corn Anticline—together with the Fort Cobb Anticline, to the southeast—could make him stupendously wealthy.

An anticline is a geologic structure that can be thought of as an underground mountain, an arched folding of subsurface strata. When a geologist looks at a contoured map of such a structure, which is based upon seismic soundings, he looks hopefully at a potential reservoir of oil and gas. The North Corn structure was in the eastern portion of Washita County, and the Fort Cobb was just across the line in Caddo County. In Grady County, which borders Caddo on the east, Ellison had observed the drilling during the early fifties of an exceptionally valuable gas well. From a reservoir of Bromide sands more than two hundred feet thick, the well produced a hundred seventy-five million cubic feet of gas daily. What if the sands grew even richer as one moved west, toward the Fort Cobb and North Corn structures? Ellison had been in the oil business since the early twenties, and had drilled wells all over Oklahoma. He had seen vivid seismic readings of the fault system that ran parallel to the Fort Cobb and the North Corn, and he believed that the Bromide would thicken greatly as the Anadarko Basin descended. Of the Fort Cobb Anticline, he once wrote: "Geologically, it is practically an impossibility to drill a completely dry hole on the Fort Cobb Anticline should the well be drilled deep enough to test all potentially oil/gas bearing formations under the area."

A well drilled into a limestone and dolomite deposit known as the Arbuckle, more than four miles down, would penetrate almost all the known producing sands, limestones, dolomites, and shales found in Oklahoma. Ellison could easily imagine a Bromide layer three hundred or five hundred feet thick along the way. He was not unwilling to consider a thousand or even fifteen hundred feet of Bromide. He could imagine multiple pay zones and vast reservoirs, individual wells that, even at late-1950s prices, could yield hydrocarbons worth twenty million dollars. Ellison was a magnificent extrapolator. No wonder Hefner admired him. There was no reason, Ellison pointed out, that the Fort Cobb and North Corn anticlines, resting beneath ninety thousand surface acres, should not produce thirty or thirty-five trillion cubic feet of gas. The structure should be worth billions. Kenneth Ellison died broke.

Starting in the late 1950s, when Ellison began in earnest to buy Anadarko acreage and to seek major partners, deep wildcats had been drilled in the Fort Cobb or the North Corn every five or six years. Ambitions seemed to run several years ahead of the requisite technology. Often the wells approached record depths, and always something went wrong: equipment would break and become irretrievably lost downhole, drill pipe would get cemented inside the well bore, erratic pressures would make it impossible to complete a well, well bores would collapse, courage would flag. Ellison remained a believer. One of his business associates at the end was M.P. Appleby, Jr., known to his familiars as Buddy. Ellison had worked with Appleby's father when they were both employed by an oil company in Tulsa. In Appleby Jr. he recognized someone with the ability to raise funds and chase oil and gas leases. Ellison's untimely demise was a great inconvenience to his only child, Clark, and to Buddy Appleby, as well as to his creditors. He was more than a million dollars in debt—mainly to oilfield service firms, but also to a couple of bankers. Clark, who had already received in trust certain leases, minerals, and producing properties, had cosigned some of his father's notes. It took eight years to settle Kenneth's estate, during which Clark and Buddy did what they could to keep interest in the North Corn and the Fort Cobb alive. Working without a formal partnership agreement, they leased acreage together and traded it for carried interests in deep wells. When leases expired, they leased the minerals again. "We're tribe to the Anadarko Indians," Buddy liked to say, referring to some of the landowners in the North Corn and Fort Cobb areas. "Every one of those kids that's college-educated down there— Clark and I paid for that."

When I caught up with Buddy Appleby, he was in his fifties and was talking about retiring. He was a wiry man with a dimpled chin, a perpetual half-smile, and white hair that he parted down the middle. Some of the energy that he drew upon when he hustled dollars and acres for Kenneth Ellison had dispersed. He had some ex-wives. He spoke deliberately, in a delicate voice. He had maxims for many occasions. One Appleby maxim went: "If you drill a successful wildcat you want to own the entire structure"—meaning that it was a wise idea to spread your money over as much acreage as possible. "You should buy two acres for every one acre you want," went another.

Clark Ellison was a courtly man, more southern than southwestern, and tweedy by oil patch standards. He was shaped like a relief pitcher—tall and a few pounds over trim—and he had a soft face. When his father died, he was twenty-one years old and an undergraduate at the University of Oklahoma, majoring in petroleum land management. That Clark did not brim with charisma was just as well. Charisma and hubris often travel as a pair, and it was a combination of the two that had tempted Kenneth Ellison to try to hold on to too much with too few resources. Clark never cared to spread himself throughout the Anadarko. If Kenneth's beliefs in the Fort Cobb and the North Corn had substance, that would be good enough.

The earliest seismic surveying of the Fort Cobb structure was done by the Superior Oil Company in the 1940s. Kenneth Ellison's map of the original Superior seismic got folded, bent, stained, and mutilated. Several major oil companies paid for seismic surveys in later years. Thanks to variable-density cross sections and six-fold computer stacks, Clark and Buddy were able to work with fresher maps. Always the same picture showed up, the same basic formation. There was definitely something down there—if only some big operators could be persuaded to drill deep enough to get an up-close look.

During the summer of 1974, Ellison and Appleby hired themselves as lease brokers. They bought four thousand acres of five-year leases throughout the Fort Cobb, and immediately proceeded to mark up and resell chunks of it to raise cash to participate in wells. Knowing that they could not afford troublesome, expensive holes, they rarely held on to more than eighty or a hundred acres in a section. "We were always wealthy men," Appleby said. "But we were short of cash." They ended up owning pieces of troublesome, expensive holes anyway: derricks toppled, drilling mud boiled and marbled into impermeability, wells blew out.

One of their most promising but most costly ventures was the Phifer No. 1, which had as its objective the Hunton formation, a Siluro-Devonian limestone four miles deep, just above the Bromide. Drilling began in the summer of 1977, and in the spring of 1978 something happened to ruin the well. The episode also appeared to ruin Ellison and Appleby, who had run out of money and whose leases were about to expire. Exasperated, they filed a negligence suit against the operator of the Phifer No. 1. The complaint was settled in Ellison and Appleby's favor and they were able to use the damages, plus some money borrowed at superusurious rates, to buy back leases in the Phifer vicinity. This time they paid two hundred fifty dollars an acre in bonuses.

Some shallower wells were by now being drilled on their acreage in Fort Cobb, but nothing as audacious as the Hunton prospect that Ellison and Appleby had in mind in northwestern Caddo County, in the same township as the Phifer No. 1, on land owned by a peanut farmer named Glenn Stevens. Getting to the Hunton meant spudding through Stevens' topsoil and farther, past the Permian and the lower Pennsylvanian and the Mississippian into the Siluro-Devonian, or, to put it another lyrical way, through the Virgil, Missouri, Des Moines, Skinner, Red Fork, Atoka, Morrow, Springer, Chester, and Sycamore formations. Of course, Ellison and Appleby had no means to get there alone, because once again they were broke. Oilfield reputations depend on results, not intentions. Technical excuses notwithstanding, Ellison and Appleby looked like losers. Logs from the Phifer convinced them that, with the right operator, they could drill a successful Hunton test. They spread their maps around town, they begged to be carried. "We were huntin' for the Hunton, baby," Appleby recalled. "And we were suckin' wind."

No one expressed interest until, one atypical day, they met Clifford W. Culpepper.

Once I did something truly graceless that irritated Cliff Culpepper. I composed a list of questions that I intended to ask someone who knew Culpepper well. Then, by mistake, I left the list in a bar, where it was found by someone else who knew him well. When Culpepper got hold of the list, he took offense and decided never to speak to me again. For some time thereafter I moved about warily, concerned that Culpepper and I were going to have a chance encounter that would cause me pain. Eventually, I eased my mind with the thought that, although I had visited him in his office and spoken with him a few times, it was unlikely that he knew what I looked like. Our eyes had never met. When you dealt with Culpepper face to face, so to speak, his eyes seemed hooded and focused—or unfocused—on something over your shoulder or deep in the outfield. Culpepper was in his late fifties. He had gray hair that fell across his forehead and one of those craggy faces that are creased like an old roadmap. His eyes might have been green. Or maybe they were brown, or gray. I really don't know. When Culpepper talked, his arms flapped from the elbow and his hands fluttered, as if he were trying to restore circulation to his fingertips. One other remarkable thing: Culpepper's handshake. In the oil patch, in the Kingdom of Okiesmo, where a handshake bound you to your word and got you what you needed—Culpepper had a handshake like cold cooked spaghetti. His fingers went loose. There was no grip. Cliff Culpepper seemed to have no handshake at all.

"We showed our deal to over a hundred people," Buddy Appleby told me. "One day, I read in the paper that Cliff Culpepper and his partner had split up. I saw Culpepper's picture. I said, 'Clark, here's a guy who really needs our help.' Clark says, 'Oh, no. You don't want to do business with him.' I said, 'Clark, how's he gonna give *us* a hard time?' " First, they made a run at Culpepper's ex-partner, who before becoming an oilman had been a high school football coach. Years earlier, this man had entered local legend when he was accused by the University of Texas football coach of spying on the Longhorns before their annual game with Oklahoma. The ex-partner looked at the Phifer logs and the Fort Cobb seismic surveys and declined to get involved. So that left Culpepper.

If Cliff Culpepper liked you—or, at least, needed to get along with you—he called you "Mister" plus your first name. Culpepper had just incorporated a new enterprise, the Ports of Call Oil Company. Ellison and Appleby became Mister Clark and Mister Bud.

"Mister Clark and Mister Bud, everything's gonna be just as clean and simple as can be," Culpepper promised when he agreed that Ports of Call would operate a well in the Fort Cobb, in Section 14-10N-13W, Caddo County. "We'll use Jack Hodges' tools on this well, and you'll never have a problem."

Jack Hodges owned drilling rigs and he owned trucks the size of DC-10s for hauling drilling rigs. He owned much oil-and-gas production. No one ever suggested that Jack Hodges had inferior Okiesmo. A friend of Jack Hodges once explained his basic philosophy: "Jack just wants to have things that are big. He's big, his kids are big, his house is big, he flies a big plane. He owns big rigs and he hauls them around with big trucks."

I recall reading a newspaper account of the wedding of Jack's daughter. The parking valets wore brocade frock coats and powdered wigs. "An eighteenth-century French garden feeling prevailed as a violinist and flutist played for arriving guests." The wedding cake was eighteen feet tall, in keeping with the eighteen motif. "Trucks and cranes, representing the family business, were drawn with icing on the sides of the cake." When Jack Hodges spent a dollar, he spent a big dollar. He pledged two million dollars to help erect a public greenhouse called a botanical tube in downtown Oklahoma City. He donated fifty thousand to help redecorate the White House, just a few weeks after Ronald Reagan decontrolled oil prices, in 1981. "The top man of this country ought to live in one of the top places," Hodges said at the time. A painted legend on the fingerboard of each of Jack Hodges' drilling rigs said "Come On, America."

"We'll use Jack Hodges' tools and we'll do just fine," Culpepper promised Ellison and Appleby. "I've never had a fishing job in my life. There won't be any problems. Mister Bud, Jack Hodges and I are very close friends. We got houses right next door to each other in Cancún."

If Culpepper wanted something from you, if he was maybe planning to slip one past you, he'd call you "Sunshine" or "Kingfish." There would be a well drilling somewhere and the phone would ring at four in the morning and you'd hear this twang, all wound up, saying, "Good news, Kingfish," or "Sunshine, here's what we're gonna do." When Culpepper wanted something that no one else seemed able to find—a special rig, a special string of pipe—he called Jack Hodges. Ports of Call would operate the well,

Hodges would make the hole, and Ellison and Appleby, in exchange for half of their acreage, would get a free trip to the Hunton. It seemed reasonably auspicious.

"When Buddy and Clark made that deal with Cliff, I was there," Jack Hodges later recalled. Eager to get involved Hodges was not, but Culpepper had been his friend for thirty years. "I saw the deal, I saw the maps. It looked O.K., but as far as I was concerned it was just another rank wildcat well. The thing had been shopped all over. Cliff was the only harum-scarum person in town who would make a deal like that, and I was the only person who could get him a deep rig. I had a rig out in the yard that was a week away from being finished and I pulled it off another job that it was headed for so Cliff could use it. From the first time I saw the acreage and the charts, from the moment Ellison and Appleby put the pants on Cliff, I knew Cliff had to drill the best well in the world to make money on it."

The terms that Ellison and Appleby exacted were quite favorable to them, considering that Culpepper was the only operator who had expressed interest in their proposal. In return for a one-half interest in Ellison and Appleby's acreage, Culpepper agreed to drill and complete a productive well—an arrangement known as "drill-to-earn." If Culpepper cared to protect himself against the risk that the well would be dry or could not be completed, he would have to sell part of his stake to other investors. "We're selling this two-for-one and a third-for-a-quarter," Culpepper would say, assuming that he and whomever he was hustling understood what that meant. It meant, essentially, that he had to promote the hell out of the deal.

Culpepper started by giving the well a name that struck him as romantic: the Tomcat No. 1. "You know, an ole tomcat goes huntin' at night," Cliff said. "I like to go huntin' at night." The name alone proved to be not irresistible enough. To sell the Tomcat No. 1, he had to make it part of a bigger package.

"We made Culpepper a *tough* deal," Appleby said. "After we first talked about it, he called us back and said he needed more acreage. So we threw in half of what we had in five other sections on the structure. Then we had to throw in four more sections."

For Ellison and Appleby, this meant a chance to get many more of their prospects drilled. For Culpepper, more acreage meant more wells to operate, more two-for-one and third-for-a-quarter hocus-pocus, more opportunities for profit. According to the Oklahoma Securities Commission, which periodically expressed interest in how Culpepper operated, his fund-raising techniques were idiosyncratic. In his happy, hyperbolic moods, he liked to say that he had drilled three hundred wells in six years, only fifteen dry holes among them. When he operated a well, he wanted to spud it, drill it, complete it, hook it up to a pipeline as fast as possible, and get on to the next one. Going to the courthouse to record mineral leases, applying for drilling permits at the Corporation Commission, sending triplicate notices to the surface landowners, petitioning for location exceptions—these administrative details never held great fascination for Culpepper. Employees of the government, he would remind associates, were "just a bunch of clerks who have created a lot of rules to take my money away from me."

It never seemed clear how Culpepper had made the money in the first place. After the Tomcat, people talked about him quite a bit and you would hear different tales. You would hear that Culpepper way back when had drilled the such-and-such well straight up and that his fortune rested upon that. It might have been the Newberry well. Or maybe the Mickey wells, the ones he drilled in the sixties, in Dewey County. Perhaps it was the Wright, the Grady County well that Culpepper borrowed six hundred thousand to drill and that ultimately returned something like fifteen to one. Some people said Cliff had made his reputation, if not necessarily his money, the time another Grady County well blew out on him. Instead of hiring Red Adair or one of those other expensive folk heroes, he had put on an asbestos suit and had gone up on the rig and shut the well back in himself.

Most facts about Culpepper were adumbrated; filling it all in required traipsing through some obscure terrain. Cliff Culpepper was born in Alabama and moved with his mother to Oklahoma in the 1930s. He had sharp memories of the Depression. There was no father around. Eighth grade was as far as he got in school. Franklin Roosevelt helped him learn auto mechanics and welding and sheet-metal work. For sixteen years, he toured the southern Oklahoma oilfields for Halliburton, the giant well-servicing company. The eighty-four-hour workweek was not a rarity. He drove cement trucks and bulldozers, sidebooms and tankers. He hauled drilling mud, frac fluids, brine, and diesel. When he saw heavy mud used as a lubricant in deep wells, he got the idea of salvaging it from the pits and filtering and lightening and reselling it. As a sideline, he was becoming an entrepreneur, specializing in dirty work.

Culpepper's skills were operational rather than managerial. Jack Hodges said, "What I guess I admired about Cliff was his gutsiness. Cliff'll roll the dice with you. The toolpushers on some of those wells Cliff was servicing would show him an electric log. Say whoever owned the well was going to plug and abandon it. But the log don't always tell the whole story. This toolpusher might see something he likes on that log and he tells Cliff about a zone they missed. So, for very little money, Cliff goes back in to some of those wells. And he gets *real* lucky. He made seven or eight wells that way. Around the mid-sixties Cliff showed up in town one day driving a Lincoln and wearing a hundred-dollar suede coat—the way he dresses sometimes you're sure he's colorblind—and he was looking for a banker."

An Oklahoma City banker I know liked Culpepper, and not merely because he paid back what he borrowed. One time, when they had agreed on a loan, Culpepper shook hands and the banker asked, "Don't you want to know the interest rate?" Culpepper replied, "I know you'll be fair with me." Once prosperity invaded Culpepper's life, the word "no" disappeared from his vocabulary. "If you play for pennies all you'll do is make pennies. If you play for dollars you'll make dollars" was his creed. When Culpepper saw something he liked, one wasn't good enough. Three wasn't good enough. He wanted six or eight or ten. It was nice to have twenty-two Ultrasuede jackets. By the early seventies, he controlled at least three trucking companies and he had interests in fifty wells. Less than ten years later, the value of the entire enterprise had expanded into the stout eight-figure range. Along the way came the Learjet, then two more, then the jet helicopter, the second home in Cancún, the third home in Baja, the seaside estate in Santa Barbara, the eighty-two-foot yacht in Newport Beach.

As an operator, Culpepper was known for his ability to drill successfully "under balance"—a technique that involves maintaining a drilling mud weight just at or below the level necessary to prevent a blowout. Erratic pressures made this a requirement in many areas, including certain deep zones of the Anadarko. Culpepper's system allowed him to operate under "controlled blowout" conditions: to absorb a sudden kick of high-pressure gas—the wild jolt that you might get from a Tomcat—without interrupting the drilling. Once he had drilled to total depth, Culpepper practiced a peculiar method of well completion. To complete a well is to do whatever will permit oil or gas to be extracted. The ideal approach is the one that leads to the greatest long-term recovery of hydrocarbons from the reservoir. Usually, the wall of the formation has to be "perforated"—literally, holes have to be punched in it. In most instances, after a steel casing has been set inside the well bore and cemented into place, a perforating gun is lowered into the hole and fired through the casing and the cement. Either bullets or jets of high-pressure gases do the actual perforating.

A conventional operator perforates a zone, produces oil or natural gas (or both) from it for as long as the economics dictate, then moves uphole to the next potentially worthwhile zone and perforates that. Culpepper was not a conventional operator. His well-completion technique was referred to in the oilfield as "grass roots to granite." He had a theory of hydrocarbon-bearing sediments that went like this: "The zone's there, you shoot holes in it, and you get hydrocarbons." The preferred method—the one that said, "Here's ten feet of pay zone. We treat it and produce it and move up. We work from the bottom up"—was not as initially impressive as Culpepper's technique. Culpepper would drill as deep as he intended, run a gamma-ray log, decide which of the zones bore hydrocarbons, and then perforate all of them at once. "Doing it that way you can get some impressive production right off the bat, but sometimes you shoot formations that shouldn't be shot," one of Culpepper's former associates has explained. "It might help you impress a potential investor, but you risk bringing in water and other contamination. Cliff just shoots it. Anything that looks like it has any porosity, any potential, Cliff shoots it. Your logs might be deceiving sometimes. Cliff shoots it."

Ellison and Appleby made the Tomcat deal with Culpepper early in 1980, shortly after the Ports of Call Oil Company was incorporated. The previous year, Culpepper and his former partner had drilled nine hundred thousand feet of holes, divided among seventy-five wells, mainly oil—as much as any independent outfit in Oklahoma. Most of this activity took place in Canadian County, immediately west of Oklahoma City, along the eastern flank of the

Anadarko Basin. Canadian County offered Culpepper a lucrative known quantity; there were none of the erratic high-pressure zones that cropped up farther out in the Basin, no exotic geophysics. An average well could be started and completed in a couple of months. Without question, Culpepper was on a roll. "It was all a matter of timing," Buddy Appleby said later. "Cliff was just coming out of Canadian County. He could do no wrong. Technically, he thought everything that applied to Canadian County applied to the Fort Cobb. He thought he was ready for deep stuff. He felt invincible. It's a dangerous feeling."

Drilling of the Tomcat began in the middle of June 1980. If everything in the Fort Cobb turned out to be as manageable as Canadian County, Culpepper and Ellison and Appleby could reasonably expect to see the Hunton sands around Christmas. When the drill bit was more than a mile shy of the Hunton, in a zone of highly porous, high-pressure sandstone—sandwiched between layers of shale—Culpepper encountered the major drawback of drilling under balance. Christmas was going to be delayed. The Tomcat No. 1 blew out.

Mud flew, gas spewed, and the well ran wild. Blowouts are good news/bad news events. Obviously the oil or gas is there, but can it be brought under control? The costly but potentially cost-effective remedy is to start over somewhere in the middle. You pour a cement plug as far downhole as possible and then, above the plug, insert a "whipstock," or wedge, that will deflect the drill bit and create a hole that slants away from the original well bore. Four months after the blowout, the whipstocked Tomcat had been redrilled to 15,385 feet.

What happened next remains open to interpretation. Poor mud circulation? Poor judgment? Natural caprice? What happened next was that the Tomcat No. 1 unloaded in a cataclysmic fashion. Metal casing had been inserted down to the 13,750-foot level, but when this blowout occurred the casing burst. The drilling rig vibrated with enough forewarning to allow the crew to escape. The earth quaked and regurgitated. It was as if Cliff Culpepper had perforated a thousand feet of open hole all at once—one of his trademark grass-roots-to-granite well completions. This time, however, nature itself had squeezed the trigger.

"It was like standing in front of ten jet engines all revved up at once," Jack Hodges said. The falling mud and shale, someone else observed, made it "look like it was raining crows."

The spectacle lasted two weeks, and toward the end the gas blew harder than ever. From an interstate highway fifteen miles north, you could see a cloud of gas and condensate and solid debris. From two miles away you could hear Beelzebub whistling. Rocketing shale would strike metal, generating sparks; the rig floor would catch fire, and flying mud would extinguish the fires. If the gas failed to disperse, the well site would be a potential bomb. If wind carried the gas southwest, it could explode a nearby town called Eakly. A blowout-control specialist named Bobby Joe Cudd kept the entire rig from catching fire, but most of the time Culpepper and Hodges and their crews, as well as Ellison and Appleby and the other interest owners, were reduced to jamming their hands in their pockets, cussing, and kicking rocks. There was enough free time to dredge superlatives: the Tomcat was either the biggest or the loudest or the most something blowout that anyone could remember. Without question, the gas that rose into the atmosphere was the most valuable. The earth had rendered something unearthly.

A temporary pipeline was laid along the ground, and pipeline companies rushed forth with contracts and offers—first five dollars per thousand cubic feet, then seven dollars, then nine. The makeshift pipeline could accommodate only half of what the Tomcat was producing; the rest had to be flared through howitzerlike vents. Consensus said that the well naturally flowed more than a hundred million cubic feet of gas a day. Overnight, lease prices in the adjacent sections went from three hundred dollars an acre to three thousand. On the fourteenth day of the blowout, the shale walls of the well bore collapsed and the Tomcat plugged itself.

Reservoir engineers who had no real foundation for estimating the Tomcat's reserves offered estimates anyway. It could produce a hundred billion cubic feet of methane, they guessed—maybe three hundred billion. Once the Tomcat was whipstocked again and successfully completed, it would be worth . . . But trying to imagine what it might all be worth missed the point. At five dollars, Ellison and Appleby and Culpepper, if he could finish the job—everyone who had bought into the Tomcat was going to be absurdly wealthy. At nine dollars, they were all headed for never-never land. Culpepper could afford more Ultrasuede jackets. The point was that there was no point. Kenneth Ellison had been correct: there was something unusual about the Fort Cobb.

Hedging their bet, Clark Ellison and Buddy Appleby accepted from another exploration company a million-dollar offer for 6.4 of their acres in the Tomcat section—1 percent of the well. When they received the check, they noticed that it had been drawn on the Penn Square Bank.

CHAPTER 11

The Tomcat blowout spawned new math and great expectations. A well that freely flowed a hundred million cubic feet of gas a day would in ten days flow a billion. If it could do that in ten days it could easily, before the reservoir was tapped out, produce a hundred billion cubic feet. At nine dollars per thousand cubic feet that would come to ninety million doll . . . no, nine *hundred* million dollars. Several "ifs" belonged in the equation, but why quibble? Veterans who had been taught to judge a well's economics by its chances of paying for itself within, say, two or three years found the new math disorienting. During the mid-1960s, when gas prices had made the big jump from fifteen cents per thousand to seventeen cents, sane oilmen weighed the possibility that they were about to become wealthy. Come the Tomcat, sane oilmen ran out and bought new electronic calculators. You needed a device with a twelve-digit display.

People who did not know better entertained the notion that deep drilling was elephant-hunting. With sufficient artillery, it was assumed, you could not miss. There were multiple pay zones. You could spend four million dollars and come out with four billion cubic feet of gas every time. If that didn't work, there was always the bigger-fool principle to fall back upon. The bigger-fool principle said: No matter what I pay for something today, there is bound to be a bigger fool tomorrow who will pay more for it and bail me out. Beginning in 1973, the rising value of oil and gas began to bail bankers out of otherwise marginal loans. Everything inflated— leasehold costs, royalties, drilling costs, material costs, labor costs, engineering costs. Geologists suddenly expected six-figure salaries, overriding royalty interests, and fancy perks. Toolpushers in the Anadarko Basin could pull down forty thou per year. Training schools for roughnecks opened and were immediately oversubscribed. By the end of 1981, more than three hundred deep rigs, plus a hundred or so with shallower capacities, were working in the Oklahoma portion of the Anadarko. The value of this capital equipment came to more than a billion and a half dollars. One widely accepted estimate was that over four billion dollars was spent that year in the Anadarko—and a billion and a quarter more elsewhere in the state. Eleven thousand miles of hole were drilled. Juggling the big numbers all day long, you still could not quantify the human implications.

During one phase, a good portion of the Oklahoma oil industry's operating capital was flowing through the treasuries of small independent companies that had grabbed the chance to sell stock to the public. Before that boomlet peaked, in early 1981—the penny stock players, it appears, had the jump on the banks by a full year—underwriters had to cull among promoters and eager investors. Certain public companies did not want you buying their stock unless you could produce proof that you were a good Christian ("The wisest & best move that thou couldst possibly make, in pursuit of good investments, is a mailing of thy good checks for substantial amounts of cash money unto GOD & SON at the above address"); believing in eighty-dollar crude oil was not enough, you also had to *believe*. A black hole opened and ingested the people who had lived in the oil patch all their lives but had never before sunk a dime into the earth—hairdressers, file clerks, chiropractors. Quite a few dollars went into overhead. Publicly raised funds decorated some sparkling new offices, places that visitors passed through exclaiming, "Hey, I like your environment a *lot*!" More than Okie mattress money was involved. There were also francs, deutschmarks, pounds, guilders. Tax treaties paved the way for English syndicates and Netherlands Antilles corporations and German limited partnerships—a rush of flight capital that traveled an oblique path through the London Stock Exchange and the Vancouver Stock Exchange and then into penny stocks or drilling fund shares, every earnest franc, deutschmark, pound, or guilder diminished along the way by a grateful promoter. As the used-car dealer population of Vancouver dropped, the independent oilman population rose. To make those investments pay, you had to find four or five dollars' worth of petroleum for every investment dollar. Speculators jumped in assuming that oil stocks selling for a dollar today would sell for five dollars within three months. Mass cupidity, a banality of greed, took hold—not sinful, just harmful. Solid citizens lost control of themselves. How were you going to survive in a cocktail conversation if you were not in on the game?

In January 1981 an oilman named Bill Saxon paid forty million dollars for 1,286 acres of mineral leases forty miles southwest of the North Corn and the Fort Cobb, where there was said to be a geologic structure as exciting as a trip to Jupiter. Previously Saxon had been doing just fine drilling oil wells in west Texas, and he had recently sold Saxon Oil stock to the public, pocketing thirty-eight million dollars in the process. His new playground was in a corner of the Anadarko referred to, interchangeably, as the Fletcher Field or the Cyril Basin. When someone asked him what he had in mind paying forty million dollars for 1,286 acres, he said, "I was ready for a little higher risk. And I wanted to give these guys with me a chance to be a one-billion-dollar company."

One Wall Street securities analyst published a research report on the Fletcher Field that predicted reserves of forty billion cubic feet of gas per square mile and seven million cubic feet of gas per day at an average price of eight dollars per thousand cubic feet. The "average" well would thus generate fifteen million dollars a year, more than a hundred million during its productive lifetime. According to even bigger fools, the Fletcher had two billion cubic feet of gas in every foot of pay zone. If there were a hundred feet of pay in a well and methane sold for nine dollars, every well would be worth a billion eight hundred million dollars. And so forth. Major oil companies flocked. Kerr-McGee Oil Industries made plans to spend a hundred and fifty million dollars in the Fletcher in 1982, then brought in Texaco as a partner. Robert A. Hefner III did not ignore what was happening southwest of the Tomcat. In 1981, he paid thirty-seven and a half million dollars for a fifteen-thousand-acre position in the Cyril Basin—a steal, he assumed, projecting that he would eventually discover sixteen trillion cubic feet of reserves. "I'll stake my reputation as an explorationist on that," he said, and he did.

FUNNY MONEY

. . .

A while ago, I had a conversation with a man on the West Coast whose career was in a brief lull—a circumstance that seemed to bother him not at all. He was half of a two-person fund-raising team that in the preceding five years had sold a quarter of a billion dollars' worth of oil-and-gas drilling fund partnerships. Because of the nature of drilling fund financing, the money that was raised actually resulted in more than half a billion dollars of oil-and-gas exploration. The two fund raisers specialized in anonymity, found their clients by word of mouth, never wrote a letter ("not even a thank-you note") without first consulting an attorney, employed a part-time receptionist, usually answered their own phones, and retained 2 percent of every dollar they minted. "A couple of small operators" is one way they referred to themselves. "If we did what we did, imagine what Merrill Lynch and Dean Witter did," one of the fund raisers said.

During a five-year stretch beginning in 1977, registered drilling funds raised twenty billion dollars—more than a fifth of what was spent for onshore exploration in the United States. "There was an enthusiastic reception by the world for oil," I was informed by a broker in New York City, who had spent very little of his life on oil rigs. "Sometimes you have to sell what people want to buy."

Boldface capital letters on the cover of every legal drilling fund prospectus said, "The securities described herein involve a high degree of risk." That was a pro forma message. Risk was not the first thing on most investors' minds. If ever a free-money proposition existed, it was the leveraged tax-shelter drilling fund. Everyone could enjoy the benefits—fund sponsors, securities lawyers, investors, bankers. The clients of the man on the West Coast had the resources to invest at least two hundred thousand dollars per "investment unit," a magnitude that attracted real estate geniuses, old-money rich folks, gastroenterologists, high-priced accountants. The smaller drilling funds, where the minimum investment ranged from, say, five thousand dollars to twenty-five thousand, brought in the ophthalmologists and dentists and attorneys. Most funds were designed as limited partnerships—heavily lawyered variations of the industry-standard third-for-a-quarter.

The most tantalizing drilling programs required a limited partner to pay in cash only a fraction of his total investment. The Penn

Square Bank was enamored of a device called a letter of credit, which is a bank's guarantee, on behalf of a creditworthy customer, that it will pay another party the face value of the letter. Historically, letters of credit have been tools of international trade but have not been widely used in risk ventures. In a leveraged drilling fund, the general partner might require of a limited partner a down payment of 25 percent, plus a letter of credit from a bank for the balance of an investment. The general partner would eventually take the letters of credit to the Penn Square Bank, where it was possible to borrow against their full amount, with the letters securing the loan. In turn Penn Square would sell the drilling fund loan to an upstream bank. From the point of view of, say, Continental Illinois, drilling fund loans had much promise. The interest rate was two or two and a half points above prime. Even if a drilling program found no oil or gas—an unthinkable possibility—the upstream bank's position was secured by the letters of credit. The administrative requirements for servicing these loans were considerable, but administrative details were supposed to be Penn Square's responsibility.

You could buy what suited your tastes. Any investor who did not feel like tying up his money with a 25 percent down payment could find a fund that required no money down. *Free money.* A letter of credit would guarantee the entire investment—cover not only exploration and overhead costs but also interest payments on the drilling program's borrowing. There was an immediate tax benefit to be realized by deducting drilling costs, and there was the assumption that future oil-and-gas income would pay off the drilling program's debts. If all went well—and why not?—an investor could plunk down zero dollars in cash in quest of a big tax benefit and a handsome profit. You could buy a share in an exploratory drilling program and go wildcatting in the deep Anadarko or you could aim for less risk and potentially less reward in an already developed field. The major oil companies and the big independents always leased more acreage than they could drill themselves. The surplus they farmed out, often to operators with the sketchiest track records. Raising funds and not sticking the money in the ground was a crime, and no one wanted to be accused of that. Tremendous pressure existed to keep pace with events. With the drilling fund money pouring in, the next challenge was to find rigs to drill it up. New rigs had to be built, which meant that more money had to be borrowed. The inordinate demand for rigs led lease brokers to decide suddenly to become drilling contractors. Thanks to the letter of credit, the small-fry Okie-type independent oilman could envision vertical integration.

The whole thing was an exercise in tail-swallowing. Rare was the potential investor who properly scrutinized the economics. If a fund had to pay an average royalty of 25 percent, and if it was predicated upon the third-for-a-quarter principle, that meant a raw investment dollar was immediately reduced to 75 percent of seventy-five cents—fifty-six and a quarter cents. If fund-raising fees and general and administrative expenses also came off the top, and if the acreage cost too much to begin with, and if a fund operator with an Exxonish fantasy had arranged to buy drilling mud, pipe, bulldozer work, and contract drilling from himself, and if, along the way, a green roughneck slipped on the rig floor and accidentally dropped a pipe wrench down a ten-thousand-foot hole, then a dollar had to work frightfully hard just to return itself, even if oil should go to sixty dollars a barrel. Prospectuses never elaborated the risks in such detail.

Entertaining science fiction has turned up in recent months in depositions taken from one-hundred-fifty-thousand-dollar-a-unit investors who have been asked to describe how oil-and-gas exploration works. Oil and gas, according to these sworn statements, hang out in big pools underground, waiting for a real estate mogul from Marina del Rey to fork over a hundred fifty thousand dollars so an oil company can sink a metal straw down there and slurp up the goo. A lawyer for one of these sophisticated investors once asked me, "What would you do if you had a lot of money and if you had to figure out something to do with it, otherwise you're in a very high tax bracket and you're going to have to give it to the government? And someone tells you that for no money down, just a letter of credit, interest payments built into the investment unit share, a rollover down the line into a straight oil-and-gas production loan, a tax deduction right now for intangible drilling costs, a chance to make a lot more money down the road, and so forth—for all of that, all you have to do is sign on the dotted line right now? And, *and*, a bank in Oklahoma City that knows the guys who are selling the drilling fund says that they are good people, *plus* they do business with Chase Manhattan and Continental Illinois, a couple of the biggest banks in the country? What would you do?"

One other thing that sophisticated investors understood about the oil-and-gas business: it was damned impressive to fly first-class to Oklahoma City, to have dinner at a restaurant called Cowboys (where you could order steak fingers and quail and fresh channel catfish and calf fries) and watch real Western ladies and range riders dance the two-step, to have breakfast at the country club, to take a quick helicopter ride out to the Anadarko to see a genuine goddamn deep rig punching a hole in the ground, and to hear from a Penn Square banker that everything would work out just fine.

CHAPTER 12

While visiting with J. D. Allen in his office one day, I sat in a comfortable chair only inches from some valuable mementos. Situated on his desk so that it confronted any visitor was a teak-framed color snapshot, and next to it sat a walnut plaque. A small silver-plated eagle—the insignia of a group of the Republican Party's most generous donors—was fastened to the plaque. In the photograph were Wayne Newton, Gerald Ford, and J. D. Allen, all dressed in black tie and seated at a banquet table. The former President's shirtfront was white, Wayne Newton's was blue, and J. D.'s was white with black-edged scallops. I studied the photograph: J. D. seated to Wayne's left; Gerald Ford to Wayne's right with his arm resting on the crooner's shoulder; Wayne's deep tan; Wayne's pink carnation boutonniere; Wayne smiling; Wayne's upper lip curled; all those teeth; J. D. bearing a potent resemblance to Wayne except that Wayne's mustache was thinner and his sideburns and pompadour were thicker; J. D. looking as if he were getting ready to smile, too. A handwritten ink message on the photograph said, "To my friend, J. D. Allen, with appreciation and admiration, Gerald R. Ford." The photograph commemorated a high moment of the 1980 Presidential campaign, the Republican Party's "Prelude to Victory" dinner—either one thousand or five hundred dollars a plate, depending upon how hungry you were. J. D. had started life as a Democrat, but by 1980 he was co-chairman of the finance committee of the Republican National Committee. He was also a co-chairman of the Prelude to Victory dinner, and that is how he came to be seated at the head table.

Beep Jennings had introduced J. D. Allen to Carl Swan and

had vouched for the younger man's willingness to work hard, but he probably underestimated his resourcefulness and eagerness to achieve. Quickly, Carl got a sense of how simple it was to slap J. D. on the shoulder and say, "Go at it, son." It was much like Beep Jennings' slapping Bill Patterson on the shoulder and telling him, "Bill, you're a banker now." Momentum accomplished the rest. Carl Swan had assets and creditworthiness, and suddenly J. D. had an alliance with Carl. If J. D. yearned to borrow from Continental Illinois, Swan and Jennings would be his calling card. If, down the road, he felt like doing business with Seattle-First, he could make his approach bearing the Continental Illinois imprimatur. And so on—to Chase Manhattan, Northern Trust, Michigan National, London, Zurich, Asia, Africa, Washington, D. C.

The Longhorn Oil & Gas Company, the primary tie that bound Carl Swan and J. D. Allen, was founded in 1977. Longhorn existed for the purpose of raising money and drilling it up. Measured against the standard drilling fund company, Longhorn looked like an above-average can't-lose proposition. A minimum investment for most of the Longhorn funds was a hundred fifty thousand dollars. (There were at least two funds per year.) The usual irresistibles figured in—low down payment, high leverage, letter of credit, immediate tax benefit, future oil-and-gas production income. J. D. and Carl, the co-chairmen of Longhorn, each owned 42 percent of the company. A couple of Cities Service veterans were hired to run Longhorn's operations and exploration. When Bill Patterson, surpassing a banker's normal obligations, was touting the beauty of Longhorn to a potential investor, he would say, according to one deponent, "We, Penn Square, are not in the business of calling letters of credit. We're in the business of lending money. If we call the letters of credit, how can we lend money?" Bill Jennings reportedly once told some prospective Longhorn investors, "This deal is too safe for me"—a remark implying that he preferred a higher risk. Between 1977 and 1982, with much assistance from Patterson and Jennings, the Longhorn Oil & Gas Company, in various ways, borrowed more than eighty million dollars. Continental Illinois lent Longhorn sixty-eight million, Michigan National was good for six million, Chase lent two million, Northern Trust lent almost two million, Seafirst put up a million, a number of smaller banks collectively lent another couple of million.

Allen's vision was unclouded. What is good for J. D., he saw, is good. Diversification, he saw, was good. A conglomeration of interrelated companies, some sort of vertical integration—that seemed plausible. During the same five-year period that Longhorn was borrowing eighty million American dollars, Swan and Allen went to the banks to finance several other enterprises. A pipe threading and fabricating firm called Texas Upsetting & Finishing—Swan, Allen, and Jennings each owned 16 percent—borrowed ten million from Continental Illinois. Denton Brothers Drilling, 80 percent owned by Swan and Allen, borrowed almost seven million from Continental Illinois and slightly less than five million from other Penn Square correspondent banks. High Plains Drilling Company, of which Swan and Allen also owned 80 percent, borrowed twelve million from Continental Illinois, two and a half million from both Seafirst and Northern Trust, a million three hundred thousand from Michigan National, a million six from Chase, half a million more here and there. The Texas Oilfield Supply Company, which was in business to do what its name suggested, borrowed fifteen million from Continental Illinois and thirty-one million from Crocker National Bank, of San Francisco. Michigan National lent more than a million. Jennings owned 10 percent of Texas Oilfield Supply and Swan and Allen owned almost 20 percent each. Texas Oilfield Supply in turn owned part of an oil company called Olympic Exploration. Swan and Allen each held a separate 20 percent of Olympic, and through Penn Square that company borrowed almost six million, mainly from Chase Manhattan and Seafirst. One assumption behind all this was that if, say, Olympic Exploration needed a rig it would hire Denton Brothers or High Plains. If Longhorn needed tubular goods, it could buy the material from Texas Oilfield Supply or Texas Upsetting & Finishing.

Becoming highly bankable, Allen discovered, meant becoming instantly popular with incipient entrepreneurs who merely needed a financial boost to set their dreams in motion. In 1979, Charles Harding, who had been a college fraternity brother of Allen's, proposed starting an Anadarko Basin exploration company called Continental Resources. Allen liked the idea and, in return for 90 percent of the equity, agreed to escort Harding to the Penn Square Bank and to cosign the company's promissory notes. Allen also agreed to let Harding and an associate run the operation day to day. Continental Resources was founded in January 1980, financed with a one-million-dollar line of Penn Square credit. Eventually, the company borrowed thirteen million from Continental Illinois, five million from Seafirst, almost two million from Michigan National. Soon after Continental Resources went into business, Allen launched Texoma Resources. Its activities were to be concentrated in the Sooner Trend, a new-oilie broad-side-of-the-barn in north-central Oklahoma. The second most heavily explored oilfield in the United States during 1981 and 1982, the Sooner Trend was where you punched holes if you were less eager to accumulate oil-and-gas reserves than you were to impress potential investors with your "success" ratio. The local geology rendered it virtually impossible to drill and not run into oil, but the geology was also such that few Sooner Trend wells were truly worth the trouble. Texoma Resources accumulated an eighteen-million-dollar bank debt, two thirds of which was owed to Continental Illinois.

Borrowing scores of millions can burden a mortal, and Allen was left with no room in his life for hobbies. In what little spare time he could muster, he started companies, which created the need to borrow more money. Continental Resources and Texoma Resources were, respectively, 90 percent and 100 percent owned by J. D. Allen Industries, Inc., which was in turn 100 percent owned by J. D. Allen. These two entities are not to be confused with J. D. Allen & Company, the J. D. Allen Drilling Company, Inc., the Allen Oil Corporation, or the Allen Energy Corporation. J. D. Allen, as J. D. Allen, personally borrowed more than twelve million dollars from Penn Square's upstream banks. J. D. Allen Industries, Inc., separately borrowed six and a half million from the same banks. Chase Manhattan gave Allen Energy six hundred seventy-five thousand. J. D. Allen & Company, meanwhile, borrowed more than two million dollars, most of which—a million four from Continental Illinois—went to pay for an airplane. Chase Manhattan also financed a million-dollar-plus airplane. The J. D. Allen Industries umbrella also took in a securities brokerage firm, a computer company that owned some IBM hardware and some oil-and-gas accounting software, and a magazine, *Dollar: The International Journal of American Investments*. These last three companies had a combined bank debt of almost a million dollars. In addition, there was a Swan-Allen Joint Venture—good for six and a half million from Michigan National and an insignificant two hundred thirty thousand from Chase—not to mention several shell companies that J. D. kept handy, including L-X Exploration, the Helix Mineral & Oil Corporation, the Midwestern Oil & Gas Corporation, and Cougar Exploration.

Along the way, J. D. hired a public relations consultant. Soon, J. D. Allen Industries began turning out self-advertisements: four-color printing, glossy heavy stock, plastic spiral binding—stuff that looked like a cross between an annual report and a linoleum salesman's sample book. Enthusiasm ran high at J. D. Allen Industries.

"Working for J. D., we were not allowed to prioritize," the public relations consultant told me. "We were expected to keep all things moving in a positive direction." Allen enjoyed putting together a deal, but he was not deeply interested in administering a business. He preferred to hire people and tell them, "This is where I want to be. Make sure we get there." If you asked Allen a question that he did not want to hear, he was likely to say, "You just don't understand corporate *fi*-nance."

Brainstorming sessions were a regular thing at J. D. Allen Industries. A consensus grew that Allen needed to diversify even further. One plan was to build a ski resort; another was to customize a submarine for offshore drilling rig repair. A Longhorn Building was envisioned—six stories plus a penthouse for J. D. Observing him, Allen's associates had varying opinions of what his goal might be.

"The best-known independent group of companies in the world," went one view.

"I don't think there's any question but what he wanted to be a billionaire, he intended to be the next Howard Hughes" was another opinion.

"After publishing, he wanted to branch into cable television. When it came to telecommunications, J. D. thought that eventually Ted Turner would fit into a small part of his shadow."

Together with some of his serious Republican friends, Allen bought a limited partnership interest in the Embassy Row Hotel in Washington. Through another Republican Party connection, he went to Asia in 1979, met some international traders from Hong Kong, had a good time, and devoted considerable energy thereafter trying to devise ways to make the experience even more worthwhile. One proposal was Longhorn International, Ltd. ("a subsidiary of J. D. Allen Industries, Inc.," said a pamphlet, "actively involved in the development of energy and energy-related ventures in China, other parts of Asia and western Europe"). Immediately after Ronald Reagan's 1980 election victory, the notion circulated through the J. D. Allen Industries headquarters that an ambassadorship would be fitting. The ambassadorship did not pan out, but J. D. did get invited on a trade mission to West Africa, sponsored by the Departments of Commerce and Agriculture. Twenty-five American executives—captains of agribiz and manufacturing—made the junket, and J. D. Allen was the only energy industry representative.

By now, Allen had discovered that pastel leisure suits and ruby-studded hammered-gold watchbands were not the only finery a gentleman could own. He had traded up to Oxxford suits and tailor-made dress shirts. His foreign travel experiences suggested to the brainstormers back in Oklahoma City that Allen should do everything possible to cultivate his intercontinental appeal, and so a path was discovered that wound from Oklahoma City to Vancouver and on to Toronto and then to London, from which it was an easy skip to Zurich and the rest of the Continent. J. D. Allen came into contact with Canadian maneuverers who could sell oil stocks or gold stocks or ham salad—whatever people might for a moment believe in—and who were connected to professional flight-capital funnelers, Swiss money managers with fiduciary heft, and English investment bankers, each of whom was interested in earning a promotional fee. Western Europeans, fearful that the Soviets might develop a sudden hankering for, say, Belgium, constantly sought ways to transport wealth to America. For years they had been exposed to the High Dollar approach, the dignified promote, but they had not really been good-ole-boyed before, had not had direct contact with many natives of Ringling, Oklahoma. You did not have to know much about the oil business to know that it was amazingly hot. During a dog-and-pony show, Allen was capable of sounding knowledgeable about the oil business. He was also capable of joking that "my belt size is bigger than my I.Q." Allen had command of the lingo. J. D. Allen was the closest thing to J. R. Ewing the average City of Londoner had seen. It was fine for him to stand there with charts and structural maps and explain why a certain oil-and-gas prospect looked good. He made an impression.

The *pièce de résistance* of the Allen-Swan collaboration was the formation of Continental Drilling. When this idea germinated, the plan called for construction of a forty-two-rig fleet, at a cost of two hundred sixty-three million dollars. At some point it occurred to J. D. and Carl that forty-two rigs might be an overachievement, so they scaled their project down to nineteen rigs, which could be built for ninety-six million. The loan closed January 26, 1982, the day after the official drilling-rig count in Oklahoma reached 882, its all-time high. Five banks participated in the loan—Chase Manhattan, Seafirst, Continental Illinois, Michigan National, and Penn Square. Swan and Allen each owned 43 percent of Continental Drilling, and each had personally guaranteed virtually the entire amount of the company's debt. A banker who attended the closing described it as "twelve guys and twenty cigars in the boardroom at Penn Square." Beep Jennings witnessed the gathering, blessing everyone present, and Bill Patterson passed out the stogies. As soon as the signatures were notarized, the borrowers and several bankers boarded J. D.'s and Carl's jets and flew to Las Vegas to celebrate. Carl Swan's pockets were full of cash. So were Patterson's. If you needed a little bankroll to start you off at the tables, Carl and Bill were good for that. The ensemble stopped over at the Aladdin Hotel, Wayne Newton's place, and everyone who wanted to shake Wayne's hand got a chance. One of the Penn Square oil-and-gas lenders sat in Wayne's dressing room and explained to Wayne how to frac an oil well with bauxite beads. Then Wayne went out and did the dinner show.

Allen and Swan and the bankers had tables right next to the stage. They drank Dom Pérignon. From the stage, Wayne said, "I'd like to introduce you to my brother," and J. D. stood up. The people in the crowd went crazy because they loved Wayne Newton and naturally they wanted to love his brother, too. Wayne looked down at Meg Sipperly, of Chase Manhattan, and said, "Where are you from, pretty lady?" When she said New York City, that was a cue for Wayne to belt out "New York, New York," more lustily than Sinatra. It was one of those amazing, gratifying nights in the merchant banking business.

CHAPTER 13

Nineteen eighty-one was a year of mysteries and marvels: my wife gave birth to our first child; the stock market analyst Joe Granville told the world, "Sell everything"; an Oklahoma City newspaper published a story with the headline "Think Tank Sees Oil Costing $333 a Barrel by Year 2000"; the Penn Square Bank cranked out a billion two in loans. In 1981, the bank's promotional theme was "Growing With Energy." An electronic teller called the Beep Machine went into operation. In the past, the real Beep Jennings had come up with some lively innovations—a T.V. ad campaign based on *The Wild Bunch;* an unusual offer for any purchaser of a million-dollar certificate of deposit (you could receive the going rate of interest or you could have a Rolls-Royce Silver Shadow)— but in 1981 the Penn Square Bank became even livelier. It became a *fun* bank. You would go see Bill Patterson, thinking you needed to borrow two hundred fifty thousand dollars, and you would walk out with a million and a half. Penn Square's most intrepid customers discovered within themselves the courage to borrow to pay interest on what they had previously borrowed. Leverage vertigo was at work—paper, dollars, illusions in perpetual disorienting motion. Concept or no concept, Patterson and Jennings must have been dazzled by how easy the whole thing was. The upstream bankers were equally surprised at how easy it was to sell money. Meanwhile, the borrowers had to cope with the novelty of having all that cash thrown at them. Borrowing to pay interest is a clear-cut symptom of leverage vertigo. The borrower is not stupid; he is just too dizzy to comprehend what has happened to the old rules. Nor is he encouraged to comprehend.

A dynamic year. In 1981, the money went out the door so fast it literally could not be counted. These were the credits that Penn Square alumni would later defend by saying, "Hey, those were good loans when we made them." Competitors got groggy shaking their heads. "In two and a half years, they put more than two billion dollars on the books. I had five hundred million," another Oklahoma energy lender once told me. "I built mine up in eight years through a lot of hard work. Even if you don't do the paperwork, how can anyone create assets that fast?"

The regulatory history of the Penn Square Bank during this exuberant phase reads like a series of memos-to-file about a delinquent pupil in a permissive boarding school—a lad who is popular with classmates but insists upon decorating the headmaster's Irish setters with linoleum adhesive, who has a cheerful demeanor but nevertheless can offer no satisfactory explanation of how the Founding Fathers diorama came to rest in the chapel belfry.

Between the time that Jennings bought the bank, in February of 1975, and its closing, in July of 1982, the Office of the Comptroller of the Currency examined the books ten times. In the eyes of the regulators, these audits revealed a steady decline in the institution's well-being. And yet, in the eyes of the public, the Penn Square Bank appeared to prosper. During 1980, for instance, its loan portfolio more than doubled—from roughly ninety million to a hundred ninety million dollars—and more than three hundred million dollars' worth of loans were sold to other banks. This had a salutary effect upon profits, which increased more than 100 percent over the previous year. Nevertheless, what the examiners found at Penn Square alarmed them. In early 1980, when the Dallas regional office of the Comptroller, in an internal report, declared Penn Square "a matter of special supervisory concern," it was said that the bank was beset by too rapid growth, insufficient liquidity, inadequate capital, and an excess of classified, or potentially problematic, loans. A much briefer examination later that year revealed more of the same. The staff appeared to be "overtaxed by business volume," and "capital adequacy was deteriorating." That summer, the bank's directors attended a meeting in Dallas with a senior representative of the Comptroller. Each director signed a formal administrative agreement to "correct all violations of law and adopt procedures to prevent them from occurring in the future." Among other things, the directors pledged to stop violating legal lending limits, to stop making loans without adequate collateral, to stop lending to poor-quality borrowers, to increase capital, to improve procedures for documenting loans sold to other banks, and to file monthly progress reports with the Comptroller.

Penn Square's own outside accounting firm, Arthur Young & Company, conducted a year-end 1980 audit and rendered a "qualified" opinion of the bank's soundness. In accountantese, that meant a less than favorable opinion. Arthur Young & Company said that insufficient reserves had been set aside to cover potential loan losses. Evidently, the Comptroller shared this belief. At the end of 1979, the total of Penn Square's assets that the examiners had classified—had found to be dubious, substandard, or noteworthy in some unpromising fashion—equaled a third of the value of the bank's capital. Although additional stock was sold during 1980 and the capital was thus increased, by the time of the Arthur Young audit the percentage of classified loans had risen to three-quarters of the bank's capital.

The examiners were back for a long visit in early 1981 and discovered "further deterioration in the bank's overall condition." During the summer of 1981, the directors were once again summoned to Dallas by the Comptroller of the Currency. A bank examiner reviewed ten areas of concern that had been cited in the formal administrative agreement. Nine of them, he said, had not been complied with. In unambiguous detail, he enumerated the specifics of this noncompliance. One of the bank examiner's superiors told the directors, "We find in our opinion—you don't have to accept it, but you ought to—that Penn Square Bank is flirting with disaster."

A conversation with Beep Jennings would not have revealed the existence of any of these dark portents. Not long after Jennings and the other directors learned of Arthur Young & Company's qualified audit opinion, Penn Square's holding company issued its annual report for 1980, which itemized the great leaps in asset growth and profitability. Jennings' message to the shareholders stated, "But figures do not tell the whole story. They indicate how much we have increased in size, but do not demonstrate how we have broadened and strengthened our capabilities and services to make this growth possible . . . the Penn Square Bank of tomorrow is happening today. So this annual report also focuses on the future: on the planned growth we have in mind for our bank."

The first page of the 1980 annual report to the shareholders, which was published in the spring of 1981, contained a boardroom photograph of five proud executives posed with a set of blueprints. The executive with the widest smile was Eldon Beller, who had recently accepted Jennings' offer to replace Frank Murphy as president and chief administrative officer of the bank. Eldon Beller was in his late fifties, tall and broad-shouldered, with a wide, imposing western face. He had a high forehead and oiled silver hair, the look of a journeyman who was perhaps on his way to an asset-and-liability committee meeting or perhaps on his way to fix a barbed-wire fence. Evidently he would smile for a camera, but more often he had a wary expression, like someone recalling an unpleasant episode in a dentist's office.

Beller's ostensible mission at Penn Square was to make manageable a bank that had outgrown everything from its physical plant to its committee structure. The job did not call for him to be a charmer, and there was nothing of the glad-hander about him. He had spent twelve years at the First National Bank & Trust Company of Oklahoma City, which at that time was the largest and most profitable bank in the state, and he had a conventional understanding of how a bank should operate. He understood that it is normal for a bank to have a loan policy and that it is normal for the bank management to see that the policy is followed. It is normal for there to be a loan review department that analyzes loans already on the books, that examines financial statements and cash flows and thus evaluates—long after a loan has been funded—whether the collateral is sufficient. In a normal bank, there is a loan committee that is taken seriously by all of the credit officers. A loan officer analyzes a credit before bringing it to the committee and then, in the committee meeting, he does a well-rehearsed song-and-dance number. The other loan officers ask questions and criticize and analyze, and then there is a vote. One aspect of Bill Patterson's magic lay in his ability to fund loans that a formal loan committee in a normal bank would welcome a chance to veto. Eldon Beller understood what is normal and he grasped that Penn Square was not a normal bank.

Nevertheless, Beller made what seemed a sincere effort. A new loan policy was drafted. It came to a hundred twenty-five single-spaced pages that specified procedures for loan documentation and review, collateral evaluation, internal loan auditing. Its language was infused with a sanctimoniousness worthy of a scout-master's lecture on self-abuse. Beller improved the loan administration function (central credit files, loan work sheets, financial statements, collateral information, mortgages, petroleum engineering evaluations); created a new committee structure, including an asset-and-liability committee, an executive management committee, an examination corrections committee, a loan review committee, a credit policy committee, and an employee benefits committee; established a loan-closing department; and hired more than two hundred people, about a third of whom had previously worked for him at the First National Bank & Trust Company of Oklahoma City.

At First National, Beller had been the senior lending officer but not the chief executive officer. Those who knew him well regarded him as an able credit analyst, skilled at dealing with customers. He did not equivocate when he decided to replace Penn Square's accounting firm—he fired Arthur Young & Company and hired Peat, Marwick, Mitchell & Company—but a natural hatchet man he was not. His duties at Penn Square called for him to occupy and administer a prescribed amount of space, to appear to be a figure of authority, no matter what the practical truth. According to his job description, as president he would "manage all of the bank's activities except the energy division." Beller had his reasons for agreeing to work for Beep Jennings. His salary plus a guaranteed bonus during his first year totaled a hundred fifty-five thousand dollars—almost double what he had been earning. Jennings offered a five-year contract that promised Beller a quarter million dollars during the final year. The two men had been only distantly acquainted when Jennings asked Beller if he wanted the job. Whatever doubts or misgivings Beller might have had about working with Bill Patterson—of whom it had been said at First National, "There was no way we were going to let [him] lend a dime of the bank's money"—he managed to contain them. When he asked about Patterson, Jennings replied, "He's been with me for a number of years and I've taught him what I know."

For Jennings, the arrangement had the desirable effect of

interposing another body, Beller's, between himself and the peri-
patetic Patterson. The reason customers left downtown banks and
went to Penn Square was that word got around that all you had to
do was go see Bill Patterson. He was like the bad girl in the
sophomore class whom all the senior boys called up for a date.
Jennings once reflected, "Our main challenge with the unique
talent of Bill Patterson was to discipline him without breaking his
spirit." One of the officers whom Beller recruited to Penn Square
explained Patterson by using a different metaphor: "Let's say you
have a whole bunch of people who are driving along at forty-five
miles per hour—some can do as much as seventy—and then
suddenly there's this one guy who's going around the track at two
hundred miles per hour. You have to slow him down, so you try to
get him down to, I don't know, one-thirty. Then from there maybe
you can get him down to one-twenty, then maybe one hundred.
It's still too fast, but at least it's not two hundred. And just when
you've got him down there around one-thirty he all of a sudden
zooms up again to one-eighty, one-ninety. That's what it meant to
try to 'control' Patterson. No one imagined that this forty-five-mile-
per-hour driver would have the ability to drive two hundred miles
per hour. Ability-wise he might not have been capable of even
forty-five. Ability-wise he was probably 'School Zone.' "

Q: O.K. What specifically caused you to begin to question his
lending activities?
A: The bizarre way in which my four-hundred-thousand or, at
least in my opinion, the bizarre way in which my four-hundred-thousand-dollar loan was handled—watching Mr. Patterson in his office on December tenth, talking consecutively on
two different telephones while he was trying to make a deal
with us.
Q: How long were you in Mr. Patterson's office on December
tenth?
A: I would say several hours.
Q: More than two?
A: Less than—plus or minus two. And they took us into a janitor's
closet to make a loan to us. Two loan officers in the janitor's
closet, which I thought was quite interesting.

Q: Is that what you found bizarre about the way your four-hundred-thousand-dollar loan was handled?

A: That, and the way he was negotiating what I considered to be three substantial transactions concurrently.

Q: But nevertheless you were willing to go forward on the loan, is that correct?

A: Yes.

—Sworn testimony of a Penn Square borrower

Above all, banking at Penn Square was expedient. A borrower did not have to make four trips to the bank to get his money. You could sign a note in blank and accomplish everything at once. The only problem was that often Bill Patterson seemed not to have time for details. Days and weeks would go by in a blur and Patterson would be so briskly in motion he would not get around to reading his mail. Secretaries, receiving instructions over the telephone, would end up signing his initials to hundreds of loan documents. Patterson, in his haste to get a deal done, might overlook this or that credit precept. Never lend people more money than they can pay back, for instance—that precept got overlooked.

As long as the upstream banks bought loans, it seemed reasonable to think of Patterson as highly idiosyncratic rather than in way above his head. Other officers or directors, or occasionally a national bank examiner, might express less than overwhelming enthusiasm for one of his loans, might observe that the size of the credit exceeded the value of the collateral, might dare to suggest a few changes. Invariably, Patterson's response was "Hey, that's a done deal"—meaning, no way was he going to renege. To be able to work both sides of the deal so effectively, to maneuver so adroitly between borrower and loan buyer—that was a remarkable skill. Patterson knew how to go to Chicago with a bunch of deals in a briefcase and return twenty-four hours later bearing commitments for ten million dollars' worth of loans. It might be ten million dollars all in one loan and the loan might be a 99 percent participation—meaning that Penn Square would lend only a hundred thousand dollars, and the rest of the deal would belong to, say, Continental Illinois. Penn Square's 1 percent loan origination fee would come to ninety-nine thousand dollars, and thus the bank would have earned, overnight, a 99 percent return on its portion of the credit. Most loan sale agreements depended upon a simpatico understanding, the equivalent of a handshake. The paperwork, the "documentation," would come later. If Continental Illinois was involved, that meant that the greatest corporate lender in the country had agreed to buy the loan. Who would dare to stand up and say that the deal was no good because a few pieces of paper were missing? The upstream bank had saved a lot of time and inconvenience and its money had gone to work, earning two points above the prime interest rate. The lender had sacrificed direct access to the borrower but in return the lender had Bill Patterson's implicit and explicit assurances that this done deal could do no wrong.

No cadre of Harvard Business School graduates did Patterson's bidding. Secretaries armed with high school diplomas found themselves being anointed as banking officers and then as assistant vice-presidents. They worked for one of the fastest-growing banks in the country, one that showed fabulous earnings, that had a long-distance sprinter—a wizard who had gone from grunt to senior executive vice-president in less than five years—running the money-making end. The bank was in the habit of doubling its size every year or so. In that atmosphere, a secretary could hope to be lending a few bucks before long. When morale sagged under the burden of the work load, Patterson would remind his subordinates that they were the source of the Penn Square Bank's profitability. Salaries generally ran 25 percent higher than those at downtown banks in Oklahoma City, and within Penn Square's oil-and-gas department they were higher than elsewhere in the bank. Most of the oil-and-gas employees regarded the remuneration as combat pay.

An administrative assistant who arrived at Penn Square about a year before the bank became extinct described a typical day. "In one day I could realistically fund ten million dollars," the administrative assistant said. "You might have had a little pre-effort. The actual line of credit would have already been established, the promissory note would already exist, and now would come the funding. Let's say on a ten-million-dollar line of credit Chase Manhattan has agreed to take sixty percent. I call and request, say, three million. That same day, the XYZ Corporation, a regular customer, might show up and explain that they have a lot of outstanding receivables from investors and they need three million. So we'll book three million on Penn Square's books for them, knowing that Michigan National and, say, Utica National, in Tulsa, have shown interest in buying that sort of credit. I'll call those banks and they'll both say that as soon as they have looked over the package they'll let us know. We'll send them each current financial statements, maybe a guarantee from the chief executive officer of the company, the loan write-up, a copy of the receivables that form the collateral. We'll send it out by overnight courier, and by the next day Michigan National might say, 'O.K., sure, we'll take the loan.' When the money comes in from Michigan National that clears the loan off our books and it brings our liquidity back up. So now, if some guy walks in and says, 'Look, I want to get in on this drilling deal, I need to borrow a hundred and fifty thousand dollars,' we can lend it to him.

"Patterson would call the office from New York or Chicago and it was like he was at the grocery store. He'd say, 'Does anybody need anything?' And I'd say, 'Yes, Bill, I need a million dollars' "— the administrative assistant named an account—" 'I need it bad.' Again, he might have discussed the credit with the upstream bank, because he knew that it was on our books and we had to get it off. Bill would call me back and say that the money was on the way. It was my job to send to the upstream bank—Chase, say—a package of documents: promissory note, financial statements, security agreements, guarantees, anything that I thought they needed. When the loan review people at Chase got to work, they might want to see the borrower's financial statement. Where it says on the financial statement 'ten million dollars worth of proved, producing properties,' they might want to see an engineering report. And I might have a copy of that in my desk but I hadn't put it in the package because I hadn't thought of them needing that.

"Everything was high-pressure. People were always running, screaming. It was like the stock exchange during a rally. Secretaries going nine miles a minute. You'd be taking telephone calls and typing at the same time. People were throwing things at you, saying, 'What's the deal on this? How do I handle this?' Other people in the bank would be calling and saying, 'You've got five million dollars that just came in on the wire from New York. What do you want me to do with it?' You'd have correspondent bankers calling, saying, 'Where's my copy of this? Send me my interest on that.' You'd have customers calling and saying, 'What the hell's my account doing overdrawn? I asked for that advance yesterday.' There was constant pressure. We were not banking those customers. We were brokering money."

No one accused Patterson of being boring. He knew how to make work fun. He could adapt. While entertaining a client in a high-toned restaurant, he redefined when it was permissible to throw a dinner roll. He kept his colleagues off balance. He had a sense of humor that made it difficult at times to know whether he was joking. When he strolled through the Penn Square Bank lobby wearing Mickey Mouse ears and smoking a big cigar, that was a joke. When he perched on a conference table among a roomful of out-of-town bankers and howled like a hound in distress—"because if you're gonna treat us like dogs we'll act like dogs"—that was only partly a joke. The whole was pure Patterson. He did not always select material that was ideally suited to his audience. There was the time he came to work wearing a Nazi Storm Trooper's helmet, there were occasions when he greeted customers wearing a Batman hat with ears that wiggled. Critics agreed that his Nazi helmet was less funny than either his lederhosen or his cap with the duck on top. Among sticklers, none of this was regarded as the emblem of professionalism. And yet, watching Patterson lend money was undeniably entertaining. Even without a costume, he could do business with two customers simultaneously—one in his office, one on the phone—while propping his feet on the desk, eating a Big Mac and fries, and taking a vitamin shot. If a visitor was feeling a little run-down, Patterson could arrange for him to get a shot, too. Patterson's phenomenal energy, his capacity for sheer hustle, redeemed him. He was on a roll.

The object was to keep smoking and joking and rolling, but it was not always possible to maintain equanimity. He could be fawningly solicitous one moment, abrasively high-handed the next. Customers whom he had lovingly courted months earlier would be permitted to languish in the waiting room for hours. Correspondent bankers would line up at the door. Patterson would give them about twenty seconds and say, "Sign here." He was dealing with transactions of ten and twenty and thirty million dollars. A new face would appear, a request for a million, and it would seem like nothing. Patterson would conclude, "Yeah. You look O.K. to me."

The first time Patterson flew to Chicago on Penn Square business was only the second time that, as he later put it, he "had been on a big airplane." Before long he was flying first-class. He learned how to make the most of an expense account. When Patterson hit high gear, he enjoyed company. Tossing a television set out of a hotel-room window in Chicago or dropping your swim trunks while para-sailing over a crowded beach in Mexico might seem like fun for fun's sake, but, really, what's the point if there's no audience? Most upstream bankers liked Patterson. If you did business with Penn Square, you covered a lot of territory. If you banked Carl Swan, eventually you got to pet Secretariat. Bank Bob Hefner and you might get invited for the weekend to France. Even if you were deskbound in New York, there were days when the telephone would ring and it would be Patterson, jet-borne twenty thousand feet overhead, saying that he was landing in thirty minutes and get ready, because dinnertime at "21" was two hours away.

Young professionals who want to do big business have to make big decisions. Just hypothetically, what do you do if you work for a bank in New York or Chicago or Seattle and last week they sent you on business to London and this week it's suddenly Oklahoma City and you look like Mr. Peepers and your plane lands and before you can claim your luggage you're introduced to four friendly females in tube tops—members of the Penn Square Bank "Entertainment Committee"—who say, "Wanna go have some fun?" What you want to do, of course, is go straight to your hotel and call your wife and say, "Hi, honey, I'm fine," and then put on your jammies and sit up in bed browsing through the Good Book that has been left in your night-table drawer by the Gideons. But big business is serious business. Pursuing a reasonable profit, reasonable people encounter occasional stress. And when it happens, what do you do? You might be a pilgrim sitting in Patterson's office, trying to get answers to twenty pressing questions while he talks on the telephone. Finally, he hangs up. Before you can ask your questions, he says, "Wanna go to Junior's?"—one of the shrines of new-oilie-ism. Sure you do. You get there, and within fifteen minutes a dozen people are at the table—half of them are bankers, half are customers, a few are both. A possible objection to what ensues is that it hasn't evolved far enough beyond the glory days of Sigma Chi, but with an attitude like that you might as well take your briefcase and go home. Some food gets thrown. When the first breadstick or escargot levitates, you think: Oh, come *on*. But then something inspired happens that distinguishes this food fight from the one two months ago in Chicago. Maybe a shirt completely covered with cocktail sauce.

After the bank closed, some journalists got busy and these exploits entered the public domain. Defenders of Patterson arose to state that too much was made of all this, besides which the facts were reported inaccurately. He had been accused of making a spectacle of himself by drinking beer out of a cowboy boot when in fact it had been champagne out of a loafer. "I've seen him stick a pork chop in the handkerchief pocket of his suit," one upstream banker told me. Another banker swore that that was another distortion—it had been a roasted quail.

December was always the busiest time at any bank in the oil patch. An oilman I know was involved in a two-million-dollar transaction that still had not been consummated when only two weeks remained in 1981. A downtown Oklahoma City banker who had made a tentative commitment on the deal was suddenly called away because of a family emergency. So the oilman and his partners took their request to Penn Square. In a single afternoon, Patterson heard their proposal, agreed to lend the money, and did so. It was a handshake, slap-on-the-back proceeding, culminating in a trip by Patterson to the cashier's window. He returned with a check for a million six hundred thousand dollars, the initial draw against a two-million-dollar line of credit. The oilman asked about the mortgage documents. "Patterson said, 'Don't worry. We'll do those later.' He knew me, as it happened, but did my corporation exist? Was I an officer? The fact is that the answer to both questions was 'no.' He didn't care. He knew who I was. That was his only saving grace. I'm a reputable person, supposedly. But I could have just as easily been Willie Sutton."

Lending money in the absence of a formal loan application;

asking a customer, for the sake of expediency, to sign several blank notes; lending additional funds to meet interest payments; looking a customer in the eye but not looking closely at his financial statement; neglecting to update reservoir-engineering reports; failing to require borrowers to have their mortgaged oil-and-gas production income sent directly to the bank each month; advancing interest payments to upstream banks on behalf of customers who had not yet sent the interest payments to Penn Square—the farther Patterson's methodology departed from the rule-book, the more momentum it accumulated. This was "character lending" with a vengeance. Patterson appeared to be an energetic young man who was eager to get ahead in the world and who had, as it turned out, been handed the keys to the bank. But what else? None of his subordinates knew all that he knew about the customers. What was true and what was less than truthful? In loan committee meetings he was capable of long-playing recitations of reservoir histories, well-by-well drilling reports, and production projections. Talking up a loan, he would say, "This note is to the XYZ Drilling Company, which is run by Bobby Dale Cox. He also has an interest in ABC Well Service and he's a partner with Lonnie Dwayne Speer in QRS Exploration. His reserves show a loan value of four million dollars and he's drilling a well in Grady County that's been logged and it's waiting on a pipeline hookup and he's got three others he's getting ready to start in Payne County next month"—and so on. Impressive presentations.

Having bought a customer's business, Patterson would do what had to be done to perform. A customer's assets, in Patterson's optimistic estimation, might be good for a twenty-million-dollar loan. If an upstream bank should look at the assets and declare them to be worth only ten million, Patterson would mobilize himself to find the additional ten million, somewhere, even if it meant waving a wand at the collateral. Once the upstream banks gave Patterson their imprimatur, challenging him became risky. "Am I crazy to be questioning this loan?" another Penn Square officer might ask himself. "Or is the bank crazy to be making it?"

Like any seasoned procurer, Patterson took care to remember which sellers got along best with which buyers, which upstream banks had dibs on which borrowers. There was a pecking order—what Continental Illinois would not buy he shopped around to Northern Trust, then Seafirst, Michigan National, and Chase—

and there were peculiar preferences. Seafirst, for instance, leaned toward drilling rigs and away from loans secured by oil-and-gas production. Of the nearly four hundred million dollars in loans that Seafirst bought from Penn Square, two hundred million went for rigs and equipment. Likewise, Michigan National had little or no expertise in lending to independent oil-and-gas operators, but it did have loan officers who understood chattel and could presumably grasp the mechanics of an accounts-receivable loan to an oilfield service and supply company. Michigan National's total loan purchases from Penn Square came to almost two hundred million dollars.

Patterson made the deals with the understanding that the paperwork would follow. According to the official loan policy, before a loan went on the books, documents were supposed to be gathered and properly executed: promissory note; mortgage; title; transfer order; formal credit memo; Uniform Commercial Code filing; financial statement of borrower; internal credit memo; etc. When a loan was participated to another bank, a copy of the promissory note was attached to the loan participation agreement. Penn Square would hold the collateral. In theory, when Penn Square was secured the upstream lender was in turn secured.

When theory and practice diverged, "documentation exceptions" became a matter for concern. Documentation exceptions included all the blanks that had not been filled in, all the trips to the courthouse that no one ever got around to making. A lender could easily rationalize that documentation exceptions were not a bad thing; they were a symptom that you were doing a lot of business. If the problem became unseemly enough, however, a moratorium might be declared. Chase Manhattan, in the autumn of 1981, refused to buy any more loans until Penn Square narrowed the documentation gap. Seafirst did the same a couple of months later. Temporarily, this tactic would work, because an inability to sell loans did not fit the Beep Jennings concept. If Patterson had made a commitment to a borrower and if Penn Square could not rely upon the upstream banks to absorb its loan commitments, it would run out of money. The week before Christmas in 1981, fourteen people from Penn Square flew to Las Vegas on a Sunday night, flew to Seattle the next morning, spent two working days at Seafirst filling in the blanks of documents, and flew back to Oklahoma City. After a not quite decent interval, Seafirst was in a position to plunge ahead.

Not long after John Lytle began to manage the midcontinent oil-and-gas division of Continental Illinois, his department began to lead that bank in "outstanding documentation exceptions." Lytle's self-defense, obviously, was the profit motive—the big spread between the cost of money to Continental Illinois and the interest rate that the friends of Penn Square were willing to pay. Lytle could cite persuasive statistics about profits: from December of 1980 to June of 1982, the volume of outstanding loans booked by his division grew from eight hundred thirty-three million dollars to two billion three hundred million. The portfolio acquired through Penn Square exceeded a billion dollars. Less than eight months into 1981, midcontinent oil-and-gas had surpassed the annual growth projection set by Continental Illinois's senior management. It was Lytle's impression that if that single department had been an independent bank, it would have been the third most profitable one in Chicago. The forty employees who reported to Lytle managed a loan portfolio that was larger than that of every bank in Oklahoma except one.

Not all the employees enjoyed the working conditions. In the late summer of 1981, a vice-president in Lytle's division, Kathleen Kenefick, sent to Lytle's superiors a memorandum that cited the documentation backlog. She wrote that the "status of the Oklahoma accounts (particularly Penn Square Bank) is a cause for concern and corrective action should be instigated quickly." She complained of a "lack of control of Penn Square Bank." Not long after submitting the memorandum, Kenefick left Continental Illinois. Although the memo implied criticism of Lytle, he agreed with its main points. Lytle later said, "Kenefick said we're way short of people, we're not organized, every loan ought to have a formal loan officer, let's not make any more loans until we catch up on the documentation exceptions. Kenefick claimed that I had no methodology. She was right. I didn't have one. I had motives. If someone had come to me and said, 'No more loans until you clean up the exceptions,' then I would have had a different set of motives."

In reality, there was no way to catch up on the documentation exceptions. Nor, it turned out, was all the missing documentation worthwhile—if, to begin with, the engineering badly misstated the reserve values or if the same collateral had been pledged against more than one debt or if an overborrower had given many creditors his "unlimited" personal guarantee. On a loan to a lease broker, the collateral might be resold two or three times before Penn Square would get around to filing its mortgage—if the mortgage got filed at all. But the Penn Square Bank was not selling documentation; it was selling done deals.

CHAPTER 14

Reasonable people can disagree about which of the Penn Square Bank's loans was the most inspired. But when I ponder the sheer miracle and joy of borrowing and spending and instantly gratifying, my own thoughts turn to Frank Mahan and William E. Rowsey III. I love the mantra-like rhythm of their names—mahan rowsey mahan rowsey mayhem rowdy—and I admire their willingness to shut their eyes and overreach into the ether.

Today, when Billy Rowsey explains what he thinks happened to his life during the boom, he refers to the Billy Rowsey of 1981 as "a young pup." At the time he was thirty years old and, as a matter of fact, more bearish than puppyish—six-two and potentially beefy, with brown hair and brown eyes. Both he and Mahan were homegrown Okie talent. Rowsey came from Muskogee, from old real estate and mineral money. During the summer of 1979 he became acquainted with Frank Mahan, and by the fall they were in the oil business together—Mahan & Rowsey, Inc., a corporation whose assets were a pair of sole proprietorships called Mahan Energy and Rowsey Petroleum. Rowsey had a fresh law degree from the University of Oklahoma and he had some curiosity about the oil business. One thing he knew: he did not intend to spend his nine-to-fives drafting oil-and-gas title opinions. Mahan was raised in Fairfax, a small Arkansas River oil town in north-central Oklahoma. Ten years older than Rowsey, he had sold drilling mud, had prospered as a small drilling contractor, had accumulated some oil-and-gas production. No one ever mistook Mahan for any breed of pup. He was shorter than average, wiry, graying, bearded, by nature less than completely friendly. He could be excitable. An

FUNNY MONEY

acquaintance described him as "one of the few people who could get kicked out of Junior's."

One of Mahan & Rowsey, Inc.'s earliest successes happened in Cleveland County, south of Oklahoma city, where, in 1980, the company leased three hundred fifty acres that turned out to be just the right three hundred fifty. The most prolific well, the Tanaka, initially flowed more than a thousand barrels of oil and six million cubic feet of gas a day. (Later it settled down to about two hundred barrels of oil and it now produces mainly gas.) In the spring of 1981, Bill Patterson and Frank Mahan met by chance at a new-oilie watering hole called Michael's Plum. Patterson said, "Let's have lunch." A week later, in the dining room of the Oklahoma City Golf & Country Club, Patterson, scribbling on a pair of cocktail napkins, wrote agreements to lend Mahan & Rowsey, Inc., four million dollars—a two-million-dollar oil-and-gas production loan, and a two-million-dollar line of credit for lease acquisitions. They did not have financial statements showing that they were worth that much, but if Patterson was lending them the money, hell, they probably were. "I might be naïve," Rowsey later said. "I'd just always assumed that you could believe your banker. But I'd never been involved with a bank like this before." A formal master loan agreement between Mahan and Rowsey and the Penn Square Bank never existed, but there was no shortage of paper. From cocktail napkins they graduated to blank notes—bunches. They signed the notes in Patterson's office and there the notes stayed. No need to summon Mahan and Rowsey to the bank for each fresh credit extension; as the occasion arose, Patterson would fill in the blanks and then ask himself which upstream bank would be the most likely loan buyer.

During a seven-month period in 1981, Mahan and Rowsey went through money at a rate that would have impressed the Pentagon. They mortgaged their oil-and-gas production far beyond the hilt, started a drilling company, revived a mud company, bought two airplanes, and placed an order for a third. Patterson sold loans of theirs to Chase Manhattan, Seafirst, and Michigan National. Mahan and Rowsey took partnership and its perquisites seriously. Each owned a Porsche and a Mercedes—on the company tab. Each owned a house in the most expensive area of Oklahoma City and a lakeside retreat in northeastern Oklahoma—

the retreats were on opposite sides of a cove. They married beautiful women who happened to be sisters. They both liked to play a game called Look at That Moose. Frank Mahan excelled at it. Say you were flying at twenty thousand feet in either Frank's or Billy's jet. Frank would point toward the window and exclaim, "Look at that moose!" and if you were dumb enough to look, Frank would surprise you by squirting ketchup at you or pouring a beer on your head. Just because Mahan and Rowsey were both Look at That Moose people does not mean, however, that they were indistinguishable. At Grand Lake O' the Cherokees, Rowsey tooled around in a sixty-thousand-dollar seaworthy racing craft called a cigarette boat; he also owned a forty-four-foot Trojan cabin cruiser. Mahan had a boat, too, but nothing quite as upscale as Rowsey's fleet. Rowsey belonged to the Book-of-the-Month-Club and subscribed to *Architectural Digest,* and Mahan did not. Mahan liked to shoot guns, and Rowsey did not.

When Mahan and Rowsey entered the contract drilling business—as Mahan-Rowsey Drilling, Inc.—they did so on the theory that the best way to avoid losing drilling prospects was to own rigs, and the best way to make money in the contract drilling business was to drill deals that they promoted themselves. They bought two secondhand rigs, ordered the construction of three others, and found financing for seven rigs in all. Chase Manhattan lent twenty-four million to Mahan-Rowsey Drilling, Inc. A Chase correspondent banker traveled to Oklahoma City, rode in a helicopter to see one of the rigs at work, and was shown a fabricating yard where another rig was under construction. A done deal—Patterson assured the man from Chase that Mahan-Rowsey had contracts to drill several wells in the Anadarko Basin and that by the end of 1981 the rigs would be sold and the loan repaid. Billy Rowsey can remember once thinking: Boy, my first hundred million was easy. But long before the end of 1981 he no longer felt that way. Patterson had scared up thirty million dollars that was supposedly secured by Mahan & Rowsey's oil-and-gas reserves. Their total borrowing soon reached sixty million dollars. Debt service was running a million dollars per month—but only if you paid it. Neither Mahan nor Rowsey ever made an interest payment. Their oil-and-gas production was bringing in less than a hundred thousand dollars a month. Their only significant income was from loan proceeds. Having got into the drilling business was looking sort of like a mistake. Patterson had to come up with a way to get them out.

Mahan and Rowsey could not accurately be described as detail-oriented. They began to overdraw their accounts, and the overdrafts ran as high as two million dollars. A new comptroller went to work for Mahan & Rowsey, Inc. One of the first things he noticed was that the books had not been posted for eighteen months. When Patterson learned of this, he in effect seized Mahan & Rowsey's checkbook. Chase Manhattan wanted to know what had happened to the collateral documents that were supposed to secure the rig loan. And why hadn't the rigs been sold, as Patterson had promised? Some of the Chase bankers, to be honest, were not personally fond of Mahan and Rowsey. A multimillion-dollar interest payment on the rigs was overdue. Dealing with dilemmas of this sort taxed Patterson's resources. The game was Musical Lending; when the music stopped, it was time to scramble for a new lender. (The rest of the rules Patterson made up along the way.) Selling a new credit would clear any overdrafts off the books and would buy time to devise new techniques for converting dross into gold. In the past, overdrafts had made it possible to "warehouse" loans temporarily—until a robust new credit package could be assembled. A twenty-four-million-dollar overdraft, however, was beyond even Bill Patterson's alchemy.

Churlishly, Chase bore down upon Penn Square from another angle. It wanted out on the Maximo Moorings note, too. Maximo Moorings, Inc., was a more novel than usual Florida real estate venture, the somehow bankable premise of which was that pleasure-boat people would rather own than rent dock space. The folks at Maximo Moorings would sell you a boat slip called a "dockominium." Maximo's master builder was Allen Senall, who had found his way in the spring of 1981 to Thomas Orr, a Penn Square commercial loan officer who operated a sideline in racehorse brokerage. (Senall also owned horses and oil-and-gas production.) Orr delivered Senall to Chase Manhattan—Chase lent three million plus—and not long afterward Orr left Penn Square. A year later only three of Maximo Moorings' six hundred dockominiums had been reserved. When Chase decided that it wished to be rid of Maximo, its Penn Square portfolio was approaching two hundred million dollars. The Penn Square Bank needed Chase Manhattan's goodwill. When Chase leaned on Senall to perform, Patterson took it personally.

In the absence of banks that would buy loans, it had become necessary to invent proxy banks. Bill Patterson was willing to volunteer for this job himself and he was willing to recruit comrades to serve his needs. To accommodate Chase—"to preserve the Chase relationship," as they say—Patterson arranged in late March for himself and two Penn Square regulars to buy Maximo Moorings, which was renamed BGP Marina, Inc. Together, they borrowed seven and a half million dollars from Penn Square—only temporarily, Patterson promised, until he ushered another buyer in from the wings. (Pressed to name the buyer, he would mention an unlikely choice, a promoter who had already borrowed twenty-five million dollars at Penn Square.)

The Maximo Moorings/BGP Marina solution would do for the time being, would permit Patterson to concentrate upon the Mahan-Rowsey rigs. He needed another musical lender, another warehouse. It was late February. The national bank examiners were due to arrive at Penn Square in mid-April. Patterson could not sell the rig loan to Seafirst because Mahan and Rowsey already owed that bank almost ten million dollars. Nor was Michigan National a candidate. Patterson had tapped that source as well. He had met with a group of Michigan National loan officers and had described at length what terrific fellows and excellent risks Mahan and Rowsey were. ("Wild sonsofbitches" was one phrase that Patterson used to commend Frank and Billy to the bankers—a tribute to their Okiesmo and all that that implied.) Michigan National responded with six million dollars, most of which was sent to Chase to cover overdue interest. Patterson knew that Continental Illinois and Northern Trust were not interested in new rig loans and were too clever to bank Mahan and Rowsey. He knew that the new owners of the BGP Marina were pretty heavily committed at the moment. Penn Square could not buy the rig loan itself because twenty-four million dollars exceeded the bank's legal lending limit by more than twenty million. Chase Manhattan wanted its money. *Chase.* Finally, the logical solution dawned on Patterson: the only party that would lend the money to pay back Chase Manhattan was . . . Chase Manhattan.

Brief half-lives—1982:

Early February: Some of the loan officers in the midcontinent oil-and-gas lending division of Continental Illinois began to ask, "What will Patterson buy back?" A loan officer named Patrick Goy drafted a list of smallish loans—less than three-and-a-half million dollars apiece, three and a half million being Penn Square's legal limit. Goy once described the loans on the list as "little tiny deals loaded with documentation exceptions." One of his fellow loan officers called them "squeaky deals, weird deals, cruddy deals, loans we'd bought to preserve the 'Penn Square relationship.' " But if Continental Illinois wanted out badly enough, would Penn Square agree to take them back? The thought that such a list existed disturbed John Lytle, the vice-president in charge of the midcontinent division. The implications were dire: the hour was late, the drilling rig count had obviously peaked, and Continental Illinois had hung out a billion dollars. Not one of the loans on the list would ever leave Continental.

Late February: Lytle dispatched Pat Goy to Seattle. During the last three months of 1981, John Boyd, the manager of the energy division at Seafirst, had bought three hundred fifty million dollars in Penn Square loans. That year, Seafirst's entire oil-and-gas portfolio had increased by seven hundred million dollars. Boyd and Patterson got along swell. Boyd liked funny hats, too—a Mao hat, a sheikh's headdress—and big cigars. Now Seafirst wanted to bring up its liquidity. Goy looked at Seafirst's portfolio, hoping to find loans that Continental Illinois might care to assume. Instead, he saw loan participation agreements, and realized that the other correspondent banks had bought loans far less inspiring than the ones Continental Illinois wished to get rid of. "It was a graveyard of deals we had turned down," Goy said later.

April: Goy was airborne, aboard an eight-passenger Learjet, on loan from a customer of both Penn Square and Continental Illinois, flying from Tulsa to Chicago. He was sitting with George Baker, the executive vice-president in charge of all commercial lending, the man thought most likely to succeed Roger Anderson as chairman of Continental Illinois. Pat Goy reported to Lytle, who reported to a senior vice-president who reported to an executive vice-president who reported to Baker. Baker managed a thirty-billion-dollar loan portfolio. Goy was thirty-five years old, amiable, twelve years at Continental, six months as an oil-and-gas lender. Anticipating delivering bad news to his boss's boss's boss's boss intimidated him in the extreme, but he told Baker what he knew. He described Continental's loan exposure in Oklahoma. He said that Continental had made production loans to people who had gone elsewhere and borrowed to buy drilling rigs or mineral leases. What if a cash drain in the drilling or lease-brokerage business hindered a customer's ability to perform for Continental? Goy told Baker what the exposure was at Seafirst and Chase—a revelation. Baker said that he would check with a friend at Chase.

Earlier that day, Baker had been the host of a luncheon in Tulsa. Each spring Continental Illinois staged a slick gathering for its major Oklahoma correspondent banks. One of the bank's economists led a symposium, a George Baker would show up to press flesh, and the Oklahoma bankers would enjoy an ego massage. The Tulsa bankers cared about what Continental had been doing at Penn Square, and during lunch they asked questions. Baker said, "We don't see any problem. We've been through all those loans. We've had a bunch of people down here working. We feel like we know what the situation is, and we're comfortable." In Baker's voice there was no equivocation, no hesitation. The Tulsa bankers kept it up, saying, "You've made a lot of rig loans and a lot of lease loans. We've seen a lot of rig deals, a lot of lease deals. Are you guys really sure you're right?" Yes, they were sure.

Also during April, for a few days John Lytle weighed an offer to become president of the Penn Square Bank. Beep Jennings thought it would be a splendid idea. Lytle would replace Eldon Beller, and Beller would get kicked upstairs to vice-chairman of the board, or something. (Frank Murphy, the current vice-chairman of the board, would retire early.) Patterson would shift from head of oil-and-gas lending to head of correspondent banking, and John Boyd, of Seafirst, would replace Patterson. As Beep saw it, this management team could work together quite well. But then other, more pressing business intruded, and Lytle declined Jennings' proposal.

CHAPTER 15

Q: When did you think the bank was doomed?
A: The day after it was closed.
—Congressional testimony of Eldon Beller

To have a career as a bank examiner in a place like Oklahoma is to endure many character-building episodes in which the key props are a small town, a little bank, a chicken-fried-steak-and-yellow-gravy lunch well before noon in the genial company of a smalltown little-bank president, and, after dark, a cinder-block motel, Wild Turkey and tap water, and a television set full of *Kojak* reruns. A sensitive bank examiner—one who is both self-interested and interested in preserving the regulatory system—learns the art of creative fudging, which is a variation on the art of going along and getting along. Enforcing every rule according to the letter does not help to preserve the system. Examiners analyze the quality of a bank's loans and they explore whether the institution has complied with banking laws. Loan quality counts. Banks do not get closed because of technical violations.

In mid-April, a delegation from the Comptroller of the Currency—four full examiners and ten assistant examiners—arrived at the Penn Square Bank, set up shop in the basement and began a general examination. In the lexicon of bank regulation, this meant a thorough review of the Penn Square Bank's management and assets. Eight hundred million dollars in new loans had been generated at Penn Square since a brief spot-check examination six months earlier. An additional eight hundred million had been booked at Penn Square or sold upstream since the previous general examination, fifteen months earlier.

The day after the examiners arrived, the Penn Square directors held a monthly board meeting. Three partners from the accounting firm of Peat, Marwick, Mitchell presented findings from a recent audit. These did not add up to a glowing rave: the rapid growth of assets continued to breed complications; the habit of rolling past-due loans into new loans without first receiving payment of interest or reduction of the principal should not be permitted; the advancing of interest by Penn Square to upstream banks on behalf of customers who were in fact delinquent in their payments would not do at all; Bill Patterson's authority was too broad and should be redefined. The official net result of the Peat, Marwick, Mitchell audit, however, was an "unqualified" opinion of the bank's soundness.

When a national bank examiner finds that a loan is in some way wanting, his duty is to decide whether to "classify" it and, if he does, to assign it to one of four categories—in descending order of gravity, "loss," "doubtful," "substandard," and "other assets especially mentioned." More than a little arbitrariness enters the loan classification process. The examiner, by his own terms and definitions, cannot make a mistake. Bankers do not enjoy losses any more than robbery victims do. Bank examiners earn less than bankers but they are compensated by being allowed to define reality for bankers, to dictate what has worth and how much.

Stephen D. Plunk, the man in charge of the examination team, had this official title: subregional supervisor for Oklahoma City and western Oklahoma for the Office of the Comptroller of the Currency of the United States Treasury. Ascending to that position had taken Plunk almost ten years. Besides seniority, one thing he had gathered along the way was skepticism of the competence of the average banker. Some of Plunk's colleagues noticed that classifying loans seemed to have a tonic effect upon him. Observing Plunk in action, several other examiners compiled a list of "Ten Things That Examiner-in-Charge Plunk Loves to Say." Number One went: "This bank has never had a real exam."

It did not take long for the relationship between Steve Plunk and Bill Patterson to sink to something less than mutual cordiality and admiration. Steve Plunk was not a Sigma Chi sort of guy. Pressing questions would arise; Plunk would put them to Eldon

Beller or Beep Jennings; Jennings would instruct his protégé to provide answers; Patterson would stall, dissemble, or disappear. The urgency of walls closing in stirred and enriched Patterson's creative juices. The occasion for bold legerdemain had arrived. While the bank examiners in the basement tried to get to know the one billion six hundred million in loans that had turned up since their last extended visit, Patterson packaged harder than ever. He would submit a loan package to two or three banks simultaneously, as if putting bait in the water. The first bank that bit it bought it. During the next ten weeks, Patterson and his assistants would create almost three hundred forty million dollars in assets. Patterson began to react emotionally to Plunk's decisions that certain loans were classifiable. When threatened, Patterson would say, "Continental Illinois will take care of that loan and then they'll take care of *you*." Plunk would persist, and Patterson would cavalierly reply, "Go ahead. Classify the loan. We'll just sell it." Patterson moved out of Penn Square and into the hands of upstream banks eight and a half million dollars of loans that the examiners had declared *losses*. By mid-May, Plunk and his fellow examiners had identified only two million dollars in losses, but within a brief period of time it became possible to imagine write-offs totaling more than fifteen million. If it came to that, a sale of additional stock would be necessary and the Comptroller would begin to muster the leverage to force Jennings and Patterson out of the bank. As the losses accumulated, the chance that the bank might fail began to emerge in the minds of some of the examiners. Speculating upon that could not have dismayed Examiner-in-Charge Plunk.

The examiners had been on the premises about a week when Patterson invented the second half of his solution to the problem of the Mahan-Rowsey rigs. The first half was Chase Manhattan; Chase Manhattan would put up the money to pay back what Mahan and Rowsey owed Chase Manhattan. To make that happen, however, it would be necessary to replace Frank Mahan and Billy Rowsey as the borrowers. Patterson asked himself which of his friends needed a favor as badly as he himself needed twenty-four million dollars. His answer was Robert A. Hefner III.

Bob Hefner, in the spring of 1982, stood prepared to express gratitude to anyone who could lend him an amount in the range of thirty to a hundred million dollars. The forty thousand acres that he had leased in the Anadarko Basin in 1981 needed to be drilled or else the eighty-million-plus dollars that he had paid for the leases would be squandered. Even more pressing, GHK and Mobil had an agreement that permitted GHK to buy back a fractional interest in successful wells that the two companies had drilled near Elk City. To do that Hefner needed cash that he did not have. When Patterson approached Hefner with the idea of forming a corporation to buy the Mahan-Rowsey rigs *just for a little while*— long enough for Patterson to find a real and permanent buyer— there was a meshing of needs. Patterson assured Hefner that the rigs would soon be sold to the permanent buyer. The vehicle for Hefner's purchase of the rigs already existed: the QOL Corporation, a shell in which Hefner retained, among other things, his house and his two airplanes. QOL stood for "quality of life." As Hefner understood Patterson, he needed only to sign a note with conditions attached—a note that would not be funded until one of Hefner's associates had satisfied himself that the collateral was sufficient and properly secured. The QOL Corporation, which did business as the No Sub S Corporation, would be the ostensible borrower but would never become the rigs' long-term owner. There would be no interest payments. Hefner had no desire to own a drilling company. QOL would function only as a loan warehouse, and in return Hefner would acquire a stronger tie to Chase's correspondent bankers. He did not want to get bogged down in Chase's oil-and-gas department; needing major money so badly, he did not have time to deal with a whole new set of petroleum engineers. Ten days elapsed between Patterson's proposition to Hefner and the closing. The QOL maneuver showed Patterson at the peak of his powers. It did not show Hefner at the peak of his.

Frank Mahan and Billy Rowsey, meanwhile, had only the vaguest sense of what Patterson was up to. Even on the day of the closing, when they met with Patterson in the boardroom of the Penn Square Bank, Mahan and Rowsey did not know the identity of the buyer. Nor did they especially care. All they knew was that Patterson had somehow managed to extricate them from horrendous circumstances. As in the good old days a year earlier, they signed whatever they were told to sign. The buyer, Patterson promised, would drop by later that afternoon to complete the transaction. The date was May 7—two and a half weeks into the bank examination. The comptroller of Mahan-Rowsey Drilling gave a deposition some months later and was asked to characterize the QOL deal from Mahan-Rowsey's point of view: "*Q:* So it was a good deal? *A:* Hell of a good deal. I'd sell another one today."

Chase Manhattan's correspondent bankers esteemed Hefner, and were pleased to have him as a customer. Certainly they preferred him to Mahan and Rowsey. Patterson and Hefner had agreed that the QOL note would come to thirty million three hundred thousand dollars. They had not agreed that Chase would finance the note without Hefner's knowledge. They had not agreed that Hefner would get stuck with the rigs. Twenty-four million went to pay Mahan-Rowsey Drilling's debt to Chase. Michigan National was made whole on the six million that had recently been lent to Mahan and Rowsey. A three-hundred-thousand-dollar origination fee to Penn Square was tacked on. Hefner did not anticipate that a million dollars' worth of Mahan-Rowsey payables would pop up at the last minute and that someone at the Penn Square Bank would use a ballpoint pen to alter a zero to a one, increasing the loan by a million dollars. That Seafirst had lent Mahan-Rowsey Drilling almost ten million dollars and received none of the proceeds of the QOL loan . . . that Seafirst held a secured lien against the rigs . . . that no buyer yet existed to take the rigs off Hefner's hands . . . that that guaranteed monstrous difficulties not far down the road—Patterson would, for the moment, isolate that information somewhere in the brainpan. When the crisis resurfaced, he would figure something out.

In mid-June, Patterson bought from Eldon Beller, for eighty-one dollars a share, a thousand shares of stock in the First Penn Corporation, the Penn Square Bank's holding company. This increased his stake in the bank to almost 8 percent. Only Beep Jennings owned a larger portion of stock. Considering that Patterson had begun life short of cash, he had not, on paper, done badly. During the May and June meetings of Penn Square's directors some recent loans to Patterson came up for discussion. Patterson owed the bank more than three million dollars. His annual salary was sixty-five thousand dollars. His financial statement showed that he and his wife, Eve, had a net worth of almost five million dollars. A million dollars of Eve Patterson's inheritance had bought shares of the First Penn Corporation.

At the June meeting, Patterson's fellow bank directors heard his account of several pending matters—a narrative that, in retrospect, seems to have contained flaws. There was a report about overdrafts, which Patterson said amounted to less than three million dollars. (The actual figure was $65.9 million.) Patterson stated that a certain loan to Mahan & Rowsey, Inc., was guaranteed by another customer. (It was not.) He said that he and the other partners in the BGP Marina expected to sell their investments to Walter E. Heller & Company in the near future. (Wishful thinking.) Describing a rig loan to Cliff Culpepper, Patterson said that the Tomcat well had been completed. (It had not.) Other directors raised questions about the bank's loans to Patterson. He had borrowed to invest in a drilling program that Penn Square had financed. Was that a conflict of interest? Beep Jennings said that this could be taken up by the bank's ethics committee (forgetting for the moment that no such committee existed).

Two days later, Jennings and Patterson joined a salmon-fishing expedition in British Columbia. Also along on that trip were the chairman of Seattle-First and half a dozen other Seafirst employees, including John Boyd, the head of energy lending; Bob Hefner's son, Robert IV; and Carl Swan and several other major Penn Square customers. Later, on being asked whether along with the salmon prospecting there had been any chitchat about the Penn Square Bank's travails, everyone drew a blank.

When the final examination of the bank began, Penn Square's capital stood at thirty-seven million dollars. When Patterson and Jennings returned from their fishing outing they were told that the identifiable losses seemed to have exceeded twenty million. Precision eluded the examiners. Patterson's ability to sell losses upstream muddied things, injected a bizarre variable into the calculation of how near or far insolvency lurked.

On June 21, a Monday, an employee of GHK saw for the first time the May bank statement of QOL Corporation. Only then did Bob Hefner become aware that the note from Chase Manhattan had actually been funded, that he had inherited responsibility for seven drilling rigs which he did not care to own. He went a little crazy. Patterson went a little crazy. Jennings tried not to go crazy. There were unhappy scenes and unhappy words. Jennings told Hefner, "Bob, you *do not* have liability on those rigs."

By the end of that week, Patterson's tenure as manager of the Penn Square Bank oil-and-gas division had ended. No longer was he free to play Musical Lenders, but he did have permission to go out and raise capital, and that also offered excitement. Early in June he had generated five million, then ten, then fifteen million in pledges to buy Penn Square Bank stock. He hit both coasts twice in one week. The night of June 27, a Sunday, he spent in Chicago, at John Lytle's home. He showed Lytle a partial list of potential investors. A thirty-million-dollar loan package would do it—thirty million to be divided among twenty subscribers, with shares ranging from half-a-million to five million dollars. The five-million-dollar pledge had come from Hefner. The next morning, supplicant, Patterson flew to the headquarters of the Michigan National Bank. Tuesday evening, he returned to Chicago.

Beep Jennings and Bob Hefner, meanwhile, had flown to Chicago on Hefner's Westwind jet. Hefner's purpose was to meet with some bankers from Northern Trust to discuss financing for GHK. Jennings went hoping to find a solid thirty-million-dollar stock loan commitment. On the ground, Jennings received two pieces of news. He learned that the Comptroller of the Currency had told Continental Illinois and the other upstream banks that many of their Penn Square loan participations were destined to be declared losses. He also learned that Hefner did not feel inclined to do him multiple favors. More or less in gratitude for the Mahan-Rowsey rigs, Hefner decided to remove his company's deposits from Penn Square. Mobil, GHK's partner in the western Anadarko, had prepaid several million dollars of operating costs—funds that GHK had invested in First Penn Corp. commercial paper. Twenty-three million dollars' worth of commercial paper matured on Wednesday, June 30, while Hefner and Jennings were in Chicago. A GHK employee went to the Penn Square Bank to make certain that the money got wired out. Part of his job was to calm the Telex operator.

That same day, in Oklahoma City, a new order from the Comptroller arrived, giving the bank ten days to raise fresh capital. On Friday, July 2, the *Wall Street Journal* reported that the major upstream banks had been told by the Comptroller that their Penn

Square loans were in trouble. That same morning, the Comptroller amended his previous order, giving the bank until the close of business that day to recapitalize. The examiners now brandished a machete, and with each stroke of its blade the capital needs grew. The first liquidators from the Federal Deposit Insurance Corporation began to arrive. Sitting inside the Penn Square shopping mall, eating a hot dog and drinking a lemonade, you could watch these people pulling up in taxis. By now, Hefner's withdrawal was no secret. Jennings delivered a statement to the press that contained the phrases "routine examination," "open for business," and "we have problem loans like everyone else." Ever the optimist, he told one of the local newspapers, "Despite the rumors that have been rampant, it's not all that tough here."

That weekend, the numbers changed by the hour. Representatives of the major banks met in Washington with Paul Volcker, chairman of the Federal Reserve Board; William Isaac, the chairman of the FDIC; and C. T. Conover, the Comptroller of the Currency. One proposal had Penn Square's shareholders relinquishing their stock and Continental Illinois taking over the bank. Another called for several upstream banks and the FDIC to assume control in a joint venture. What stood in the way of all such options was a blind calculation. Even if you could exactly predict loan losses and fix the value of Penn Square's assets, you could not measure Penn Square's uncertain liabilities. Whoever bought Penn Square's assets would also be asked to inherit a black bag labeled "Contingent Liabilities." Outstanding loan commitments seemed to be in the range of four hundred million dollars. Those commitments, along with the knowledge that there would be fraud claims against the bank, made the contingent liabilities a wild card. There was no way to look inside the black bag and discern the value and meaning of its contents.

Inside the Penn Square Bank, a reasonable reaction—panic—obtained. And why not? The regional bank examiners, the chicken-fried-steak-and-yellow-gravy crowd, had never seen anything this big before, had no experience with a bank closing, much less a full-scale liquidation. A strange brew: the big boys in Washington, D.C.; a separate council within the Federal Reserve Bank in Kansas City; the liquidators assembling in Oklahoma City; the regional bank examiners inside the Penn Square Bank; Jennings and his fellow directors and officers and attorneys huddled in their bunker; the upstream bankers stranded in Michigan, Seattle—the merchant-banking outposts. . . . It was as if a bunch of chemistry students, their vision restricted by safety goggles, worked busily away in a laboratory, each one conducting a different experiment, each within its individual limitations not dangerous . . . But then the experiments cross-pollinated, fumes migrated from one lab station to the next . . . There was no teacher in the room to supervise, just a bunch of callow chemistry students. KABOOM! KABOOM! BOOM! BOOM! BOOM!

Four of the five upstream banks—all except Michigan National, which had excused its people for the Independence Day holiday—conducted a weekend photocopying marathon inside Penn Square, gathering the loan documents that they had previously managed to live without. But even at Continental Illinois, which had the most forewarning, no one seriously expected a liquidation. John Lytle placed a bunch of documents on an airplane in Chicago Saturday night. Sunday, the Fourth of July, was a beer-and-balloons family day in his neighborhood on the North Shore. Monday was a day off. Monday night, by phone, he received instructions not to come to work for a while. At Chase Manhattan, when the lawyers were summoned and Penn Square was mentioned, their initial reaction was that "some bank in Philadelphia had a problem." The official closing took place at 7:05 p.m. on Monday, July 5. A senior staff person from the Office of the Comptroller of the Currency entered the boardroom, adjacent to Beep Jennings' office. Eldon Beller was there, as were two of the bank's attorneys. Jennings was given a list of charge-offs totaling forty-five million dollars: on the basis of the examiners' conclusions, the bank was insolvent. Then Jennings was handed the order to liquidate the bank. Beep read the list and the order and said very little. The thought occurred to him that half of the charge-offs were still good loans. Or perhaps he was mistaken. Jennings went home, assembled his family, and shed some tears. "There is bad news and there is good news," he said, demonstrating once again of what stuff he was made. "The good news is we no longer have an estate-planning problem."

CHAPTER 16

It happened that on July 6, 1982, the day after the Penn Square Bank went out of business, the Vice-President of the United States was scheduled to address a political luncheon in Oklahoma City. Heedless of the local wind conditions, he delivered his prepared text. "I believe I bring some good news," proclaimed George Bush, effervescing. "The recession has been deep—deeper than we anticipated—but the recession is over. I can tell you that recent economic indicators show that the recession has bottomed out, economic recovery is underway and gaining momentum." The room was full of Republicans—J. D. Allen, that stalwart, sat in his usual spot at the head table—and they were slow to applaud. Wrong timing, perhaps. Definitely the wrong place.

A few weeks later I was having dinner with friends at a restaurant in Oklahoma City. We were drinking frozen margaritas and eating chicken-fried steak presented in a nouvelle cuisine manner. One of my friends, an interior decorator, said, "We had a good town started." He shook his head. "But it blew up." Plenty of people in Oklahoma City simply did not see how a national bank—indeed, a Beep Jennings enterprise—could be put out of business just like that. Absorbing what it all might mean posed a challenge. An easy first reaction was: "This is just one of them things that'll happen, I guess."

The complication was that this thing had only begun to happen. The instant that the Comptroller of the Currency and the chairman of the FDIC agreed to close and liquidate the bank, Penn Square's stockholders were wiped out and the uninsured depositors stood to lose a bundle. Money brokers—professional

143

megabuck jobbers who, for a fee, steer pension and credit union funds in the direction of the highest "prudent" yield—had invested a hundred twenty-five million dollars in Penn Square certificates of deposit. In this manner, an impressive proportion of the loans that the Penn Square Bank made and sold were funded by individuals who to this day do not realize that the bank existed. Looking at the immediate debris, a cynic could ask whether anyone was truly worse off than before the boom. These victims—weren't their wounds self-inflicted? Was it not as if a church congregation had committed arson upon its own house of worship?

The Penn Square Bank deserved credit for prolonging the good times and for exacerbating the crummy ones. Nationwide, the tally of active rotary drilling rigs peaked in December 1981 at 4,530. The high point of the Oklahoma rig count—882, up and running—was not reached until a month or so later. From there it was a free fall. By the spring of 1983, the count was down to 232. With the decline in the rig count came a decline in the cost of exploration—contract drilling, pipe, mud, supplies—as well as a redrafting of the rules. Banks began to advertise escrow services for joint drilling ventures—a sacrilege in a business where in the past an oilman's word presumably sufficed to make him creditworthy.

The newest oilies had started with nothing, had borrowed everything, and, on the correct theory that the worst they could do was break even, had spent their borrowed funds with alacrity. I collected vignettes:

There was the million-dollar Toronado. A big New York bank, it was said, held a million-dollar participation on a loan to a lease broker. When the borrower failed to perform, the big New York bank sent someone down to Oklahoma City to find out what was going on.

"What happened to the leases?" the banker asked.

"I never bought 'em," said the borrower.

"Wait a minute. What do you mean you never bought them? Our agreement with Penn Square says that that loan is secured by those leases, the unlimited personal guarantee of the borrower, and other personal property, including a 1980 Oldsmobile Toronado. What happened to your unlimited guarantee?"

"I'm broke."

"What happened to the money?"

"It got spent."

" 'It got spent!' You mean to tell me I've got a million bucks tied up in a 1980 Toronado?"

"Hell, no. I sold that car last year. You haven't got a goddamn thing."

A new strain of Okiesmo emerged. Although it might no longer be feasible or tasteful to brag about how much you were preparing to borrow or how many aircraft you owned, Okiesmo could also thrive upon hopeless stoicism—"My bankruptcy lawyer's better than yours" . . . "I'm hogtied tighter than you" . . . "I'm runnin' for pres'dint of the CIO. That's 'cause ever'body I see I owe." Beyond the garden-variety crash-and-burns were the exotic flora. I read in the newspaper about an oilwoman named Donna Rose Willis, who ran a few drilling ventures, including one called Tycoonette. When she filed her bankruptcy petition, the liabilities included the potential claims of everyone who had invested with her and might someday feel inclined to sue her. The total came to two hundred sixty-five million. A lot of these unhappy investors had heard about Mrs. Willis through church; they were mostly Nazarenes. When the investors' names turned up in print, many came forward to complain that Mrs. Willis did not owe anywhere close to what she claimed she did. She had just made up the big numbers, it seemed, to embarrass those people.

As the mundane-bizarre tales proliferated, I would write notes to myself: "Remember to ask So-and-So how he came to owe the FDIC almost a million bucks." How charmingly naïve! In time, with the litigation building steam, my standards rose and I refused to be distracted by any lawsuit that involved less than eight figures.

Reading the newspapers, following the reports of bankruptcy filings, gathering hearsay, I encountered familiar names. I noticed which former Little League baseball teammates from my boyhood in Tulsa were on the ropes or close to it. The shortstop owed twenty million but remained afloat. The left fielder, owing more, had run off the road and into a deep ditch. With envy and empathy and a sense of relief, I developed a suspicion that if I had been living in Oklahoma during the boom the only thing that would have kept me out of permanent trouble would have been leg irons and a cell in a preventive-detention facility for probable deadbeats. Still, I was haunted by the knowledge that I could have borrowed five million during the boom, buried it in the backyard, and, come the bust, dug up four million and carried that over to the FDIC, which would have gladly settled for eighty cents on the dollar.

The bankruptcy bar was, of course, the place to be. Suddenly, bankruptcy lawyers, the ambulance chasers of the corporate legal fraternity, occupied center-aisle seats in the orchestra section. Literally. Amarex, Inc., a publicly owned exploration-and-drilling-fund company, the seller during a four-year period of a hundred sixty-five million dollars in subscriptions, a major customer of the Penn Square Bank and of Continental Illinois, held a creditors' meeting in the Civic Center Music Hall. During 1983, bankruptcy filings rose at a faster rate in the United States Bankruptcy Court for Western Oklahoma than in any other jurisdiction in the country. Oil-and-gas employment declined by a third; the state-wide unemployment rate doubled. Within a year of the bank failure, more than a hundred and fifty companies that had banked at Penn Square, with debts to the FDIC totaling three hundred fifty-two million dollars, filed for bankruptcy.

The closing of the bank precipitated a softening of the local market for polo ponies and racing thoroughbreds and quarter horses. One of Penn Square's busier customers, Kenneth E. Tureaud, had to give up not only his horses but also his three airplanes (including John Wayne's old Jet Commander), a box of rubies and emeralds, 155 Picasso etchings, eleven condominiums, some Florida oceanfront, twenty copies of a Salvador Dalí print called "Chevalier Surréaliste," and a couple dozen LeRoy Neiman prints, paintings, and drawings. Tureaud's bankruptcy was messy. The man and his various enterprises had at least fifty-one bank accounts. He was one of those out-of-staters who could smell a friendly bank from two thousand miles away. I asked an attorney who had studied Tureaud's career to explain his methodology, and the answer was: "Very simple. He borrows money and he doesn't pay it back." (When Bill Patterson had promised his fellow investors in the BPG Marina that a permanent buyer would be along any minute, one prospect he mentioned was Ken Tureaud—overlooking that Tureaud already owed Penn Square and its correspondent banks twenty-five million dollars.) If you wanted to nitpick, you could criticize Ken Tureaud for being too much of a Renaissance man, not enough of a specialist, not a purebred oilie. Tureaud had been around the real estate game for years, had dabbled in precious metals, but his greatest idea by far was Acry Dent ("the Quonset huts of false teeth"), and when I think of him—always with fond sorrow; he died in an automobile accident in 1984—I think not of a would-be wildcatter but of a visionary who wanted to do whatever he could to lift up the 40 percent of the earth's population that is toothless.

Anyway, Tureaud's horses went on the market. One February night I drove out to the Oklahoma City fairgrounds to witness the dispersal. The air was chilly but the sale barn felt cozy. Five hundred people had squeezed into bleachers that could have comfortably accommodated three hundred. A lot of the onlookers wore scarlet or purple or electric-blue satin jackets with script embroidery on the back: "Mr. Thunder Moon," "Oklahoma City Nite Rodeo." Surveying the gathering, you could not necessarily tell who had money. The lawyers and the CPAs were identifiable because their tweed jackets had leather elbow patches. I saw western women in real tight Levi's and western men in pearl-gray Stetsons. I heard conversations that went like this:

"Harr yew?"

"Hey, how you doon there, buddy?"

"Well, whadya know, boy?"

The dialogue might have progressed further, but someone would always point out that the western men were blocking the aisle. So they would tell each other, "Hey, gooda seeya." They had huge hands with broad, flat fingers, and they wore silver-and-gold belt buckles so heavy they stooped slightly as they shuffled on.

Before the bidding started, I walked past the horse stalls. I spent a long time admiring Cute N Blonde, a beautiful three-year-old palomino filly. She wore a halter with red ribbons and had red wool pom-poms in her braided mane. Her white tail had been brushed out full. The number "14" was stenciled in white paint on her left hip. I had difficulty accepting the idea of something that gorgeous being sold in distress.

"Bankruptcy practice is real simple," a lawyer told me. "Only two ways you can go: reorganize or liquidate. The tricky part is getting the cases." Now that part had become less tricky because there were cases to spread around—many varieties, some marginal, some not-so-close calls. The mainstream oil-and-gas Chapter 11 petition listed on the liability side a bank or two; three or four pipe-and-supply companies; three or four well-site service companies, ranging from Schlumberger to Mac's Welding in Wewoka; a hotshot service; a mud company; a drilling contractor; an accountant; two diesel suppliers; an engineering firm; working-interest owners; an airline charter service; MasterCard; the Internal Revenue Service and the Oklahoma Tax Commission; and attorneys. The creditor who owned the hotshot outfit was a poignant case indeed. Hot-shotting is oilfield errand-running. You call a hotshot company when you need right now to move a nipple or a flange or a float shoe from a supply yard in Oklahoma City to a well site a hundred twenty miles away. The hotshot outfit was owned by a good man in his late thirties who had borrowed money to buy a couple of trucks, would have mortgaged his house if for some reason he had not been living in a trailer, had opened a dispatching office and hired three or four women to keep the books and talk on the phone and four kids right out of school to work the midnight-to-dawn jobs. Business was great. It looked like time to branch out, maybe buy a couple of tank trucks and start hauling brine or diesel. Then the entire state's credit froze and overnight everyone's receivables became uncollectibles, and the hotshotter realized that he was a victim of a new disease called liquidity gridlock. The only thing left to do was to consult an attorney. You added up your liabilities, and if you had assets you had to go through the formality of proposing a way of paying back some of the money. The Okiesmo wags said: "It's a great time to be in the oil business if you're not broke."

Ancillary industries percolated. You could sign up for weekend training seminars with titles such as "Creditors' Rights in the Oil Patch" and "Bankruptcy: A Look at Chapters 7 & 11 from All Angles." This was a lawyers' relief fund, a fifteen-year annuity. The FDIC, in the name of Penn Square, sued most of the names in the phone book. And vice versa. The directors and officers of Penn Square got sued by credit unions and drilling fund investors. Peat, Marwick, Mitchell, the bank's accountant, was sued by, among others, credit unions and money brokers. Not every oil-and-gas operator had followed every letter of the securities laws. Others had drilled dry holes. If a Penn Square connection existed, the natural thing to do was to holler fraud and sue. Everybody and his dog sued Longhorn Oil & Gas, Carl Swan, and J. D. Allen. If the FDIC or an upstream bank that had lent money to a drilling fund operator tried to call an investor's letter of credit, the investor rushed to court and demanded a restraining order. Litigants spread all over the map, and when their attorneys started showing up at the federal courthouse in Oklahoma City the place developed a distinctly charcoal-gray tone, as if a morticians' convention had settled in.

Oklahoma City had by no means enough lawyers to handle all the new business. It spilled over to Tulsa, Houston, Dallas. Then there were the polished retainers of the various upstream banks, litigators who specialized in "workouts," which is the art of making a borrower's insufficient assets satisfy the claims of creditors. The dislike of the opposing lawyers for one another was naked. One of the few things that they could agree upon was that a custom-designed hell should be built for the Federal Deposit Insurance Corporation. The FDIC lawyers and liquidators did not mind taking extreme stands and refusing to yield. They would define "reasonable" and then they would sit and wait for their adversaries to capitulate. As receiver of a bankrupt estate, the FDIC operated upon the premise that the receivership should be served first and last. The FDIC would do whatever was deemed to be "in the best interests of the receivership." No one at the FDIC knew how oil-and-gas financing worked; no one acknowledged the importance of cash flow; no one understood the classic and unavoidable pyramid of the typical oil-and-gas borrower; no one seemed to care how a loss of credit would damage the value of collateral. Wherever cash or collateral could be found, the FDIC intended to be at the head of the line. Later, when the damage became evident, the liquidators would shift blame to the Comptroller of the Currency, who had permitted a monster to mature at the Penn Square Bank and then had given the FDIC people so little time to prepare for the task of unraveling and liquidating. Over all, negotiating with the FDIC seemed far less enjoyable than doing business with Beep Jennings and Bill Patterson in their carefree days.

One afternoon several months into the liquidation, I sat in a third-floor office in the bank. The office had once belonged to Beep Jennings, but its current occupant was a senior career employee of the FDIC. His name was Thomas Procopio and his title was "chief liquidator." By the time of this meeting, I was well aware that if the FDIC were a person you could not invite it to a gathering of strangers and expect it to make a bunch of friends. I was aware that the day after the bank closed, Procopio's predecessor as chief liquidator had circulated an edict instructing Penn Square's former employees, now suddenly on the payroll of the FDIC, to turn in their "From the Desk of . . ." memo pads—a gambit not likely to set a tone of trust—and that this man had enjoyed making remarks such as "I don't have to be reasonable, and I'm not going to be." As I chatted cordially with Procopio, however, he did not strike me as unreasonable. He struck me as a lumpish, fortyish guy who had a graying beard and an informal manner and a decent sense of humor. I noticed that on a shelf behind his desk there was a photograph of a gorilla with the caption "Patience My Ass . . . I'm Gonna Kill Something," but I took that for irony. I was caught off guard, therefore, when not long into our conversation Procopio told me that he regarded the Penn Square Bank as "the core of evil."

I asked him what that meant.

"They didn't want to play by the rules," Procopio said. "They didn't want to stay in their environment and be a good shopping-center bank and serve the needs of their community, which is why they were given a charter in the first place."

A colleague of Procopio's named Paul Heafy had joined us. "This bank was the rich spoiled kid on the block," Heafy said. "I supervise ten people who used to work for Penn Square and now work for us who make more than I do. These guys didn't even bother to repair things that broke. They'd buy an IBM Selectric typewriter and if anything went wrong they'd stick it in a closet and buy another one. They had a closet full of those typewriters.

They filled that one up and then they filled another one. They ended up with two closets full."

"I know there are good people in the oil business in Oklahoma," Procopio said. "I think some of them banked here. They are people who got in on the boom and built up a business without having any business sense. A good bank would have recognized that about them and helped them keep their accounts in order. There were some of those people who can just smell oil, you know. They're very good technicians. But they're not very good managers of people and their destinies."

The conversation proceeded in this vein for about half an hour. After Heafy left the room, Procopio and I stood at the window. The view was to the north. We could see the parking lot beneath us, then a broad field of weedy red hardpan, a creek bed, a stand of young cottonwood and blackjack oak and redbud trees, a line of stockade fences, and a row of houses. "I think about my forty-three thousand dollars a year," Procopio said, referring to his government salary. "And then I think about the guy who used to be in this office, who was making five hundred thousand. He had this big little city in the palm of his hand and if he had only wanted to go the straight and narrow this bank would have become what he wanted it to become."

I wanted to ask Procopio how he had come up with the figure of five hundred thousand—I thought it was too low. I knew that his "core of evil" theory contained flaws, but I did not know how to respond. As we spoke, a dozen or so FDIC investigators were in the basement and next door, in what had formerly been the Penn Square Bank oil-and-gas department, examining thousands of documents, assembling files, trying to figure out what had happened from the outset. When these investigators came up with something provocative, they would refer it to the United States Attorney for the Western District of Oklahoma, who would share it with the FBI, hoping to make it presentable to a federal grand jury. I thought: Did the Comptroller of the Currency have nothing to answer for? Were the upstream banks, with their master plans for growth, without culpability? Was not greed a universal instinct? How did evil enter the picture? In my mind, "evil" implied bad men with big ideas. Did the government seriously believe that whatever had happened at the Penn Square Bank had been *planned*? Did not the dementing mess downstairs indicate that Beep Jennings and his subordinates lacked the smarts to close a loan properly, much less premeditate and execute an international financial swindle? Did the government have a sinister theory of why Penn Square, a merchant bank, had sold loans? Well. In the land of oil-and-gas, in the wake of boom and bust, one's moral barometer broke easily. Perhaps a juicy conspiracy theory merited a counterconspiracy theory. Who had dispatched these spiteful bureaucrats with their vinyl briefcases and their lower-crust credit cards anyway? Perhaps the people who wanted to punish a friendly, God-fearing oil-and-gas lending bank in the American heartland were charter members of the cabal that controlled the money supply and met for lunch every Thursday inside an ivory tomb somewhere along the Boston–New York–Washington mega-lopolitan corridor. Once you had crossed the threshold into the core of evil, many fantasies became plausible.

On the way home from Procopio's office, *nè* Beep Jennings' office, I stopped at my neighborhood supermarket to pick up some things for dinner—about ten dollars' worth. While I was standing at the checkout counter, an elderly gentleman who was wearing a blue baseball cap turned to me, held out his Winners' Jackpot Double Bingo ticket, which he had not yet punched, and said, "You want twenty-five thousand dollars? Here." I accepted it with gratitude and with the implicit understanding that should the two of us ever meet again at that same Safeway checkout counter, I would try to remember to pay him back. At home, there was a postcard from some people in Connecticut, typed neatly and mailed first-class. It suggested that I turn my tax dollars into liquid gold. It said that piling up profits was a matter of knowing what to do when, that I could win $100,000 in the U. S. Gov't oil lottery, and that the lottery was a well-kept secret. I could be rich tomorrow, there was no obligation, each day I waited could be costing me a fortune, and if I would send my phone number to Connecticut someone would send me a confidential report titled "The Oil Crisis: Myths and Facts." I sent my phone number and I am still waiting.

CHAPTER 17

After the Penn Square Bank closed, I kept a tally of other banks that failed or came near to failure, particularly banks that had lent to the oil-and-gas industry. Fresh corpses turned up regularly and the intensive-care wards of the banking system stayed full. Soon, one of every twenty-five banks across the nation had earned a spot on the FDIC's "problem list"; the list had grown far beyond its previous peak, which it had achieved in the wake of the recession of the mid-1970s. Six weeks after Penn Square, the Abilene National Bank, in Texas, a somewhat smaller institution, failed and was sold to a Dallas-based bank holding company. During the winter of 1983, the United American Bank of Knoxville, Tennessee, failed and was sold, and that failure rearranged the fates of a chain of almost twenty banks in Tennessee and Kentucky. During the first quarter of 1983, the ten largest banking companies in the country averaged more than a 17 percent increase in problem loans over the previous quarter. Later that year, the First National Bank of Midland, Texas, a major oil-and-gas lender, with assets three times as large as Penn Square's, failed and was bought by another Texas bank. Then InterFirst, of Dallas, announced the largest quarterly loss in American banking history—two hundred and forty-nine million dollars. The First National Bank & Trust Company of Oklahoma City announced a quarterly loss of fifty-eight million, which, as a percentage of assets, was even worse than InterFirst's. By the beginning of 1984, the FDIC's list of problem banks had risen to 617, a post-Depression record. It seemed reasonable to wonder whether there were not still other Penn Squares in Dallas or Houston or New Orleans or Denver or right there in Oklahoma City. Prudent oil-and-gas bankers—the ones who had never lent against collateral less solid than discounted petroleum reserves with proved production histories—found themselves staring at losses that months before no one had imagined imagining. Where, precisely, was the core of the evil?

The upstream banks dispatched workout teams to Oklahoma City—rotating crews whose job was to secure collateral, to assume management of loan accounts that had previously been the responsibility of Penn Square, to renegotiate loan terms and repayment schedules, to advise whether to sue, and to duel with the liquidators. This tedious and often demoralizing labor was made even less enjoyable by the bank's having failed during a typical Oklahoma summer. Torpid days dawned when the attorneys and workout troops did not feel inspired to behave politely. Extended Penn Square duty seemed like a hot and dusty Siberia. One August weekend when even your teeth felt scorched, an associate with Milbank, Tweed, Hadley & McCloy, the New York law firm representing Chase Manhattan, discovered that the only entertainment in town was a concert by the ancient rock group Crosby, Stills & Nash. The local cultural deprivation offended the lawyer, and the avidity of the audience at the concert appalled him. He said, "Now I understand how Penn Square happened. Too much enthusiasm."

The upstream banks had trouble admitting to themselves just how shaky many of their Penn Square loans were. Continental Illinois had bought loan participations whose face value equaled half of its capital. Seafirst had gambled more than half. Michigan National's participations came to three fifths of that bank's capital. The figure for Northern Trust was 31 percent. Chase Manhattan, on the other hand, had bought some howlers but had risked only 6 percent of what it could afford to lose.

In several respects unconnected to Penn Square, however, Chase Manhattan did not enjoy a prosperous spring and summer of 1982. A firm called Drysdale Government Securities collapsed in a heap of fraud accusations, owing Chase more than two hundred and eighty-five million dollars. A smaller government securities dealer, Lombard-Wall, failed, with an unsecured debt to Chase of forty-five million dollars. An oil-and-gas refiner, GHR

Companies, filed for bankruptcy protection, owing Chase one hundred and twenty-five million dollars. Bad news in banking does not breed confidence. Chase Manhattan's workout officers and lawyers could not abide the thought that the bank had lent money to Penn Square customers only days before the joint fell apart. When it came to Penn Square, the feeling was: Let's hose down this dog and get out of town. Ultimately, Chase wrote off more than three quarters of its Penn Square portfolio. If the Chase correspondent bankers had had more of a head start, the losses might not have been so easy to swallow. From early 1981 to mid-1982, Chase had managed to buy two hundred twelve million dollars in Penn Square loans. While fun was still being had, some of Chase's money salesmen had fantasized about one billion dollars in loan participations.

Designating culprits did not consume much time. A fortnight after Penn Square's failure, half a dozen Chase correspondent bankers, from foot soldier to executive vice-president, became unemployed. Next the lawyers focused upon delinquent customers and upon the bankrupt estate. Chase sued the FDIC for more than seventy million dollars, alleging fraud, deceit, and misrepresentation of collateral. The FDIC fought back, accusing Chase of having extorted ("unlawful economic coercion") almost twenty million dollars in principal and interest that Penn Square had forwarded on behalf of nonperforming customers. Then Chase, Continental Illinois, and Seafirst in effect sued themselves. More precisely, the banks' shareholders, in the name of the corporation, sued certain of their own former bank officers, alleging mismanagement of their Penn Square dealings. Banks routinely insure against costly "errors and omissions" by employees. If the plaintiffs could prove negligence by the defendants, Chase and Continental might each recover a hundred million—and Seafirst seventy-five million—of the dollars that had been risked and lost in the oil patch.

Michigan National bought less than two hundred million dollars in Penn Square loans. By the end of 1983 more than a hundred million had become losses or anticipated losses. The bank omitted a quarterly dividend payment for the first time since 1941. Relatively speaking, the impact of this was much more serious for

Michigan National than the loss of an even larger amount was for Chase. No one at Michigan National got fired in the immediate aftermath of Penn Square. Rather, a we-had-*no-idea* strategy seemed suitable. These Oklahoma bankers *lied* to us, went the company line. We were *mugged,* we were *bamboozled.* Everything that Michigan National had invested in Oklahoma, it seemed, had grown out of deep admiration for Continental Illinois. A copy of a letter materialized in Michigan National's files—one that John Lytle, of Continental, had written to Bill Patterson in early 1981. The letter, which was self-congratulatory in tone, referred to a meeting between some Continental Illinois bankers and some Michigan National bankers. Lytle described the Michigan National people as "pleased with the package of credits that we put together" and "growing both in confidence and understanding of oil-related lending." In closing, Lytle thanked Patterson for his help and proposed "that this is a service, that working together, we can provide to others."

To get some of its money back, Michigan National hired F. Lee Bailey to sue Continental Illinois for fifty-seven million dollars.

Seafirst announced shortly after Penn Square's liquidation began that it expected to write off roughly a third of the four hundred million dollars in loans that it had bought. With no assistance from Penn Square, Seafirst had hustled an additional eight hundred million in energy credits. Before the write-offs, the bank had a net worth of just under six hundred million. Four hundred employees—out of eight thousand—were laid off or reassigned. John Boyd, who had been the manager of Seafirst's energy division, resigned, and his boss, John Nelson, the executive vice-president who managed the world banking group, took early retirement. William Jenkins, the chairman of the bank, told the *Wall Street Journal,* "I should have retired last year." A member of the bank's board said, "I really don't know in the pit of my stomach whether it's half as bad as they've told us or twice as bad." Twice as bad, it turned out, was not the half of it. Within six weeks of the Penn Square closing, Jenkins decided to retire. When he departed officially, at the end of 1982, he took with him the president and the vice-chairman, and the three took, collectively, a million eight hundred thousand dollars in severance benefits.

A new chairman was hired, a former chief executive officer of the Wells Fargo Bank. During his first month at Seafirst, the new chairman set up a one-billion-five-hundred-million-dollar line of credit with twelve major banks. Nevertheless, Seafirst's condition deteriorated through early 1983. More layoffs were announced. The executive dining room was closed. By spring, the capital was down to a dangerously low fraction of the bank's total assets. It seemed predictable that once the results of Seafirst's 1983 first quarter became known a run on the bank would occur. To restore liquidity and to inject the fresh capital necessary to sustain the enterprise, a merger was required. Which is how BankAmerica came to own the Seattle-First National Bank. This was no small blip on the charts. Penn Square had broken the nineteenth-largest bank in the United States and had provoked a merger that created the largest bank holding company in history.

Loan losses are lamentable but unavoidable. Among bankers there is an inbred tendency to react to fiscal humiliation as if one had spilled gravy on a tablecloth or neglected to send a hostess a thank-you note. Willard Butcher, the chairman of Chase Manhattan, told a meeting of shareholders in the spring of 1983 that the Penn Square experience had been "difficult and certainly a source of acute embarrassment." Richard G. Jaehning, the president of Seafirst, told the Banking Committee of the House of Representatives, "At this point, Seafirst is a little bruised and more than a little embarrassed, but we hope and expect a vital recovery." Jenkins, before retiring as chairman of Seafirst, said, "We're alive, healthy and kicking but hurt, chagrined and very embarrassed."

A banker in Oklahoma City told me of a meeting in Chicago with Roger Anderson, the chairman of Continental Illinois, roughly a month after Penn Square closed. The two men chatted amiably for a few minutes, and Anderson said, "Well, I guess that Penn Square deal's about to blow over down there." The Oklahoma City banker was shocked. "I told Anderson I thought there was plenty more blowing to come. He asked me some questions. I had gone there to tell him that we wanted to help him, that we knew more about the Oklahoma oil-and-gas lending market than Continental did. We knew about some of their energy credits and we might be able to tell them some things, help them look out for some risks that they might not have been aware of. I had a feeling that the guy just didn't grasp the situation. He was reacting as if maybe the trust department had a bad year, or something. I never heard from him again. I lost my sympathy real quick."

Barring undue pressure from the regulators, banks are free to make their decisions about whether loans are performing or nonperforming, potentially valuable or worthless. A nonperforming loan is one on which interest is not being paid or one that has been renegotiated (the terms, interest rate, or maturity has been refigured) or one whose collateral has been foreclosed upon. During 1982, Continental's nonperforming loans rose by a billion dollars, of which almost six hundred million came from Penn Square. The first anniversary of the Penn Square failure had not yet arrived when it became clear that Continental had suffered serious permanent damage. More than two hundred fifty million dollars in Penn Square loans was written off. A bank that had deliberately grown to become the number one commercial lender in America was, with astonishing celerity, eliminated from the competition. Prestige and momentum vanished. The three hundred million in lost capital not only represented a loss of income, it prefigured an upheaval of the institution.

Less than two months into the workouts—August 28—Continental began a housecleaning. John Lytle was fired. His boss took early retirement and his boss's boss resigned, as did Pat Goy, the young vice-president, who, five months earlier, had passed the flying time from Tulsa to Chicago with George Baker, the executive vice-president in charge of all commercial lending, and had explained to Baker his misgivings about the Penn Square–Continental Illinois relationship. When Goy was summoned to his August 28 meeting with Baker, he did not expect to be dismissed; in fact, he assumed that he was about to be promoted and placed in charge of the workout offices in Oklahoma City. He prepared for the meeting by outlining a staff budget and a list of personal moving expenses. "My wife was crying, thinking about leaving our friends in Chicago and moving to Oklahoma City," Goy later said. "But I told her that it would be good for us and good for the bank. I had made up a moving budget, and I remember that there was a new expense item—draperies. I told my wife, 'I don't care what they say, I'm gonna get the drapery allowance.' I think they allowed two thousand for draperies and I knew that I was entitled."

Instead of the drapery allowance, Goy was given a one-paragraph letter—his resignation—and was instructed to sign it. "I looked at George Baker and said, 'Are you sure you've got the right guy? How about if I leave the room and come back in and we start all over? Remember when we talked on the airplane in April? Maybe you've confused me with someone else.' But, no, they meant me."

Three months later, George Baker was gone. At the end of 1983, John Perkins, the president of Continental Illinois, and Donald Miller, the vice-chairman and chief financial officer, announced that they would be leaving the company. Then, in February of 1984, Continental's directors forced Roger Anderson to retire. The chairman floated out with an immense, billowing golden parachute: a three-hundred-fifty-thousand-dollar annual pension and a consulting contract, good for two years, at not-quite-fourteen grand per month. A special supplemental payment made the entire severance package worth five hundred fifty thousand dollars a year.

Anderson would thus not be present to witness firsthand the worst of Continental Illinois's problems. The worst had not yet begun.

CHAPTER 18

To qualify for the first annual *Forbes* survey of the four hundred wealthiest individuals in America, one had to muster a minimum net worth of one hundred million dollars—an amount that is known in Texas and Oklahoma as "a unit." The name of Robert A. Hefner III appeared on the list, which was published in September 1982, and his net worth was estimated to be a unit and a half. The dedicated professionals at *Forbes* had spent a year researching the topic of excessive wealth. By the time their information appeared in print it was obsolete. Hefner had not merely slipped a rung or two in the plutocracy. According to the accepted definition of net worth as the difference between assets and liabilities, a true appraisal of Hefner's net worth in the fall of 1982 should have been preceded by a minus sign. Liabilities were accumulating all about him in deep drifts, and the value of his assets was evaporating. Nowhere near enough cash was coming in, and the credit picture looked quite unpromising. The single advantage that Hefner held was the one that had sustained him from the beginning—debtor's leverage, the ability to go through terrific sums of borrowed money at a speed that made him bankruptcy-proof.

Within six weeks of Penn Square's closing, Hefner's primary banks and trade creditors formed a committee. Among the GHK trade creditors were the Parker Drilling Company, the well-service companies Halliburton and Schlumberger, Dresser Industries, the Kerr-McGee Corporation, and two large suppliers of pipe and oilfield equipment. The banks were Continental Illinois, Seafirst, and Northern Trust. Chase Manhattan, which had financed Hefner's investments in a thoroughbred horse-breeding enterprise and other non-energy-related pursuits, did not formally join the original group of creditors. In time, with accumulated interest, the bank debt of The GHK Companies stood at two hundred forty-four million dollars, and GHK owed trade creditors an additional ninety-eight million. Altogether, Hefner was responsible, either as a direct borrower or as a general partner, for debts totaling four hundred sixty-one million dollars. There was also a disputed bank debt in the range of fifty million dollars—an amount that included Chase's loan against the seven drilling rigs which Hefner had inadvertently bought from Mahan-Rowsey Drilling, Inc. To place himself in a position to repay any of it, Hefner first needed to borrow more money to drill up the acreage that he had leased in the Anadarko Basin with the help of his original overborrowing. Unofficial rumor had it that the grand total of GHK's debt was closer to six hundred million dollars, but who really knew? When you dealt with The GHK Companies, which was an aggregate of partnerships, you could never be certain whether you were addressing Hefner personally or The GHK Company or The GHK Company, Ltd. or GHK Exploration Company or the GHK Gas Corporation or Gasanadarko, Ltd. or Westwind Properties or North Block Gas, Ltd. And which partnership or corporation owed what to which banks? Some creditors could not recall having seen audited GHK financial statements that were less than three years old. Some creditors were convinced that the truth was unknowable.

In terms of personality, Bob Hefner added up to more, *far more,* than GHK was or was likely to become. He had an impossible debt burden, and none of the proposed solutions could make anyone whole. He had his share of lawsuits—these in addition to fifty million in liens filed against him by the end of 1982—but he had also cultivated a remarkably forgiving audience. His trade creditors, investors, and bankers all recognized that they would have to sacrifice much to salvage anything from the Hefner workout, and his genius lay in having left them with no other choice. A workout plan was signed March 31, 1983, which led several of the parties to refer to it subsequently as "The April Fool's Eve agreement." It was not that everybody there was a fool. If gas went back to nine dollars a thousand, if the sun rose one day in the west, they would all be in the clear.

Diverse factors had delivered Hefner and his creditors to this impasse. In 1980, Hefner's farmout agreement with the Mobil Oil Corporation had provided him with thirty-two million dollars in cash, plus a commitment from Mobil to drill two hundred million dollars' worth of deep gas wells in the Anadarko Basin. So pleasant was this experience that Hefner decided to try to pull off another deal just like it. His lease acquisitions in the Anadarko Basin during 1981 cost more than eighty million dollars. By 1982, he had again run out of cash. The leases had three-year fuses. GHK owned interests in 208 wells that were being drilled the day the Penn Square Bank closed. Of that total, GHK operated twenty-three wells. While drilling, the daily operating cost of a well averaged twenty thousand dollars. If cash became available, Hefner could think of a way to spend it. In 1981, he had borrowed a hundred million dollars from Continental Illinois and an additional thirty-four million from other upstream banks. Hefner needed money on his terms—long terms. Not only did he remain unafraid of debt, he seemed unable to live in any other circumstance. The failure of the Penn Square Bank, however, was a circumstance that he had not anticipated.

Soon after the Penn Square Bank became extinct, Hefner had a dream in which he was hovering above the earth, floating comfortably, enjoying the view, until God came along and slapped him in the face with a four-by-four. God said, "Take that, and remember it before you decide to come out here next time." Meaning that Hefner had overextended, had tried to outsmart reality, and even he knew it. The endless need for operating capital had induced him to try to accommodate Bill Patterson by signing the QOL note. Seafirst, which held a lien against the seven drilling rigs that ostensibly formed the QOL collateral, seized the equipment and sold the whole mess at auction for twenty cents on the dollar. As a result, Seafirst lost most of the thirteen million dollars it was owed by Frank Mahan and Billy Rowsey. Chase Manhattan, however, had traded a dubious twenty-four-million-dollar credit for a dubious thirty-one-point-three-million-dollar credit. The QOL fiasco generated a Chase Manhattan lawsuit against Hefner, a Hefner countersuit, bad publicity, lousy karma. Hefner believed that he was his own harshest critic. A dream about God slapping him with a four-by-four was a form of self-criticism.

Not that Hefner gave up trying to outsmart reality. He remained gaudily quotable. To make points, he invoked Darwin, Einstein, an Italian mathematician named Cesare Marchetti, and himself. His favorite quotation from himself was: "To the extent that mankind is eternal, resources are infinite." At no time did he cease to sermonize and philosophize in the name of methane. "Men walked on the moon in 1969," he would say. "And for the first time human beings could actually look down upon the planet and stare at its finiteness. The Club of Rome wrote about the 'limits to growth' in 1972. The Club of Rome wasn't dangerous, just wrong. Methane is pervasive. We have an earth that is still outgassing substantially, and we can depend with confidence that methane will be the fuel of the next several centuries."

Hefner stayed in motion, campaigned shamelessly. Without Penn Square, where could money be found? He looked for surrogate bankers—for new deep pockets. He seemed indefatigable. I observed him once during a twenty-four-hour rotation through the District of Columbia. ("Well, we can't drill, we might as well be in Washington.") Among other reasons, he made the trip because Congress was threatening to decontrol all natural gas prices in a way that would have discriminated against Hefner's beloved deep gas. Washington had become a frustrating place. After supporting Jimmy Carter in 1976, Hefner had not only switched to Ronald Reagan in 1980 but also become a Republican Eagle—a ten-thousand-dollar donor in his own right—and a proselytizer who recruited ten or twelve other Eagles. And now Hefner could not persuade George Bush to give five minutes of his time—whenever, wherever—to some people from the Bank of Tokyo who seemed eager to invest a billion dollars in American industry, including, perhaps, natural gas exploration. A conversation with the Japanese ambassador was one item on Hefner's Washington agenda. He kept appointments with a senator from Idaho and a congressman from Indiana and a congressman from Michigan, lunched with a senator from Kansas, dined with a congressman from Oklahoma. He literally lobbied in the Senate lobby, cornered a senator from Louisiana, a senator from Oklahoma. He attended a meeting of the National Petroleum Council and listened to a speech by the Secretary of Energy. At the Japanese Embassy, Hefner and the ambassador discussed nuclear power (Hefner was con, the amabssador was pro), natural gas cogeneration (Hefner said his industry was a great place to invest money, there were plenty of bargains), and golf (the ambassador was avid).

"And you are from what state? Colorado?" the ambassador asked.

"Oklahoma."

When Hefner and the ambassador shook hands and parted, the billion dollars from the Bank of Tokyo was still in Japan.

Whatever disappointments might come Hefner's way, Elk City, Oklahoma, would always have citizens who loved him. Minus the methane that lay beneath it, Elk City might have been just another bunch of road signs on the way to Amarillo—one of those places where you could buy cactus jelly and genuine handmade Indian pottery, turquoise and copper, hats, belts, knives, mounted long horns, rattlesnake skins, souvenir plates of the fifty states; a trading post where you and the kids could see a live buffalo or spend a night in the safari campground. With free-market methane, it turned out to be a place to spend a billion or so bucks quickly.

Elk City's population—twelve thousand—made it a borderline metroplex by Oklahoma standards, but three-quarters of those people had not been living there ten years earlier. There had been an oil boom during the nineteen-fifties, but it bore no resemblance to the monster that Bob Hefner fostered. Along the roads leading out of town, equipment and service contractors erected cinderblock field offices: pipe and valve and tool suppliers, drillers, truckers, rig skidders, tubular inspectors, blowout troubleshooters, roustabout agencies, mud companies, fishing specialists, dozer operators, tank transporters, waste haulers, welders, perforators, wire-line loggers. Next came Pizza Hut, Long John Silver's, Mexican fast food, and "luxury condos." Wise citizens knew better than to complain. When the lease brokers showed up this time, offering mineral owners a thousand and then fifteen hundred and then twenty-five hundred and eventually four thousand dollars an acre in bonus money, the wheat and cotton farmers must have felt divinely redeemed. Rising equipment and fuel and fertilizer costs had got them wondering why they even bothered anymore. But when deep-gas prices made things start happening so fast, if you still owned your land and your mineral rights you looked like a wizard by virtue of having survived. Uncultivated surface in this part of the Anadarko Basin had a wavy, erratic relief that gave it the look of a vast strip mine that had been poorly reclaimed. The topsoil was red, unpromising, full of more clay than nutrients. To a farmer who had broken even four years in a row, a lease bonus of two hundred thousand dollars for eighty acres probably seemed less a windfall than simple justice.

The bonuses and the Monopoly-money royalty checks that sometimes followed failed to uproot reality in Elk City. It was against the law to put on airs. The architecture was Prairie Clapboard, painted white. If you lived in town but happened to own, say, a hundred and twenty acres of minerals outside of town and someone came along and leased it and drilled a producer and now your royalty check every month equaled your annual salary, the social code said that you were allowed to plant fresh sod where the weed patch used to grow, add brick borders to the flower beds, repaint the white clapboards and maybe add a dark trim, trade up to a nicer Chrysler, and stick the balance in a CD down at the bank.

One day, after the boom had died, I went to Elk City to see the friend of a friend. Driving into town, I passed the Robert A. Hefner III Municipal Airport. I was on my way to see a man who felt more than a little grateful for the existence of Bob Hefner. His name was Huff Kelly and he ran a one-horse oil-and-gas operation out of a ground-floor office in the rear of one of Elk City's three commercial banks. Huff Kelly used to be part of a group that had controlled the bank. When the group sold it, as the boom peaked, the deposits totaled sixty million dollars. Two years later deposits were down by six million dollars but the bank remained profitable. Kelly had kept his seat on the board of directors. He was a short, neat, gray-haired man with a high forehead, chipmunk cheeks, and an imperturbable manner. He wore a white shirt and a beige necktie. His eyeglasses had square lenses and silver wire frames. He played with an unlit cigar.

Entering Kelly's office, I passed the desk of a middle-aged copper-haired woman whom I took to be a receptionist. The office was done up in the modest western contemporary style. There was dark wood paneling, comfortable teak and oak furniture, a couple of floor-to-ceiling windows that offered a view of Third Street, Elk City's main east-west thoroughfare. A large map covered most of one wall. It showed all the oil-and-gas activity within the eleven Oklahoma counties that are part of the Anadarko Basin. Any square-mile section in which drilling had begun or was about to begin was shaded with green pencil. Orange shading denoted a producing well, blue a dry hole. There was plenty of blue, but orange and green predominated, and the orange was spread all around the map. Next to the map was a bulletin board. A picture postcard of Susan Powell, who was Miss America of 1981 and who came from Elk City, was pinned to the board. Some plaques for distinguished citizenship decorated the wall behind Kelly's desk. The "out" box on his desk contained a check for $1.67 and a plastic flyswatter.

Huff Kelly and I chatted for almost an hour, during which the copper-haired woman casually wandered in and out—to look up this or that lease on the big map, to help Huff recall the name of someone's bankrupt well-servicing firm, to contribute her thoughts about the true value of the dollar. It took Huff a while to get around to formally introducing us, and by then I had gathered that she was not a receptionist. She was the bank's senior vice-president and cashier. Also, she was an important customer. She wore a rose-colored blouse and blue slacks and no jewelry. With a few baubles, she could have easily blended into the mah-jongg crowd that my mother used to run with. Huff said that his daddy and her daddy had migrated to western Oklahoma from West Virginia and had begun to accumulate minerals in 1929. Her name was Martha Ann Kelly and she was Huff's first cousin.

At one point, Huff mentioned Martha Ann's ten-acre one-eighth royalty interest in a well near the Texas border. She stepped over to the map and pointed it out for me. Ever since the Oklahoma Corporation Commission had issued new rules that had the effect of reducing gas purchases by the pipelines. Martha Ann's income from that particular well had fallen by 90 percent. It now brought her only three hundred dollars a month. When Martha Ann was out of earshot, Huff mentioned that her oil-and-gas production earnings the previous year had been four hundred fifty thousand dollars. This led to a general discussion of some of the God-given benefits of inhabiting the earth above the Anadarko Basin. Martha Ann rejoined the conversation. She asked me how many millionaires I thought there were in Elk City. I said I had no idea. Martha Ann said that she wasn't sure either but if you lined up the townspeople, the ones dressed in the most worn and faded overalls would turn out to be the wealthiest. We got around to the local florist and mineral owner who had decided to use his new riches to build Elk City's first health club and spa.

"We're both charter members," Huff said. "But that place doesn't stay open enough hours to make money yet. They've been closing it on weekends."

"That hasn't affected me," Martha Ann said. "My back's been acting up lately."

"They need to add a swimming pool," Huff said.

"I don't miss the crowds that were in this town two years ago," Martha Ann said. "There was no place to put them. We had people living out by the lake, living in the park, living in their cars. The traffic was so bad it got to where I wouldn't try to drive my car across all four lanes of Third Street. If I needed to get to the other side, I'd make a right and then down a block and then a left and another left, go two blocks out of my way. Now you can cross Third Street again. We had girls thumbing rides out at the edge of town. Then we had girls in shorts and high heels thumbing rides. There were hippies walking up and down Third Street. We had what sure looked like the Hell's Angels here, too. We don't have any of that stuff anymore. Some of these stores were so crowded I'd walk right in and see all those people and walk right out."

The phone rang. It was a friend of Huff's asking whether he knew what was going on in Section 23 of Township 11, Range 23, in Beckham County. Martha Ann walked over to the map and found the answer, and then she went back to her desk. When Huff finished with the call, we talked for a few more minutes, during which he used the flyswatter to defend his work station against some invaders. When the phone rang again, I decided that it was time to say good-bye. On my way past Martha Ann's desk, I saw that she was studying the Elk City phone directory, a slender tome. "I'm looking for millionaires," she said. "I don't know about the people that have the supply companies. I'm just counting the mineral owners, the ones I know about who we've banked. I'm only through the A's and the B's. I've counted forty-seven."

Between the long-term potential and the short-term economics of the Anadarko Basin—between the field and the furnace—distortions persisted. In 1981, when pipelines bid up the price of gas to nine dollars per thousand cubic feet, wells got drilled for economic rather than geologic reasons, shallow pay zones got passed up in favor of deeper but more-expensive-to-reach reserves, a well like the Tomcat would come along and encourage everyone to abandon common sense—it was all a perfect setup for the chaos in the natural gas marketplace that came on the heels of the Penn Square Bank failure. A securities analysis published by one major brokerage firm early in 1982 noted that "the deep Anadarko Basin remains the most exciting exploration play in the country" and that "gas contracts are economically protected in a multitude of ways and competition for gas supplies remains strong." By autumn, gas purchasers—mainly the pipeline companies—were abrogating contracts left and right and with impunity. The year began with 450 rigs working in the Anadarko Basin, spread over Texas and Oklahoma, and by Christmas the rig count was down to half that. In November, the Kerr-McGee Corporation abruptly halted drilling—just yanked the bits and pulled the rigs—on eleven deep exploratory wells.

The similes changed. No longer was deep drilling like elephant-hunting. Now it was "like picking apples with a helicopter," "like dangling a string of spaghetti from the top of a ten-story building to try to thread a darning needle at ground level." The gas, of course, was still down there, but the haste of the boom had overtaken the technical expertise of many of the players. Then, Okie independents who had successfully completed deep wells got caught between the bankers and the pipelines. By the spring of 1983, "take-or-pay" eight-dollar deep gas was selling for three dollars fifty cents a thousand cubic feet. A take-or-pay clause said that a pipeline had to pay a certain price for a certain amount of product, whether or not the pipeline took delivery. The flip side of take-or-pay was "market-out." A market-out clause enabled a pipeline company to reduce gas purchases or lower prices if the market—the supply and demand—suddenly made a contract uneconomical. Life was unfair. Pipelines discovered that they could market-out even when a contract contained no such provision. The producers were forced to sell gas at a loss. They would not have drilled if they had known that the gas would bring three-fifty rather than seven-fifty or nine-fifty, but even the uneconomical lower price beat no cash flow at all. A gas producer's prudent banker might have evaluated natural gas reserves by projecting a price rise to the equivalent of sixty-dollar-a-barrel oil. Even with no price rise, loan losses should have been avoidable. Even with a drop in price, the losses should not have been severe enough to cause panic. What no bankers foresaw, however, was that the pipelines would simply stop taking and paying for the gas that they had agreed to buy.

Heaped atop the shambles of the marketplace were questions about what Congress would do next. Decontrol all gas prices? Recontrol deep gas? Natural gas was being imported from Canada and liquefied natural gas was coming in from Algeria, both protected by take-or-pay contracts. But who was brave enough to abrogate a take-or-pay agreement with a foreign government? The price that consumers paid for natural gas remained high. Domestic producers, meanwhile, had financed their exploration with collateral that suddenly had no market. That another gas shortage was bound to come along in five or six years offered no consolation. Too much gas at too high a price—a contravention of the law of supply and demand. You could hear the heavy clanging of doors as the experts who had predicted exactly the opposite of what was happening clambered back into their think tanks. From backstage came a falsetto whine, a chorus of fair-weather free-marketeers fretting over the prospect that oil, then selling for twenty-nine dollars a barrel, might fall to twenty dollars a barrel; that the price-fixing conspiracy—OPEC—that had once committed the nation to "the moral equivalent of war" might disintegrate; and that industrialized economies East and West might disintegrate along with it.

CHAPTER 19

"**J.** D. Allen is generally not paying his debts as such debts become due" was one of the observations contained in an involuntary bankruptcy petition filed in Oklahoma City in early February 1983. Three banks—Crocker National, of San Francisco, Continental Illinois, and Seafirst—collaborated on this petition and they noted that the debtor was on the line to them and others for an amount "in excess of $300 million." Not long after this filing, Jerry Dale Allen responded with a petition of his own, seeking to amend his bankruptcy from involuntary to voluntary, identifying the exact amount owed as three hundred seventeen million dollars, and requesting six months to negotiate with his creditors. The day after this news became public, Allen told an acquaintance, by way of explaining the fix he was in, "The problem is these people in the oil business today are out of touch with reality."

During a creditors' meeting that resulted from Allen's own get-together with reality, one of his attorneys made a brief but stirring speech. All of Penn Square's major upstream correspondent banks sent representatives to the meeting. They did not have one another's best interests at heart. "Everyone here wants to blame someone else, and no one seems to understand what happened," said Allen's attorney. "You bankers say, 'None of this is our fault. Just give us our money back.' But what you're forgetting is that you told J. D. Allen that his signature was worth millions. And then he walked into the bank and signed his name more than three hundred times. He signed lots of blank notes. And you encouraged that. Who's to blame?"

Had J. D. Allen assumed that the money he borrowed was free?

Or had he simply failed to keep track of the grand total? Contained within those questions were implications that defied easy unraveling. Stretching, I could contemplate the marvelousness of the J. D. Allen saga—how, say, one day you're sleeping in your car and then, just a little piece down the road, you're three hundred seventeen million in debt. I could understand how you might meet Carl Swan, a successful entrepreneur who is loved and admired, and how you might get Swan to cosign a personal note, and how in the process you could meet some big-time bankers, turn a couple of high-dollar deals, and pretty soon find yourself borrowing big-time money on your own signature. Once that happens, it is not unreasonable to go from being a Democrat to being a holier-than-the-Pope Republican. Then, if history makes a few weird turns, Ronald Reagan can get elected President of the United States and you can find yourself on airplanes to Africa and on banquet daises with the likes of Gerald Ford and Wayne Newton. I know how a snowball works and how a young stud from Ringling, Oklahoma, can get appointed by the Secretary of Energy to the National Petroleum Council. Momentum I can fathom. One element of the J. D. Allen equation I still do not grasp, however, and that is: How can a fellow's liabilities all get mistaken for assets?

None of J. D.'s tribulations did Carl Swan any good. Swan's chronic cosigning finally caught up with him. A financial statement prepared late in 1981 said that his net worth was eighty million dollars. During the next few months, it began to look not that solid. He told friends that he had been raised on a truck driver's salary and he could live on one again if he had to. Upon the closing of the Penn Square Bank, Swan, as a director, acquired some serious contingent liabilities. Even before that event, his horizon had begun to cloud over. The Longhorn Oil & Gas Company—which meant Carl Swan and J. D. Allen and the company's securities brokers and lawyers and accountants, and Bill Jennings and Bill Patterson and other Penn Square officers and directors, about fifty defendants in all—began collecting lawsuits from Longhorn investors around the country, about eighty plaintiffs in all. "This deal is too safe for me," Bill Jennings was said to have once told some prospective investors. Then, to his and everyone else's unpleasant surprise, Longhorn's various drilling programs failed to discover sufficient oil and gas. That oversight led the banks that had lent Longhorn money to try to collect against the limited partners' letters of credit. To avoid having this happen, the investors decided to sue, alleging securities fraud. Several Longhorn drilling programs headed for bankruptcy court.

Allen's insolvency was tough to penetrate. To one degree or another, J. D. Allen, a.k.a. Jerry Dale Allen, was also J. D. Allen Industries and J. D. Allen & Company and the Allen Energy Corporation and Continental Drilling and Continental Resources and Texoma Resources and Diversified Oilfield Services and Texas Upsetting & Finishing and High Plains Drilling and Cimarron Drilling and Denton Brothers Drilling and a dozen or so Longhorn Oil & Gas drilling programs and another dozen or so real or paper entities. I took myself to the courthouse and perused the bankruptcy file. I saw that Allen wanted to be protected not only from Chase Manhattan and Continental Illinois and Seafirst and Northern Trust and Michigan National, he also wanted the electric company and the dry cleaner and the tobacconist to back off. I saw that he was paying forty dollars a month for medical treatment at the Center for the Whole Being. I saw that he had requested eight thousand dollars a month for personal living expenses and I saw a petition filed by one of his creditors that said, "If the debtor wants income on which to live, he should get a job and earn it." I saw that the proverbial bottom line amounted to a hilarious number, but I still awaited a deeper revelation of how it had happened. So I paid several visits to Allen himself.

J. D. Allen conducted most of his business in the Oil Center, a pair of twelve-story boxes on a service road next to an expressway, less than a mile from the Penn Square shopping mall. His suite was on the eleventh floor, next door to Carl Swan's and eleven floors above the still-surviving Junior's, the restaurant where in happier times Okiesmo's finest had wined and dined and occasionally flung dinner rolls and anchovies.

The first time I went to see Allen, not long after the filing of his bankruptcy petition, he wore a neatly tailored gray pinstripe suit and a custom-fitted white shirt and an all-silk club tie. He smoked a long thin cigar and drank iced tea and told me that he would be ready for some *hombre-a-hombre* just as soon as he got all his problems straightened out. That meant settling the three hundred seventeen million in liabilities and resolving the Longhorn litigation. All this, he said, would take about sixty days. He laughed at odd moments, a high-pitched heh-heh. The next time I went to see him, he spoke of some deals he was promoting in Africa, where he was trying to find work for Continental Drilling's rigs. When I asked how he went about such a task, he explained, "I know the leaders of several African countries." He mentioned some African countries, but he did not mention any leaders by name. One day Allen promised that he would eventually recite his thoughts and feelings about the behavior of Penn Square's upstream banks. Although we never did get around to that, I inferred his thoughts and feelings when I later read in the newspaper that he was suing Continental Illinois for one billion two hundred million dollars, accusing the bank's top executives of conspiring to seize and destroy J. D. Allen Industries.

As a rule, before I was allowed to see the man himself I was required to sit a while in the waiting room, which I did not mind a bit because it gave me a chance to read *Drilling: The Wellsite Magazine*—catch up on the latest in downhole technology—and to admire the abilities of the receptionist, a young woman with blond hair who knew how to operate a telephone that had a forty-eight-button console. ("Now what was your name again? And who was it you was wantin' to talk to? And who'd you say you was with?") One time, waiting for Allen to become available, I chatted with an assistant who told me that as soon as Iraq and Iran got serious about bombing refineries, the oil business would bounce back. The next time I dropped in, this member of the brain trust had moved on. At J. D. Allen Industries, bankruptcy meant retrenchment, and retrenchment meant fearless prioritizing.

The lettering on the glass entrance to Allen's suite said "J. D. ALLEN INDUSTRIES" in characters about five inches high. In the reception area there were brass overhead light fixtures, beige carpeting, a sofa with that nubbly oatmeal-toned upholstery, a small Persian throw rug, three silk bird drawings and a Chinese war scene on silk. Against another wall stood an Oriental red lacquer cabinet from the Early Pier One Dynasty. Inside were some brass goblets and brass trays. The furnishings in Allen's inner office were elegant. Among the contents of one glass display case were a porcelain vase, a glass egg, a couple of porcelain tigers, a bronze casting of a longhorn skull, and a wooden box the cover of which was shaped like Ronald Reagan's cowboy hat. The room also contained a big walnut desk, an ornately carved mahogany sideboard from China, some hunting scenes, a yucca, a rubber plant, and some ferns. A gilt-framed English horse painting gave the place a little Paul Mellon touch. All around the room, almost always autographed, were photographs of Allen in the company of various Republican luminaries: George Bush ("With warm best wishes"), Howard Baker, Gerald Ford (twice, including "To my good friend J. D. Allen with best regards"), Bill Brock, John Connally (with wife), Alexander Haig. Ronald Reagan stared at a visitor from several directions. There were three shots of Allen and the President—two at poolside, one at the White House—and a pencil portrait of Reagan on one wall. Marie Osmond smiled while she posed with Allen. And perched on the shelf of a breakfront was a black-and-white glossy head shot of the actor Hugh O'Brian, inscribed: "J. D. you are a super guy. See you wherever the waters run deep. Hugh."

My final conversation with Allen took place not long before Christmas of 1983. By then, his bankruptcy petition had grown some mold and no workable plan for repaying the three hundred seventeen million had been devised. For a change, the receptionist sent me right in to see him. Allen said he had just returned from England, where he had gone to talk to some major-money people about getting his rigs working in the Sudan. We chatted about the weather (awful windy) and briefly vivisected the national banking system (awful bad). Before ten minutes had gone by, he apologized for not being more fun to talk to. He was still tired from his trip. Plus, he had really tied one on the night before. A secretary entered the room and handed him a packet of Christmas cards to sign. He said that a lot of people were counting on receiving cards from him, it just meant a lot to them, so he was doing it. He signed while we talked. J. D. Allen's autograph was oversized and earnestly legible, and with a flourish at the end he drew an oval around the entire signature.

When I asked how he felt about his fiscal dilemma, he became philosophical.

"It's like football," he said. "You might hand the ball off and not score a touchdown and end up saying, 'I regret that, not trying the quarterback sneak.' If you think you're never gonna play another game, never get to run that play again, you might be sorry. But I'm not done playing this game."

I recalled that right after the 1980 presidential election loyalists within the J. D. Allen organization had drumrolled a campaign to get him an ambassadorship. "A post he would feel comfortable with," went the company line. "Maybe Luxembourg or Ireland or Ivory Coast, one of those places." Looking back, did Allen feel that things might have turned out more happily if he had pursued public service full time?

"I'm too blunt to be a politician," he said. "You're in a fishbowl. If I wanna go out and get drunk, I'm gonna go out and get drunk. If I wanna raise some hell, I'm gonna do that. If you're a politician you can't do that. You can get away with that stuff if you're an ambassador to a little country because it's not an elected position. I didn't much care where I was ambassador, except that I didn't want some place like France or Britain, where you're in a fishbowl and you're never gonna accomplish anything because each of those places is like a bureaucracy in itself."

When I reminded Allen that he was a man of action, he perked up.

"I'm an entrepreneur, a deal maker," he said. "If I don't like someone I tell 'em to kiss off and I walk out. I know how to say, 'Hey, this is my idea and it's a helluva deal and it's gonna make you a helluva lot of money and if you don't like it, then so long.' All along I've expected to be successful. People were always saying to me, 'Goddamn, J. D. You've got all these oil companies.' And I'd say, 'I always expected to have 'em.' Being successful and making money just comes natural to me. I'm an idea person and a deal person. That's what I do best. I come up with an idea and make it happen. That's what I'm good at. I've never really considered school degrees to be useful. I like practical experience. I think that's where you learn, by doing it. I've never been a textbook person."

We were interrupted by another visit from the secretary and then by a phone call and then Allen picked up where he left off, saying, "I doubt that anybody has created the number of companies that I did in my time. I wanted to help people that were trying to get started. When I first started out I made my knuckles black and blue knocking on doors. I wore out shoes. I didn't want to tell people with an idea, 'You're too young, come back when you're old,' or 'Come back after you've done it.' I never liked it when people told me that."

I studied Allen—his thin dark mustache, his round dimpled face, his round and indistinct physique. That day he wore a plaid western shirt, ostrich boots, blue jeans, and a belt with a silver buckle studded with turquoise pieces the size of shooting marbles. He was thirty-six years old. Like his great friend Wayne Newton, he looked no age at all.

Another ten minutes passed, and it felt like time to go. The last Christmas card had been signed. On Allen's desk sat a copy of a Christmas memento that he had sent to friends a couple of years earlier. It was poetry-as-a-paperweight, an engraving frozen in Lucite, titled "The Wildcat," signed by J. D. Allen ("Have a prosperous year"):

> *Running high and looking good*
> *Just like wildcats do and should.*
> *Fifty feet and sometimes higher*
> *It fills the owner's soul with fire.*
>
> *Although there's stretch in every line,*
> *It's running high and looking fine.*
> *The driller often slips a string*
> *But that is just a trifling thing.*
>
> *They cut a sand line, make a splice,*
> *But only do it once or twice.*
> *They use a steel line in a pinch—*
> *The driller's never off an inch.*
>
> *Geologists now come take the dope*
> *And with a shining microscope*
> *They study sand and shale and lime.*
> *To think this out takes lots of time.*
>
> *With their colossal brains they ponder.*
> *Mouth-opened farmers stand and wonder.*
> *Lease brokers stand in line and wait.*
> *He speaks, "She's running high, looking great."*
>
> *A thrill that shakes the very ground—*
> *They're gone before you look around.*
> *Royalties and leases sell,*
> *She's running high and looking swell.*

Three months have passed—another scene.
The rig is gone, the grass is green.
The gaping slush pit, cracked and dried.
An optimist, here, fought and died.

So thus it is with wildcat wells,
They're spudded in with clanging bells.
When plugged and shouts of joy have died,
You wonder who in hell has lied.

Knowing that the poem was older than J. D., I asked him who had written it.

"I did," he said, arching his brown eyebrows, letting out a heh-heh. "Babysitting a well one night in my car, it just came to me."

When we shook hands, I wished him happy holidays and told him I hoped another boom would come his way soon.

"I didn't get into this business during the boom," he said. "I started out when oil was three dollars a barrel. I wasn't in on any short-term deals. I wasn't after a quick buck. If I had been I would've gone public and sold out. But when you get to be a public company you're trying to make dividend payments rather than trying to make the company grow. I'm a growth person. If I'd sold out I coulda made a fortune, but I don't regret not having done it. I can still do it. It's no big deal. The oil business went down. The gas business went to hell. I'm probably the only person in this whole deal that's young enough to make use of this disaster. Hell, I haven't hit the prime of my life. I loved wheelin' and dealin'. And women. Oh, I love women. I have no regrets. I'll build another empire. It won't take me long. It didn't take that long to do the last one."

CHAPTER 20

The beauty of the Tomcat gas well was as mixed as its blessings. Blowing out, rocketing methane from sixteen hundred feet of open hole, it possessed the fierce, sublime, deafening wild beauty of nature out of control. And it possessed an earthy Okie beauty, raw and luxuriant. The vapor that disappeared into the Oklahoma sky in the winter of 1981 was money, maybe the first installment of a billion dollars. At night, ignited, its astounding flares were worthy of any self-respecting war zone. The possibility that the Tomcat could be controlled gave it a mythical aura. The aura enveloped in instant legend Cliff Culpepper, the president of Ports of Call Oil Company, which operated the Tomcat. It enveloped Clark Ellison and Buddy Appleby, the prospectors who had traded with Culpepper a huge slice of their leasehold in the Fort Cobb Anticline, the geologic structure that the Tomcat tapped. The aura attracted to the ninety thousand acres of the Fort Cobb real dollars, funny dollars, and real funny shitkickers who would offer to sell you a deed to one square foot of Anadarko Basin minerals. Beyond the mythical aura lay the reality that the Tomcat could not be controlled, and that made the well a wonderful metaphor.

Starting out, the Tomcat was more than just another pretty gas well, and then odd fate and circumstance made it voluptuous. "People were looking for a Cinderella," Jim Niles, one of Cliff Culpepper's associates in Ports of Call, has reflected. "Ports of Call was a brand-new oil company and Cliff Culpepper was a western Oklahoma success story. Then you had Buddy Appleby and Clark Ellison, who'd been out there prospecting all those years, although mainly Buddy and, before Clark, his daddy. The Fort Cobb was a part of the Anadarko that hadn't been real hot because everybody was paying attention to the Fletcher field, farther south. The Tomcat was a well that had been looking extremely good if the gas sold for five dollars, and the next thing we knew we were talking to the pipelines about ten dollars. Those reporters who wrote stories about it heard that it was blowing a hundred twenty million cubic feet a day and they figured out that it could pay for itself in a week. They didn't want to hear that it wasn't all hooked up, or that even the gas that was hooked up had to be diverted and burned for hours at a time while you cleaned out the vents. Those details were too complicated. The utilities fed the whole deep-gas mass hysteria because if they could get gas dedicated to them, they could expand faster, they could justify building more pipelines. I had calls from pipeline companies that I'd never heard of, wanting to buy Tomcat gas. You'd have thought it was magical gas."

Initially, Buddy Appleby and Clark Ellison and Cliff Culpepper agreed that, for Culpepper to earn a share of the acreage that surrounded the Tomcat, the Ports of Call Oil Company had to drill a producing well in the Hunton formation, about four miles deep. After making this deal, Culpepper leased from others more acreage, until he controlled two thirds of the 640-acre unit in which the Tomcat was situated. Ports of Call still owned more than a third of the well when the big blowout occurred. At that point Ports of Call could have farmed out every acre and banked a few million, but Culpepper preferred the idea of obscene profits. Some optimists had promised that there were two billion cubic feet of gas per foot in the pay zones of the Fletcher field, southwest of the Fort Cobb. Why not in the Fort Cobb too? All you had to do was drill and complete the well.

Cliff Culpepper grew up shoeless poor, no-daddy-around-the-house poor, in the 1930s. Later, he had a life that he could enjoy. In Santa Barbara, he came across a thirty-two-thousand-square-foot cliff dwelling that had been an important location in the film version of the Harold Robbins masterpiece *The Betsy*. He bought it furnished, for three and a half million, just as the rig count peaked. It sat on four acres above the Pacific. I like to imagine Culpepper, the sovereign of that promontory, staring at the western ocean and thinking of the ways in which this beat Dust Bowl southern Oklahoma. When things rolled right, he had an ability to transmit enthusiasm. In Santa Barbara, he would listen to people complain about the offshore oil rigs. From the shore, you could hear them. "That's music to my ears," Culpepper would say. "You don't drill for oil, you can't drive your car. You don't drill for oil, there's lots of things you can't do."

The biggest Tomcat blowout, the one that lasted fourteen days, began January 27, 1981, seven months after it was spudded. The well was supposed to have reached the Hunton by Christmas of 1980, and it was a mile short of its destination, in the Morrow-Springer sands, when it unloaded. It had blown out four months earlier, and it would blow out twice more—four times in all. Ellison and Appleby amended their deal with Ports of Call. All that Culpepper had to do was complete a Morrow-Springer well. He never got there. The Tomcat went through two operators, two drilling contractors, three well bores, three whipstock attempts, thirty-two million dollars. It went on for three years and created seventy thousand feet of hole in Caddo County, Oklahoma. When it was finally completed, in May of 1983, Ports of Call had been in bankruptcy for six months. In distress, the company's interest had been traded down to 3 percent. Bankruptcy was also the destiny of Robinson Brothers, the drilling company that succeeded Ports of Call as operator of the Tomcat. Robinson Brothers went from nine hundred employees to nine. (Continental Illinois had put up most of the money that Penn Square had funneled to Robinson Brothers—sixty million dollars.) The Tomcat flowed ten million feet of gas a day. That could bring three dollars a thousand cubic feet—not quite the ten-dollar gas and the hundred twenty million feet a day of the wonderful blowout. The well stood a vague chance of breaking even in seven or eight years, rather than in a week or ten days. The trajectory of the Tomcat delineated the inevitable path of the deep-gas delirium. The Tomcat turned out to be a tar baby. It mocked, it hectored, it moralized. Greed is a mortal sin, it seemed to say. Greed is innate. Look what happens when you behave greedily in the presence of an awesomely valuable thing.

The FDIC held a claim of only one and a half million dollars in Ports of Call's bankruptcy. The total debt came to thirty-eight million. The company's assets actually exceeded its liabilities, but the assets were not very liquid. Ports of Call had spent twenty-four million dollars on the Tomcat. Culpepper owed himself a lot of money. He owned separate companies that had sold the Tomcat its pipe and air charter service. His son, Mike, had sold it dozer work and diesel oil. One of Ports of Call's main trade creditors was the Glomar Drilling Company. When Glomar filed for bankruptcy, it owed the FDIC twelve million dollars, a debt that had been personally guaranteed by Culpepper. (Howard Hughes had used "Glomar," and Cliff liked the sound of it.) Another Culpepper venture, Hobo Drilling, was sued by Seafirst after falling behind on its loan payments. Six months after Culpepper bought the house in Santa Barbara, he deeded it back to the original owner, relinquishing his million-dollar down payment.

One morning a while after the Tomcat was completed, my telephone rang and it was Cliff Culpepper calling, suggesting that I meet him at his office in half an hour. I said "Great," and then I made myself presentable and hustled over there—to a seven-story building on a dismal commercial strip across the avenue from the largest western-wear store in Oklahoma City. Although Culpepper still held the title of president of the Ports of Call Oil Company, in bankruptcy his responsibilities were more or less limited to monitoring the fellow who monitored the field operations. I arrived at his office on time, but he had disappeared. An oil well about fifteen miles west of town was having some salt water disposal problems, and Culpepper had dispatched himself in that direction. Salt water disposal had been one of his specialties ever since his truck-driving, brine-hauling days back in the forties.

After I had waited in a reception area about forty-five minutes—long enough to do a close textual analysis of an entire issue of *Sunbelt Executive: The Guide to Business Pleasure and Wellness Decisions*—Culpepper showed up. He wore a blue cotton sports shirt and blue beltless trousers. He did not look as if he had been occupied with pleasure and wellness decisions. He looked tired and weather-worn. His lined face sagged and the forelock of his gray hair lay down around his eyebrows. Although he was only fifty-eight years old he could have passed for an experienced pensioner. I gathered that he was trying to rebound from an illness. There had been reports a few months earlier that he had

had a stroke, although Culpepper himself was not convinced. One night, his wife, Mickey, summoned an ambulance. Cliff told the attendants, "Nothing wrong with me. Just a little bad vodka. Never mind. Sit down, boys. Mix yourself a drink." It might not have been a stroke that made Cliff look so spectral. It might have just been God's wear and tear. Or he might have been under the influence of the vile parts of insolvency.

Culpepper's office was not spacious—maybe eight by ten, a significant scaling down from the days when he had done his decision-making in a thousand-square-foot chamber that had the feel of an auditorium. The old place had been equipped with everything but a conference table; the reason there was not one of those was that Culpepper did not much believe in conferring. The furnishings of the post-bankruptcy Ports of Call ran toward ocher Herculon, with scatterings of laminated oak. A Sony videocassette recorder and a Hitachi television set rested on a table in Culpepper's cubbyhole. He loaded the recorder with a cassette and turned on the TV. I leaned against his desk and watched about twenty minutes of unedited footage. The video showed the Tomcat No. 1 blowing out and the audio sounded like a fleet of garbage truck compacters singing *The Messiah*. Along the way, Culpepper offered a laconic narration: "They skidded the rig off it . . . Thar . . . Hear it ten mile away, see it twenty mile away . . . Couldn't shut it in without busting the pipe . . . Spent maybe four hours away from there in two weeks . . . Five seven-inch joints of pipe . . . Solid arn . . . All lit up . . . Red Adair . . . Christmas tree . . . Moving the derrick off . . . Skiddin' the rig again . . . We knew the gas was down there, see . . . Lotta people thought this was the biggest well in the United States . . . Three lines was blowin'. . . ." A couple of times the well caught fire. Flying shale would strike metal and generate a spark. Then flying mud would put out the fire. The camera work was static—testimony to the spellbinding effect of the blowout. The site had been bulldozed and then rained on by debris that made the whole thing resemble moonscape. Now and then the camera would pick up a tableau that looked terrestrial—a group of men huddled in the distance, or half of a yellow Camaro.

"I haven't seen this in a long time," Culpepper said toward the end. "Since we went into Chapter Eleven, it's been kind of a sore spot."

Affixed to the wall behind the television set were a pair of oil-and-gas maps. One showed Caddo County, where the Tomcat and its offsetting wells were drilled, and the other showed Canadian County, where Culpepper had enjoyed much success before Ellison and Appleby crossed his path. Several times, Culpepper repeated, as if he were still trying to digest the experience, "This was one of the largest wells ever was in the United States." On the opposite wall, tacked to a bulletin board, was a poster with block lettering at the top that said: "HOW TO DELAY PAYMENT FOR TWELVE MONTHS." ("Lose invoice and ask for copies, three times. . . . Claim that goods went to wrong address. . . . Computer not working. . . . Accountant has broken right arm. . . . Accountant is sick. . . . Accountant is dead. . . .")

When the tape ran out Culpepper temporarily ran out of things to say, but with a bit of prodding he began to utter thoughts on foreign affairs and how that stuff connected to problems that people in the oil-and-gas business were facing. An associate of his once told me that Culpepper was not opposed to the idea of bombing the Panama Canal, if that's what it would take to interrupt supply routes. "Yeah, bomb it," Culpepper had said. "It'll take them Mexicans a year to fix it." In 1980, Culpepper had read the Oklahoma City newspapers and had gained the impression that some of the local people—J. D. Allen and that crowd—had a direct line to the White House. He had donated many of his well-deserved dollars to the Republicans that year, but then Ronald Reagan had let him down. Saudi Arabia was another sore spot. Trying to deal with the federal government on this foreign-oil-import thing was a big frustration, because "when the Saudis drill a well they've got three thousand feet of producing sand and we've got ten to twenty feet," he said. "It costs the same to drill a well here as there. How are we gonna beat that? We cain't. There's no way we can produce oil and gas and compete with the reserves Saudi Arabia has. And you know the government's going to buy oil from Mexico or Algeria or Canada or whoever to reduce the world monetary bank debt. We need some tariffs on that foreign oil and gas. I didn't like Carter 'cause he was too dumb. I thought when

Reegun won, I felt like we had a President. If I was elected President somebody'd assassinate me because I wouldn't pay for a dollar of Arab oil. We cain't compete with their reserves. It just don't make sense, buying oil from Saudi Arabia. Hell, all your Palestinians are over there. You know, six out of ten doctors in Kuwait are Palestinian. It just don't make sense us helping them, or helping the Japanese. I want the Japanese to sit in their Toyotas and watch their Sony TVs. 'Cause we aren't gonna buy 'em. The Japanese, all they eat is a bowl of rice a day and we cain't compete with them. I don't think every American should eat a bowl of rice a day. I don't like rice. Try to tell that to Reegun, though. It's like fighting a dead horse in the mouth."

I asked Culpepper why he thought the party had ended.

He said that good help was hard to find. Too many drilling crews on deep rigs weren't properly trained, and on top of that they were lazy. "If a fellow could wear a hat and stand up that was good enough," he said. "Two years ago there was no honor out there in the field. Those roughnecks, when it come time to put on a new drill bit, if they seen a rig across the way they quit here and signed on over there to work. They don't want to work. It might take twenty hours to change a bit. They don't want to lift and move that pipe." Some crews stuck scarecrows on the rig floor so that when the company man drove by he'd look up there and think they were working—Culpepper said he'd seen that. I asked him where he'd seen that and he said, well, he'd heard about it, so it must have happened. Furthermore, goddamnit, these fly-by-nights thought a well blowing out was a picnic or something. "Roughnecks like to see 'em blow out so they can stand over there and watch 'em. Then they don't have to do any work. Why do people go to a horse race or a rodeo? They like to see a spectacle.

"I know we were running a hundred miles an hour but I didn't know in Texas and Algiers and Mexico and them other places they were all doin' the same thing. Hell, cocktail waitresses stopped hustling drinks and started hustling pumps, equipment, draw works. You've got the Feds with all kinds of rules and regulations you got to abide. I knew if this ever got to be a good business the politicians would stick their noses in it. They must've smelled the money and figured there was some way they could mess this up. They did a pretty good job so far. When the Penn Square Bank went down one thing led to another and just certain things happened and we couldn't weather the storm.

"Around here we had to go on a computer, and if you want to find out what's going on you hafta talk to one of those programmers and they only talk programmer language. You never know where you stand with those guys. Someday I'm going back to the old system. That's one paper sack there for bills paid. One paper sack over there for bills owed." He pointed to opposite corners of his desk and then, with his fingertips, lightly patted the edge of the desk, six inches from his belly. "Any money left over goes in the sack right here."

We would have talked longer, but another visitor showed up, a salesman for a large drill pipe supplier. He wanted to show Culpepper a photograph of his three-month-old grandson and he also wanted to discuss a couple million dollars that Ports of Call owed his company. Before I left, I noticed that Culpepper's desktop calendar was open to 1992. Perhaps, deep inside, he was more of an optimist than he was letting on. The last thing he said was "If I can get all my problems over with, Ports of Call problems, I'm gonna drill some wells."

"Mister Clark and Mister Bud, everything's gonna be just as clean and simple as can be," Culpepper had promised Clark Ellison and Buddy Appleby in early 1980, before the Tomcat No. 1 was spudded. Hundreds of interest owners and contractors were parties to the Tomcat experience, and the postmortem dwelt heavily on the question of blame. When I went to see Ellison and Appleby one day not long after my visit with Culpepper, however, I found that they bore ill will toward no one. Their operating principle had forever been "Never drill with your own money," and it had at last paid off. After originally leasing 337 acres in Section 14, Township 10 North, Range 13 West, of Caddo County, they were down to a twenty-eight-acre carried interest in the completed well. Along the way, they had deposited a million dollars and then some in the bank. They were both solvent. Clark Ellison had stakes in forty-seven producing wells. Buddy Appleby had interests in forty-five. They still wanted to drill thousands of feet deeper than the Tomcat had ever gone—to the Hunton formation in the Fort Cobb Anti-

cline and to the Bromide and Arbuckle in its neighbor, the North
Corn. They wanted a good look at every stratum under the crust.
And they understood that they might never get the chance. They
had a deep-gas exploration proposal—a hundred million dollars,
nicely depicted with a multi-hued bar graph—that would be a
cinch to finance just as soon as Mars invaded Saudi Arabia.

"I don't think you'll ever meet two guys who wanted to win the
game they were playing more than Clark and I wanted to,"
Appleby said.

"And we were doing something that had never been done,"
Ellison added softly.

"And the banks wouldn't let us in the door."

"My dad took care of that."

"All along, we've been in this for the money," Appleby continued. "Kenneth Ellison was, and we are. There might be people
who think we got to the office every morning at six o'clock for
altruistic reasons, but they're wrong. We did it for the money. But
we tried not to be greedy. We always felt it was good to have other
people in on our deals. You don't want all your acreage in one
section. We kept our maps clean and we spread our information
around. We'll still show our maps to anybody who wants a look. We
believe in clean maps and we believe that they should look nice.
We never fold them. We roll them up. The money we spend on the
tubes we store those maps in is worth it. We want people to be able
to read our maps. I want our maps all over town. I want people to
know what we know. I'd like to pin them up on the bulletin board
at Safeway.

"We're not angry with anyone, but we're not having much fun
right now. Neither one of us likes to work this hard. Our families
don't want to run this business. They just want our money. I've got
a boy fifteen years old. I've spent thirty-eight years in a hotel room.
I wouldn't wish that on my worst enemy, much less my son."

Clark Ellison mentioned a rumor that Cliff Culpepper wanted
to drill some Redfork wells—ten-thousand- to twelve-thousand-
foot tests—in the Anadarko Basin. "We'd still do business with
him," Appleby said. "If we could get a contract drawn up that
pleased Clark and me we'd both sign it. And Cliff'll sign anything.
I could get him to sign today's newspaper."

That meant, in other words, that Ellison and Appleby had not made a mistake when they asked Cliff Culpepper to operate the Tomcat?

"Hell, no," Buddy Appleby said. "That blowout made people pay attention to the Fort Cobb. Nine offsets got drilled, we got carried free in every one, and they're all producers, all except one. The Tomcat gave us credibility. As far as we're concerned, Cliff Culpepper made us."

CHAPTER 21

Eventually the Justice Department became committed to the proposition that, mainly, it was Bill Patterson's fault. The government even went as far as to suggest that Bill Patterson had a wormy, corrupt soul. For more than two years the United States Attorney for the Western District of Oklahoma talked to Penn Square's former employees and customers and victims, to the FDIC and the FBI and the IRS, and to grand jurors. On the first anniversary of the bank failure, the FDIC announced that its investigation had uncovered 340 possible criminal violations. Six months later this number had risen to 451. Another six months passed and a federal grand jury in Oklahoma City indicted Patterson on thirty-four counts.

Friends and associates of Patterson, heedless of what the Feds insisted, believed almost unanimously that even if he had violated a few hundred banking laws he would never have done so for personal gain. One line of defense had it that Patterson was perhaps crazy and, if so, probably dumb-crazy. "Smart-crazy is I steal three million dollars and I hide it real well," a friend of mine explained. "While I might go to jail for a couple of years, when I get out the money'll still be there. Dumb-crazy is if you have to go to jail and you've got nothing to show for it. Dumb-crazy is when you do it for the thrill, to be a big shot." Even if loans were kited, notes altered, bad credits sprinkled with monkey dust to make them shine like triple-A-rated debentures, what did that imply about motives and intentions? That Patterson was a criminal mastermind? Might it not imply that Bill Patterson was average? He had an instinct for salesmanship, of course, and evidently there were odd creases in his gray matter. But didn't his case above all illustrate the colorful consequences of a man with no remarkable talent getting in over his head to a remarkable extent? Averageness was a trait that Patterson's lawyers intended to emphasize to the jury.

Crazy, dumb- or smart-, is a matter of context. By the time Patterson was indicted, in the summer of 1984, the Penn Square Bank failure had become the costliest in United States history. The upstream banks had charged off more than half of their Penn Square loans—more than a billion dollars' worth. Of the loans that had not yet been declared losses, the majority were nonperforming. Penn Square's shareholders, of course, had lost their entire thirty-seven-million-dollar stake the day the bank closed. The FDIC, in assuming liabilities that dwarfed the bank's assets, stood to lose a hundred twenty-five million dollars in the course of the liquidation. The claims from uninsured depositors and from general creditors would approach a quarter of a billion dollars. Not to be overlooked but most difficult to quantify were the costs of the failure to a numberless constituency of innocents who never saw or set foot inside the bank, who never lent or borrowed a dime. When Penn Square evaporated as a credit source, the customers who were unable to arrange financing elsewhere not only went broke but also took with them these innocents—small, unsteady dominoes way down the line—who ended up losing their solvency or their jobs or, at the very least, their hopeful assumptions. When the FDIC (and then the Department of Justice and then Congress and then the Department of the Treasury) descended on Penn Square to inspect the wreckage and appraise the damage, the impulse to lay blame at a distant doorstep was universal. Time passed and the consequences of Penn Square resonated—louder, broader. In a just and proud society, someone should have to answer and pay for the mess. The context expanded; the mess gained amplitude. Did the contributions of a Bill Patterson or a Bill Jennings grow or diminish? What would a jury of Oklahomans think?

The federal investigation was a remarkable tease. Every few months, word would leak that indictments would be returned "next month." Then—nothing. For almost two years, nothing. A brief stir occurred in January of 1984, when Thomas Orr, a Penn Square vice-president, pleaded guilty to one count of tax evasion and one count of conspiracy to commit bank fraud. Orr was the commercial loan officer who lent money to horse breeders and who brokered horses at the same time. His weakness was the bread-and-butter kickback. Some of Orr's customers made Bill Patterson's new oilies look like the editorial board of the *Harvard Business Review*. Bill Price, the United States Attorney, told the press that the Orr pleas constituted a major development and that the government would crack the whole case open any minute. But the Orr matter was in fact an irrelevant holding action. In the spring of 1981, more than a year before the failure, Orr had left Penn Square. Whatever his sins, they had had almost nothing to do with the closing of the bank. Later, Price offered a bold explanation of what was taking so long. Penn Square, he said, was "the most complicated banking case in history." He went on, "If you polled every prosecutor in America, I think you'd find that this is the toughest case in the country right now to prosecute."

Patterson, meanwhile, remained hard to reach during business hours. I remember hearing that one day, when Patterson had been working at the Penn Square Bank just a few months, an officer in the installment lending department invited him to lunch. Afterward, as they walked through the shopping mall back to the bank, Patterson asked his colleague whether he knew anything about the lawn service business. Were any of his customers in that line of work? Yes, the installment lender said, he had a couple of customers who did that, and they seemed to make out pretty well. Patterson said, "You know, I'm kind of thinking of doing that myself on the weekends." The remark puzzled the other fellow: Why would a bank officer want to do that? But then he forgot the conversation and did not think about it again until he heard, a few weeks after Penn Square closed, that Bill Patterson, the former senior executive vice-president in charge of energy lending, had begun a new career mowing lawns. The longer it took the U. S. Attorney and his grand jury, the more I was tempted to call Patterson and invite him over to do some yard work.

The Bill Patterson trial began the second Monday in September of 1984. About a week later, by which time the government's case was half presented, I happened upon Beep Jennings during my early-morning constitutional. He was out for a walk with his

Yorkshire terrier, Chaucer. Jennings wore chinos and a Wind-breaker and a slouch hat and he could not have seemed more jaunty. I spotted them from a block away, dog and man, bopping along. In the crisp and silvery light at 7 a.m., Jennings radiated bonhomie. I was reminded that to know him and not like him meant that you were demanding unreasonable terms. You were missing the point.

Jennings had reason to feel jovial. Down at the courthouse, the U. S. Attorney was doing him an inadvertent but sizable favor. To make a case against Patterson, the government lawyers had fallen into the habit of asking witnesses whether Mr. Jennings was present on specific occasions when Mr. Patterson allegedly forged notes, distorted collateral, and misrepresented and prevaricated in the smiling faces of correspondent bankers. Invariably, the answer was that the bank chairman had been nowhere near the scene of the purported offense. "If Mr. Patterson is not guilty, then nobody is," the U. S. Attorney let slip at one point. It had become apparent that a prosecutor would have a difficult time indicting and convicting Beep Jennings.

Up close, the Jennings good cheer intensified. Seeing Beep and the loyal Chaucer out for a stroll reminded me of an afternoon a few months earlier, when I had met Jennings at the Beacon Club for drinks. The Beacon Club occupied the penthouse of the First National Bank & Trust Company building. A wise investor could clip coupons on the banking floor, at the mezzanine level, and then ride an elevator to the twenty-ninth and change there to a private elevator that ascended a couple more floors. The Beacon Club bar was done up with brown vinyl on the armchairs, wood-grain Formica on the tabletops, crepuscular lighting, and picture-window views of many of the major downtown parking lots. Near the bar was a Mexican wall hanging with a dead bird stuck in the middle. At the Beacon Club, the Okiesmo Grand Masters, their midriffs hyperextended, gathered to test their martini tolerance. Between hoists, the aperçus ran from "Know the difference 'tween a genius and an idiot? Twenty feet uh hydrocarbon-saturated sand" to "What Oklahoma needs right now is a fair sheikh."

That afternoon Jennings wore a gray suit, a pale green button-down dress shirt, and a red club tie, and he had taken a seat at a table near the entrance, situated so that almost every member through the door gave him a warm hello. It was great to see Beep, they said, and Jennings, all white hair and veteran-toastmaster gusto, said that it was great to see them. We had been in the Beacon Club for about an hour—Jennings and I and one of his attorneys, Charles Green—when one of Green's partners, glowing as if he had been sitting in the Beacon Club since breakfast, stopped by the table.

"Is this the way you do business?" the second attorney asked.

"I'm here with our favorite client," Green said.

Jennings tilted his head upward and regarded Green's partner out of the corner of his eye, then turned and faced me squarely. His jaw tightened. He lowered his chin and, in his most sincere and sonorous voice, said, "And I *needed* the money. So I *took* it."

We all thought that was a funny joke.

Although Jennings might never run out of friends, he did have woes. His daily routine no longer revolved around a global merchant-banking scheme and an ever-rising drilling-rig count. It revolved around depositions and meetings with his creditors. The usual plaintiffs were suing him—the FDIC, credit unions, drilling fund investors, money brokers, Frank Mahan. There had been a time when Jennings appraised his share of the Penn Square Bank's stock at eight or nine million dollars. That was before the Comptroller of the Currency wrote the bank's capital down to zero and beyond.

An examination report filed by the Comptroller in 1979 referred to the chairman as "principal lending officer on a majority of the bank's credits." Another report, in 1980, observed that "Mr. Jennings appeared to function as the guiding force behind the bank's oil-and-gas activities." Jennings' best defense was that he had been a lousy manager, that he had had no idea what Bill Patterson had been up to until it was too late. He had been busy traveling: in the company of Bob Hefner and Carl Swan and J. D. Allen—to London, Paris, Zurich, Munich, Brussels, trying to expand his network of loan buyers. He had been busy investing his own money: in a new airline, a drilling fund, an oilfield supply company, a gas pipeline, three hotels, oil-and-gas exploration, precious-metals mining, gypsum mining, commercial real estate (including the doomed PennBank Tower, the new home that the shopping-center bank would never get to occupy). He joined partnerships that borrowed from Penn Square's upstream banks, and he personally borrowed upstream: from Continental Illinois, more than a million; Chase Manhattan, more than six million; Seafirst, seven hundred sixty thousand; and Michigan National, a million-and-a-quarter. In other words, Jennings had apparently been far too preoccupied to run the bank. He had invested heavily in Amarex, a large drilling fund operator and a major Penn Square customer. The price of a share of Amarex had gone from fifty dollars to fifty cents. Recently, some domestic adjustments had become necessary. To raise cash, Jennings had sold his home-stead, a five-thousand-square-foot farmhouse which came with several outbuildings, two hundred acres of prime real estate, and a herd of Angus cattle. It brought more than three million dollars. Jennings' damage appraisal indicated that since the bank failure he had dropped between ten and fifteen million dollars. His bankers would not all be getting back a hundred cents on the dollar.

"My present living expenses are approximately what my utilities used to be," Jennings said, fingering a bowl of Beacon Club popcorn. "I have two cars, each of which is four years old and has more than seventy thousand miles on it." Jennings and his wife had moved into an apartment that rented for four hundred dollars a month. "I want you to understand. The family is not destitute. It might sound like I'm poor-mouthing because I sold a place for more than three million dollars and I'm living in a four-hundred-dollar apartment. Well, I'm proud to do that and I'm comfortable and I still have my friends."

Finger-pointing had some therapeutic value. To make clear how he felt about the FDIC, Jennings would tell the story of what happened when he returned to the Penn Square Bank on behalf of the Bank of Healdton, the original Jennings family shop in southern Oklahoma. The smaller bank had bought seven million dollars' worth of Penn Square loan participations. Jennings made his first visit back to Penn Square about three months after the FDIC invaded the premises. As he passed through the lobby, he was greeted by some of the great guys and gals who had once worked for him. The chairman of the FDIC now signed their paychecks, but they were touched to see the Beeper, their old commander, and they greeted him warmly. As soon as the FDIC's chief liquidator heard about this, he circulated a memorandum to the effect that Jennings and other former officers had been hanging around the bank, and if they did not cut it out the FDIC would seek a court injunction barring them from the building.

"It is these inhumanities that disturb a sensitive person," Jennings said. "I sure wish the FDIC would settle with me on a percentage of my net worth. They'd owe me three hundred thousand dollars."

In Jennings' mind there was no question that, if they'd been given a fair chance by the Comptroller of the Currency, Continental Illinois, Chase Manhattan, and Seattle-First would have taken over Penn Square. Because Penn Square was the first major energy bank to be liquidated, it was also destined to be the only liquidation of its kind. If the bank had been allowed to survive another year, if the pervasiveness of the oil-and-gas bust had been evident to the regulators, if it had been clear that Penn Square was only one of many banks that had funded the boom, many things would have been different.

"But they didn't give us enough *time* to straighten the situation out, to make that transition," Jennings said, slapping the arm of his chair. "I understand how Patton felt. We were out in an area that we couldn't defend. We were under heavy attack. We were taking a shelling and we needed to get our planes in the air to knock out those enemy positions. We sent a message to the main command post that we needed four more carloads of fuel. And we had to have it immediately or the sonsofbitches were going to blow the place up. We needed to buy time to evacuate. We were saying, 'Three months—give us three months to define those "contingent liabilities" and we'll make an orderly retreat. But first send us the four carloads of fuel.' Instead, what happened? The supplies never came, reinforcements never arrived. We got hit by an attack squadron. They tore up our airplanes before we could ever get them off the ground. I spent forty-five years in the banking business. This is a helluva climax to a banking career."

The popular dime-store psychoanalysis of the bank failure cast Bill Patterson in the role of "the son Beep never had." Among its defects, this theory failed to identify the cement in the bond, and it neglected to explain why Jennings had been such a permissive father. When I raised the subject, Jennings' tone shifted to High

Beeperese. "I can state very clearly my feelings about Bill Patterson," he said. "I'm very disappointed in his actions. And I'm going to make another statement: I'm disappointed in *myself* for failing to take action earlier to remove him and possibly to save him. I'm not bitter. I'm just disappointed. I'm embarrassed that I didn't do something earlier. But, good God, it happened so *fast*. And he constantly said that he'd respect the policies of the bank. I thought he was learning and maturing. In 1979, I first said to Bill, 'I hope someday you can become the president of this bank.' By the fall of 1981 I had substantial doubts that he would ever become the president of the bank. I remember thinking, within a few months of that: I just want my bank back."

A whiff of nostalgia had crept into Jennings' voice—a longing not for the past per se but for the future that he had once envisioned. Actually, aside from having been driven to the verge of personal bankruptcy, Jennings was to find that things would work out better than the worst scenarios might have indicated. Back in 1972, when he had been executive vice-president of the Fidelity Bank and had done business with the principals of the Four Seasons Nursing Centers—opportunity seekers who went on to be charged with having manipulated one of the all-time great stock market frauds—he had been described by government investigators as an "unindicted co-conspirator." If "Four Seasons" no longer rang a bell in anyone's memory, why, in another ten years, should "Penn Square"? It would just be an air-conditioned place to shop. Even though Jennings' banking career was history, if anyone should ask whether he had ever been indicted he would be able to say no. He had begun to think about a new future. He was thinking of getting involved in merger brokering and real estate, and—more High Beeperese—"And I intend to work for the stabilization of the Bank of Healdton, which is owned by my mother and wife and children and the officers of the Bank of Healdton."

The Okiesmo Grand Masters were ready to depart the Beacon Club until another five o'clock rolled around, and so was Beep Jennings.

"My chief failing is that I'm a very trusting person," he said, squinting. "One, I tend to believe that people will do what they say they will—probably to an unrealistic extent. Two, as an executive in the banking industry, I tend to delegate authority without effective safeguards. I would plead guilty to that. I probably shouldn't have been in the banking business. At least not during the last ten years. I doubt that my philosophy is consistent with the structure of the American banking system. A regulator will argue that anybody can be generous with other people's money. But that's missing the point. I believe that, beyond lending money, a banker has to encourage and create opportunities. Concern for a customer and a desire to see him succeed are not inconsistent with a sound credit policy. I think I'm a damn good credit man and I'm a damn good collector. I know that people have said that I committed the cardinal sin in banking: I put all the eggs in one basket. I think we permitted the bank to grow at a pace that we simply could not accommodate but, having said that, I might qualify it by saying that we were *seriously* trying to curtail the growth of the bank. I would say also that I'm a better banker than what Penn Square indicates."

The courtroom for the Patterson trial was a large, air-conditioned, soundproofed chamber on the third floor of the Federal Building in downtown Oklahoma City. Its walls were done in institutional pale green paint, and fluorescent lighting gave the atmosphere a cool lime tinge. Above the jury box hung four oil portraits of federal judges from the Western District of Oklahoma. The spectator benches and the wall paneling were oak. Behind the judge's roost was floor-to-ceiling paneling decorated with a dozen brass stars.

The judge was Lee West, a stocky, pink-faced Jimmy Carter appointee. During his five years on the federal bench, West had established a reputation for fairness and straightforwardness. He had the demeanor of a veteran city editor and a low tolerance for dillydallying. In presenting the government's case, U. S. Attorney Bill Price maintained that he would be telling the story of the bank failure, that the jury and the public would at last understand what had happened at the Penn Square Bank, and that they would come to see Bill Patterson as the party primarily responsible. Judge West, upon learning, a week before the trial date, that the government wanted to call a hundred and twenty witnesses to make its case, sternly indicated that he preferred justice to proceed more swiftly than that. The government complied by dropping nine of the thirty-four indictments. In the remaining counts, Patterson was accused of six instances of wire fraud, seventeen misapplications of bank funds, and two false entries in Penn Square's books.

The prosecution case lasted two weeks; the defense, when its turn came to call witnesses, needed one hour and fifteen minutes. U. S. Attorney Price presented the government's side with help from two assistants, Susie Pritchett and Teresa Black. When the Penn Square investigation began, Price's office had been deep into a long-running inquiry into the mores of Oklahoma's county commissioners, who had an institutionalized custom of accepting gratuities from contractors who did county business. ("Why do you think they call 'em commissioners? 'Cause they work *on commission*.") Having recently placed under medium security most of the county commissioners in the state, Price might have approached the Patterson trial with the feeling that he was on a roll. As the trial progressed, however, that feeling probably faded. Price was a prematurely gray, pleasant, and pleasant-looking man in his mid-thirties who had more trouble conveying moral outrage than conveying earnestness. He rambled and plodded in an earnest, agreeable way. When the judge, more than once, chastised him for redundancy or for leading a witness, Price dropped his head and hung his tail between his legs in an earnest, obedient way. Assistant U. S. Attorney Pritchett, a short, fortyish, gray-haired woman, also had mannerisms that annoyed Judge West. She was relentlessly cheerful—often past the brink of smugness. She had a brisk and deliberate style that indicated either efficiency or portentousness. All three of the government lawyers knew how to ask the same question four times in a row.

Intending to deceive, Patterson had manipulated a fraudulent game of Musical Lending—that was the essence of the government's case. The evidence dissected several such loans. To cover up bad credits, it was alleged, Patterson took illegal advantage of good customers. He shifted loans from bank to bank, and he shifted the ownership of collateral from this shaky borrower to that creditworthy close friend of Penn Square. In these endeavors, he took advantage of the quaint willingness of many customers to sign blank notes. Under oath, a number of customers recounted how they discovered that they had "borrowed" distressing amounts. This close friend testified that Patterson had stuck him for two million dollars; the next one had unwittingly borrowed three million. Bob Hefner got in the way of thirty-one million three hundred thousand dollars' worth of Mahan-Rowsey Drilling's obligations. Joe Dan Trigg, a devoted longtime pal of Jennings, wound up on a four-million-dollar note to buy oil-and-gas properties from Saket Petroleum that were worth less than four million dollars. One witness quoted Patterson as having said, "Saket has a new partner and he [Trigg] doesn't even know it."

Maximo Moorings, Inc., the Florida "dockominium" venture that Patterson agreed to take off Chase Manhattan's hands and renamed BGP Marina, was the subject of two indictments. The prosecution wished to make Maximo/BGP Marina a useful moral example of the depredations that will result when your banker keeps a file of blank notes around for just-in-case situations. Hal Clifford, a bluegrass musician-turned-oilie, testified that he had agreed, very temporarily, to assume part of the BGP Marina loan only because Patterson had promised that another buyer would be along any minute to assume the entire loan. The other buyer never did materialize. The original documentation of the BGP Marina loan described the collateral as "oil-and-gas mortgages," which appears in no dictionary or thesaurus as a synonym for "dockominium." One clutch borrower, J. D. Hodges, testified that he never did promise to invest in BGP Marina. Just the same, he ended up with more than two million of the deal. Many friends of Penn Square became aware of their phantom loans only after the bank closed and they received past-due notices from the FDIC.

Of all the charges against Patterson, the wire-fraud and false-entry indictments arising from the sale of Mahan-Rowsey Drilling to the QOL Corporation appeared to stand the best chance of producing guilty verdicts. Hefner, who owned QOL, testified that he had never intended to buy the rigs, that no formal sale agreement existed, that he had never authorized the funding of the thirty-one-million-plus Chase Manhattan note. Hefner added that he was convinced that the QOL transaction had become the pivotal factor in the decision by the regulators to liquidate rather than to try to arrange a sale of the Penn Square Bank.

While cross-examining one of the government's most impressive witnesses, a former Mahan-Rowsey accountant named Randel Dunn, Patterson's attorney Burck Bailey did a nice job of clouding the issues. Instead of addressing the accusation that Patterson had deliberately committed fraud, Bailey dwelt on Mahan and Rowsey's chronic reluctance to behave like altar boys. Bailey's attack was swift and effective:

"Mr. Dunn, just to put it in a simple way, Mr. Mahan and Mr. Rowsey lied to Penn Square Bank, didn't they?"

The government witness agreed.

"And they lied to Bill Patterson, didn't they?"

"Yes."

"Constantly?"

"Yes."

"And they lied to you, didn't they?"

"Yes."

". . . And when Bill Patterson found out each time he had been lied to, he was absolutely outraged, wasn't he?"

"Yes, he was."

"In fact, when he declined to lend more money to Mahan and Rowsey they threatened to kill him, didn't they?"

"There was one instance when Mr. Mahan said that."

Later, the jury heard from a Penn Square employee named Bill Kingston, whom Patterson had assigned to monitor the Mahan-Rowsey accounts. Kingston recalled an afternoon in June of 1982—the Penn Square Bank was by then breathing only with the aid of a respirator—when Frank Mahan, in a lather, showed up in the oil-and-gas lending department. The bank had failed to honor some of his personal checks, and this had offended him deeply. That Mahan's overdrafts already exceeded two million dollars and seemed headed for Penn Square's legal lending limit did not mitigate the insult he felt. Patterson and Kingston happened not to be on the premises, so Mahan had to content himself with making messes of several people's desks. On his way out, he announced that if he had his way Patterson and Kingston would be dead by morning. Patterson's attorney did not want the jurors thinking that Mahan might only have been indulging in playful hyperbole. He wanted them thinking that even if Patterson had got rid of more than thirty million dollars' worth of Mahan-Rowsey obligations by selling their drilling company's assets to Bob Hefner, he had done so not with an intent to deceive Hefner or the Penn Square Bank but, rather, with an intent to avoid assassination.

Because Mahan and Rowsey were not on hand—the government still hoped to indict them and therefore preferred not to use them up as prosecution witnesses—there was no way to know whether Mahan would have denied the whole episode or would have acknowledged and defended his actions. I, for one, wished Frank Mahan had been in the courtroom. Friends of mine who knew him had told me that he was not averse to amusing gunplay. There was, for instance, the story about the night that someone put a few bullet holes in one of Billy Rowsey's pleasure boats. That was the same night that the Grove, Oklahoma, police were summoned and Frank Mahan said, "See? I was aiming at that bottle over there and I missed every time." I think it would have been neat to hear him tell that story under oath, not because it had any bearing upon the charges against Patterson but just to give the jurors a break from the tedium.

The first morning I sat in on the trial, it occurred to me that the jurors—twelve regulars and four alternates—looked like bank tellers. I imputed helpful attitudes to them. Several chewed gum. They were the exact eleven ladies and five gentlemen I would expect to run across if I went out to the Penn Square Mall at three o'clock on a Thursday to buy flashlight batteries or a pair of house slippers. The women had home permanents. No one dressed fancy. The numbers that popped up during the testimony—what numbers! The jury would have had a much easier time grasping the evidence if someone had just knocked a few zeros off those numbers. Each juror earned thirty dollars a day for his trouble.

I tried to imagine a defense attorney's dilemma. Would Patterson come off as an egomaniacal young punk? Or could he be portrayed sympathetically, as a tool and a scapegoat? As the proceedings dragged on, the jurors looked more bored than baffled. At the end of one afternoon, which I had spent listening to an FBI agent recite a bunch of mind-glazing numbers and feeling sorry for the jurors, I walked from the courthouse to my car and encountered a lawyer friend, a bankruptcy specialist named Hargis. I regarded Hargis as an expert on the case—not because he is such an accomplished courtroom flamer (although that happens to be so) but because Patterson had recently helped to install a new sprinkler system in Hargis's front yard. ("He did the work. And I know I'll never have a problem. I've got a warranty.")

Hargis had not sat in on any of the trial, but I knew that that would not stop him from having a strong opinion on the outcome. Of the jury, he said, "These people can't continue to live in this town if they don't convict Patterson." I pointed out that some of the jurors lived as far away as Stroud, Oklahoma, halfway up the turnpike toward Tulsa. Hargis said that was even worse for the defense. "Those people in Stroud, all their in-laws and cousins worked for little oilfield service-and-supply companies that went out of business after the bank closed. If they decide that Patterson didn't do it, then they have to figure out what *did* happen or none of their relatives are ever going to talk to them again." That made sense to me. I decided then that Patterson was headed for the slammer, and I had regrets. If only he had studied harder in college, I thought, he could have got into medical school and avoided this heartache. I felt bad for Patterson's wife, Eve. She seemed nice. She was my age, a concerned mother, a loyal mate. "Wonderful gal," Hargis said during our street-corner conversation. Just as he said this, down the block came Patterson and his lawyers. They gave us a smile and a big hello, and Patterson went out of his way to shake Hargis' hand.

If details became a burden for the jurors, there were nevertheless refreshing moments, opportunities to focus upon broader themes. One such moment arose during Eldon Beller's testimony. Listening to Beller, the president of the Penn Square Bank, I was reminded of the corollary to Murphy's Law that goes: "If more than one person is responsible for a miscalculation no one will be at fault." When the House Banking Committee had held hearings immediately after the Penn Square closing, Beller testified that he had no control over Bill Patterson and, therefore, no control over the management of 8o percent of the institution's assets. Two years later, the U. S. Attorney gave him a chance to elaborate.

Price asked, "What caused the failure of Penn Square Bank?"

"I've had quite a while to think on that one," Beller said. "To begin with, the unwillingness of Bill Jennings to properly supervise Bill Patterson and the energy department as was his responsibility. And his time he spent during the day doing things other than supervising the bank as CEO, chief executive officer. And his unwillingness or apparent disregard for the new president who

had been brought in to clean up the bank—this was me—or give
him the sufficient backing or backup he needed to get the job
done. And Bill Patterson's reckless lending that has been alleged.
The decline of the energy business so abruptly, so suddenly, in
such a complete collapse that it brought down good companies
with good credit. It was without precedent. The Comptroller by
their inefficient and ineffective lack of a follow-up examination of
the bank. Brokers who put hot money into the bank as fast as they
could. And the greed of upstream banks like Continental Illinois
and Chase Manhattan, who were certainly derelict in their duties
in qualifying their credits and funding loans and who allowed this
thing to pyramid. And, finally, me, because I was hired to save it
and to the degree to which I wasn't able to save it I accept
responsibility for its failure. No one thing caused the collapse of
Penn Square Bank."

"Are you a friend of Mr. Jennings?" Price asked.

"No."

"Do you blame Mr. Jennings?"

"Yes."

"What do you think the actions of Mr. Jennings and Mr.
Patterson have done to your life?"

"Destroyed it."

Beller was perhaps the only witness against Patterson who appeared to go about his task more in anger than in sorrow. Many of
the others, no matter what they said on the stand, maintained
fondness for the defendant. Bill Patterson, they testified, was "an
ebullient, outgoing, hardworking guy"; he was "very likable, very
considerate of his employees"; he was a terrific salesman,
"hardworking, didn't work banker's hours." Patterson appreciated
the kind words. Often, as a recess was beginning and the jurors
filed out of the courtroom, he would approach a witness, smile,
and extend a handshake. Patterson would stand there and engage
his accuser in conversation as if it were all cocktail chatter.

To convict Patterson, the government would have to prove not
only that he had *defrauded* the Penn Square Bank but also that he
had done so with *intent*. Therefore, a key element of Patterson's
defense was that he would never have intentionally defrauded the
bank because he was its second-largest shareholder. After Penn

Square closed, Patterson had told friends, "Well, that's the last time I'll every buy any bank stock." In court, he was not quite so droll. The day that he took the witness stand, Patterson resembled a successful young white-collar professional more than a professional crabgrass exterminator. He wore a blue blazer, gray slacks, a light blue shirt, and a maroon necktie. His brown hair was neatly brushed. He was not tall but he had broad shoulders, the build of a small-college running back. Because his mouth was asymmetrical, only his left front teeth showed when he spoke. A mainstream Okie twang moseyed through his deep, dry voice. He often grimaced and tilted his head, as if straining to understand the question or, even, his own answers.

Over all, his performance was quite splendid—a blend of obfuscatory brilliance and dreadful ignorance. On the one hand, he claimed a spot in the great chain of know-nothingism. He was a victim of the invisible "they," a pawn in the hands of other bankers and lawyers and sinister number-crunchers. For a naïf, however, he was deft at recognizing a prosecutorial trap, at anticipating how one question could lead him into a blind alley five questions hence, and under cross-examination he frustrated Price. He mustered sufficient selective recall and billowing fog to qualify for an executive position in any circumlocution office. Four times during his testimony he shed tears. One crying jag occurred when he said, "I'm broke, I've got five million dollars in judgments against me." Three times during his Penn Square career, he said, he was hospitalized for exhaustion and dehydration.

There were master strokes, such as when he noted that his first trip to Chicago to sell Continental Illinois a loan was only the second time that he "had been on a big airplane." Another, on becoming a loan officer: "It was kind of all brand-new to me. I learned how to do past-dues, overdrafts, how to work on loan sheets, how to look at a financial statement." During cross-examination, when the prosecutor produced a transcript from South Oklahoma City Junior College that listed a number of courses in which Patterson had been enrolled—Principles of Banking, Money and Banking, Accounting 1, Analyzing Financial Statements—and asked why the defendant had previously stated that he had "never attended any banking school, had never taken any courses," Patterson replied, "I didn't take the courses. I just went to the finals." Were it not that his in-laws now helped to support him and his wife and their three children, "we wouldn't be able to eat."

Eve Edwards Patterson did not miss a minute of the trial. Because the air-conditioning made it chilly inside the courtroom, most days she wore a sweater. With that draped across her shoulders and a handbag hanging from one of her arms, she seemed prematurely middle-aged. She was a pale, dark-haired woman in her early thirties—attractive but definitely not glamorous. Other than a gold Rolex watch and a wedding band, she wore no jewelry. Eve Patterson's brothers, a pair of well-built, solid-looking citizens named Carl and Eddie Edwards, shared her vigil. Bill Patterson's mother, Patricia, sat through the government's entire case, then happened not to be present when her son testified. She usually had her jaw locked. I never saw her smile. She had a face as plain as dry toast. During recesses, she chain-smoked. Her gray, close-cropped hair and her eyeglasses gave her the look of a parochial-school teacher.

As the trial proceeded, Patterson's attorney Burck Bailey regarded with more and more disdain the voluminous exhibits that the government offered as evidence. Bailey, the president of the Oklahoma County Bar Association, was slender, gray-haired, and handsomely tailored. He had an elegant way of waving a hand in front of his eyes, in bemused disgust, each time Price or one of his assistants approached the court clerk with another document. His cross-examinations lacked enthusiasm. As the government's case grew redundant, Bailey slipped deeper into minimalism. I could not tell whether his failure to animate meant that he was demoralized or surpassingly confident. It turned out he was saving some juice for the closing argument. Bailey began this peroration by telling the jurors how great they were. He said, "You bring good judgment, experience with life, and common sense." He said that the jury system represented "the most sacred ideals" of the country and he quoted from Tocqueville, who shared that opinion. He spoke softly to a fault. There were long dramatic pauses, expressions of exasperation and dismay. Splaying his fingers and then bringing his hands together, he said, "The government's case turns the facts on their head. No one gave more to Penn Square Bank than Bill Patterson." He said that he had not routinely objected to the hearsay testimony of the prosecution witnesses because the hearsay rules belittle the intelligence of jurors, because "you know when a lawyer is putting words in the mouths of witnesses."

Hitting his stride, Bailey showed vigor and rhythm: "They asked Bill Patterson to do impossible things to make themselves rich or richer. . . . They charge Bill Patterson with a felony for lending money to Mahan-Rowsey—if that isn't the *most* offensive charge! These people plundered the bank. And the person who got robbed is being charged with the crime. . . . There's no logic to the government's case. It's simply throwing mud at the wall, hoping something will stick. . . . It's just so unfair and so unjust to lay all of this on Bill Patterson. They want to charge Mr. Patterson with every conceivable possible picayune flaw that occurred out there. . . . Where is the evidence of criminal intent? It doesn't exist. It's a spurious charge. There's just nothing here, is there? . . . *That's* fraud? These charges are offensive." Of Bob Hefner, Bailey said, "He is a person of incomprehensible wealth. His net worth is four hundred and forty-six million dollars. He's wanting more lines of credit, more money to buy up all the lease rights in western Oklahoma. He wants as much as Bill Patterson can get for him. He always has." The government sees that "the case won't fit under one statute, so they say maybe we'll try to place it under three statutes and maybe the jury can be bamboozled into sticking him with one of them."

About halfway through, Patterson began to cry. His blazer was green, his slacks were beige, his shirt was white, his necktie was blue with white polka dots, and his face was bright red. He sat with his hands resting on the defense table, his left hand atop his right, then his fingers interlaced, then back the other way. He seemed to be taking all this quite seriously.

When the government's last licks came, Price spent forty-five minutes further testing the jury's endurance. He began by saying that Patterson was "treated like a king in all the money centers of this country," and continued, "A man on a giant ego trip. . . . He can't let loose of the dream that he's going to be the biggest banker in the world. . . . It's a gigantic shell game, a gigantic bubble that keeps getting larger and larger, and it's based upon deceit." Those were the most memorable metaphors. From there, he hiked off into the factual thickets, trampling syntax every step of the way.

The jurors received legal instructions from Judge West on a Tuesday afternoon and, along with their good judgment, experience with life, and common sense, retired to deliberate. Twenty-four hours later, they returned and said that they had found the defendant not guilty on twenty-three of twenty-five counts. Patterson did his finest crying yet when he heard that news and he cried even more the next morning, when the jury acquitted him of the last two counts. It was true that a few matters of concern still hung over his head. The FDIC had sued him, as had a number of credit unions, unhappy drilling fund investors, money brokers, and former Penn Square customers. And there were those civil judgments against him which totaled five million dollars. A new grand jury had been impaneled in Oklahoma City, and although Patterson had nothing to fear there another grand jury was conducting business in Chicago, trying to figure out what had gone wrong at Continental Illinois. For the moment, at least, a huge cry of relief felt right. His wife and brothers-in-law cried along with him, and Burck Bailey cried, too. It lasted more than half an hour and would have gone on longer if the judge had not kicked everyone out of the courtroom. The catharsis so exhausted Bill Patterson that he could barely walk as he left the courthouse. It was all he could do to climb into a car and be driven home. When he got there, he went right to bed. Not until four hours later, when he woke up, feeling refreshed, did his wife tell him that the grand jury in Chicago had just indicted him sixteen more times.

CHAPTER 22

In 1967, when John Lytle was thirty-two years old and had worked eight years for the Continental Illinois National Bank & Trust Company, he and his wife, Sharon, bought a house in the town of Northfield. The trip to downtown Chicago from the Lytles' four-bedroom, two-bath white-painted brick Colonial, on a leafy cul-de-sac, to the granite-and-marble-and-limestone headquarters of Continental Illinois, on La Salle Street, took twenty-eight minutes in ordinary traffic. In Northfield there were broad lawns, shady lanes, white picket fences, and quiet mornings, afternoons, and evenings. The house cost sixty thousand dollars. The Lytles did not yet have children, but they planned to start a family soon, and Northfield appealed for that reason. Next door was an undeveloped lot inhabited by tall old oaks. There was room to expand. Lytle's annual salary from the bank was thirty thousand dollars.

The sixteen counts of the Chicago indictment against Bill Patterson named John Lytle as a co-defendant. Each was charged with conspiracy, five misapplications of bank funds, and ten wire frauds. A third defendant, Jere A. Sturgis, a real-estate salesman-turned-oilie from Enid, Oklahoma, was indicted on two counts of wire fraud. Sturgis did not bank with Continental Illinois. From Penn Square and other correspondent banks, however, he borrowed sixty-five million dollars and, according to the government, he coveted more. The government based its case on a pattern of facts that originated in the summer of 1980, when Patterson lent Lytle twenty thousand dollars, unsecured, at a rate of interest below prime. The borrowing increased for a year-and-a-half, until

207

one of Continental's auditors discovered, inadvertently, that Lytle owed Penn Square five hundred sixty-five thousand dollars. Lytle's superiors were impressed by his sincerity when he said he did not feel that he was in a conflict of interest. The loans from Penn Square, he explained, typified how Oklahoma bankers treated their friends and special customers. Lytle thought he was doing both Penn Square and Continental a favor. Roger Anderson, the chairman of Continental Illinois, participated in the decision to reprimand Lytle rather than demand his resignation. John Lytle had been a loyal and hardworking employee, his motives appeared innocent, and, besides, he managed a terrifically profitable division. Through Penn Square, he had managed by that point to acquire more than eight hundred million dollars in loans—assets that were meant to yield an average annual return of almost 20 percent. Part of the proceeds of Lytle's loan from Penn Square he invested in improvements to his home, and part—one hundred sixty-five thousand dollars—he invested in eleven shallow oil and gas wells that were drilled and operated by Sturgis. In January of 1982, at Continental's insistence, he paid off his Penn Square loan. Beep Jennings and Bill Patterson made this as painless as they could. Most of Lytle's debt was refinanced at another Oklahoma City suburban bank. Additional credit was extended by the Bank of Healdton, which Jennings' family owned. In March of 1982, Lytle decided to reduce his debt, and sold the oil and gas properties back to Sturgis, in the process almost tripling his money. To pay Lytle, Sturgis borrowed from the Penn Square Bank. When, a year later, Sturgis filed for personal bankruptcy, his debts exceeded a hundred million dollars. Scrutinizing the Patterson-Lytle-Sturgis connections, the federal prosecutors alleged a kickback.

There were several charges in the indictments that did not relate directly to Sturgis. At issue were loans that, it was alleged, Continental Illinois should never have made. By the time of the indictments, Continental's write-offs of Penn Square loan participations totaled five hundred fifty million dollars. Three hundred twenty-five million more had been classified as nonperforming. In other words, 85 percent of Continental's billion-dollar Penn Square portfolio had gone bad. The government wanted to prove that at the root of Penn Square's relationship with Continental

Illinois there existed a sinister link between John Lytle and Bill
Patterson. Arraignment took place eight days after the indictments
were announced. Lytle did not enjoy being fingerprinted or posing
for a mug shot. Patterson seemed to take it in stride. Standing
before the judge, he turned to Lytle and whispered, "Hey. This is
nothing!" Lytle disagreed. Each charge carried a potential penalty
of five years in prison. Furthermore, it gave him much discomfort
to contemplate his former employer's interest in seeing him convicted. No longer was he a hardworking middle manager who
tended to be rather spotty when it came to operational details. He
had become a bounty hunter's dream. Continental Illinois owned
an insurance policy, a fidelity bond, that protected it against losses
arising from criminal behavior by its employees. The claim value
of the policy was a hundred million dollars. Lytle, convicted, could
be worth that badly needed amount to what was left of the
Continental Illinois National Bank & Trust Company.

In early May 1984—four and a half months before Lytle's indictment—a run began on the deposits of Continental Illinois: an
outflow so severe that, within ten days, the Federal Deposit
Insurance Corporation and a consortium of twenty-eight healthy
banks were forced to intervene with a combination of credit and
capital totaling seven and a half billion dollars. When the Penn
Square Bank closed, deposit balances in excess of a hundred
thousand dollars became worth about sixty cents on the dollar. By
contrast, the FDIC was willing to guarantee all of Continental's
deposits, regardless of the size of an account, in order to keep that
bank open. There was also revolving credit at the Federal Reserve
Bank of Chicago. The FDIC and the consortium of banks increased their assistance, until they had extended fourteen billion
dollars' worth of emergency credit to Continental. Yet the run
continued. To raise cash, Continental's holding company sold its
London merchant banking subsidiary, its credit card business, its
leasing and residential mortgage-servicing divisions. Foreign operations in Bahrain, Belgium, the Netherlands, and Switzerland
were closed or sold. The bank staff was reduced by two thousand.
In 1981, the year that Continental bought five hundred fifty
million dollars in loans from Penn Square, the bank's assets were

valued at forty-seven billion dollars. Three years later, the bank was seventeen billion dollars smaller.

By early June it was evident that Continental Illinois could not survive without a permanent guarantee of federal support. During the first six months of 1984, deposits fell by twelve billion dollars. A quarterly dividend payment was omitted for the first time in forty-eight years. The price of Continental's stock aimed due south. Big banks—First Chicago, Citibank, Chemical Bank—looked at the books and decided not to buy Continental. The Bass brothers, of Texas, and the Pritzker family, of Chicago, looked and decided the same thing. By mid-July no potential private investors remained. The results for the second quarter of 1984 showed that the bank had lost one billion one hundred sixty million dollars—*the worst three-month performance ever reported by an American corporation.* Only the United States government could afford to own Continental's diseased assets. Finally, in late July, two years and three weeks after the Penn Square Bank failed, the government in effect bought Continental Illinois. For three and a half billion dollars, the FDIC acquired the weakest assets in the Continental portfolio, loans that had once had a face value exceeding five billion dollars. Half of these assets were energy loans. The FDIC also invested a billion dollars in fresh capital. In the complexity of its details, the FDIC's takeover matched the unwieldy magnitude of Continental's problems. In the financial community there was a semantic discussion: Had the bank, in practical terms, *failed?* (The stockholders had lost 80 percent of their investment and stood to lose the rest if the loans acquired by the FDIC continued to decline in value and collectibility.) Had the bank been *nationalized?* (If not in the strictest legal sense, it had nevertheless been de facto nationalized.) Howard Baker, then the majority leader of the Senate, said that the Continental crisis would cause Congress to "review the entire banking system." The chairman of the House Banking Committee saw in Continental irrefutable evidence that deregulation of the banking system had gone too far. Testifying before the Banking Committee, C. T. Conover, the Comptroller of the Currency, contended that if Continental had been liquidated (à la Penn Square) it would have taken with it scores of smaller institutions—perhaps hundreds. *The Wall Street Journal* quoted a bank industry analyst who described Continental's decline as "the most significant domestic banking event since the Depression." Of the bank that Roger Anderson and his loyalists had built, only a shadow remained.

I went to see John Lytle on a bright, clear, frigid morning during the interval between his indictment and his trial. From O'Hare to Northfield, I happened to share a limo with a neighbor of the Lytles who had met Beep Jennings and Bill Patterson and J. D. Allen and Carl Swan and other Okiesmo potentates in the summer of 1981, when Sharon Lytle threw a surprise birthday party for her husband. On that occasion there was genuine Oklahoma barbecue served on the Lytles' front lawn and a real country and western band parked in the driveway—unusual for the North Shore. The neighbor said the Penn Square guests had seemed like a fun bunch of people.

I arrived at Lytle's house just as he was about to run some errands. We hopped into a gray Peugeot station wagon and headed for a nearby bank where he had opened an account after being fired by Continental. In 1981, Lytle's twenty-second and last full year at Continental, he received a sixty-nine-thousand-dollar salary and a fifty-six-thousand-dollar bonus. Three days after becoming unemployed, he started his own oil-and-gas financial consulting business. His clients were former Penn Square customers. "Consulting" meant trying to avoid formal bankruptcy. He did this for a year and a half—stalled creditors, hustled receivables, tried to help overextended oilies find refinancing—and earned more per hour than he ever had as a banker. Eventually, some of the clients shuffled off to bankruptcy court anyway. Next he hooked up with a high school friend, an independent oilman who operated in Oklahoma, putting together small drilling deals. This was less rewarding than consulting had been. Lytle had an ample net worth, but most of it was tied up in his homestead. The house that he had bought in 1967 had grown by sixteen hundred square feet. He owned the tall oaks and the empty lot next door. Now the time had come to consider liquidating family assets. Lytle had been forced to sell a vintage Corvette. And the empty lot was back on the market.

When we pulled up in front of the bank, Lytle left the motor running and ran inside. He wore a green down ski jacket and brown Glen plaid wool slacks. He was forty-nine years old. Even with his gray hair he could have passed for thirty-nine. When he came out of the bank he was smiling. "This bank has been really nice to me," he said. Then he laughed. "Of course, whenever I walk in there they act like maybe they should do this"—he threw up his arms, palms out, stickup style—"but then the vice-president comes over and shakes my hand, asks how I'm getting along." Not that the friendly vice-president would lend him money. Lytle could not even swing a loan using the Peugeot as collateral. No banker in Chicago wanted to have to explain why John Lytle had appeared to be a good credit risk.

We drove to a parochial school where the youngest of Lytle's four children, Patrick, attended kindergarten. Normally, Lytle's wife would have gone on this mission, but she had a lunch date. Back at Lytle's house, we sat in a study where there were bookshelves, a desk, a telephone answering machine, green leather armchairs, a green leather hassock, and a mullioned picture window. Snow had fallen the previous night. From the study, a short hallway led through the kitchen and into the family room. Logs glowed in the fireplace there. The room was cozy, full of natural light. Patrick sat at a long table, ate peanut butter, and watched cartoons on television. When Lytle showed me the room, he said, "This is the Penn Square addition." It was a quiet early afternoon. Conversations with Lytle, while not exactly solemn, never struck me as zippy. We talked desultorily about this and that. Until the formal case against Lytle went to trial—an event that lay many months down the road—there was, in a way, not much to say. Either John Lytle was going to wind up a convicted felon or he was going to be looking for a job.

Lytle could ponder Bill Patterson's federal trial in Oklahoma City. Had the jurors simply rejected the facts as recited by the government's sixty-one witnesses? Were the facts adequate but was the criminal statute itself missing? Was it that, regardless of whether Patterson had harmed the Penn Square Bank, the government could not prove he had done so intentionally? Did the jurors regard Patterson as culpable but resent that the Comptroller of the Currency was not indicted along with him? Under whose nose had the Penn Square Bank grown rancid? Why the grand piety and the punitive impulse? Certainly someone had jerked levers inside the bank in the Penn Square shopping mall. And the bank had collapsed, and mind-boggling havoc had ensued. But what were the crimes and what constituted fitting punishment? Patterson's banking career inspired profound thoughts about what one ambitious young man can accomplish in this land of opportunity. Being acquitted in Oklahoma was, in a sense, testimony to the stunning amplitude of his achievement. Remarkable stuff—the Penn Square Bank, Seattle-First, Continental Illinois. All along, the Penn Square Bank and the oil-and-gas boom had been driven by a vast myth-spawning mechanism, and the Oklahoma jurors understood that. Patterson-as-Iago was just another myth. Would a Chicago jury, however, seeing Patterson and Lytle seated together at the defense table, see a different reality?

By the time Sharon Lytle returned from her lunch date, her husband was overdue for an appointment with his attorney. As we drove toward the city, he remarked that her lunch companion had been the wife of Dwight Chapin, who was Richard Nixon's appointments secretary. For committing perjury in connection with the Watergate investigation, Chapin had spent eight months in prison. He now lived in Winnetka and was making out all right in the public relations business. The Chapins had told the Lytles to expect the worst during the trial. Nevertheless, Lytle was not pessimistic. He expected to be acquitted. If he overlooked that the Continental Illinois Bank had journeyed to the margin of oblivion, he could think of circumstances for which he was grateful. It occurred to him that, back when the good times were rolling, he might have borrowed twenty million dollars. He had avoided that, hadn't he? Things might indeed have been worse. As we exited the freeway and entered the Loop, Lytle spoke appreciatively of the parishioners of his church. Ever since the indictment, people had come forth with offers of assistance: "Money, help, whatever you need, we'll do what we can." One friend volunteered to buy Lytle's furniture. Lytle said thanks, but the family still wanted to sit on it. The friend said, well, if Lytle wanted to sell it now and buy it back later, that would be fine. "I appreciated the gesture," Lytle said, waiting for a stoplight to turn green. "I guess what the guy was really offering was to make me a fully collateralized loan."

CHAPTER 23

Bob Hefner, in his capacity as chairman of The GHK Companies, received a letter during the summer of 1983 from Robert L. Parker, the chairman of the Parker Drilling Company, one of the largest contract drilling firms in the world. It was Parker Drilling's unenviable distinction to have become one of the largest trade creditors of GHK. For more than a year, GHK's bankers and trade creditors had been trying to reorganize the company's debt, and during that time the outlook had progressively deteriorated. The so-called April Fool's Eve agreement—the debt repayment plan negotiated in the spring of 1983—had proved to be a product of desperately wishful thinking. One purpose of Parker's letter was to recapitulate just how bad things were. He recited the specifics of the dilemma that confronted Hefner and the people to whom he owed money: GHK's long-term debt totaled three hundred twenty-five million dollars, which meant that interest costs, at a rate of 12 percent, were running close to forty million a year; GHK's oil-and-gas revenues, estimated on the basis of conditions then current in the depressed natural gas market, were only eight million a year; the most recent unaudited financial statement showed that the company had assets of two hundred twenty million, of which only seventeen million was cash; accounts payable approximated ninety-three million; GHK had a negative net worth of minus two hundred ten million. Parker's analysis of GHK's situation was summed up in this statement: "We conclude exactly what you said to us in our office—you can't go on like this financially."

More than a year later, the natural gas marketplace was still greatly depressed and the old debts, plus a fortune's worth of new interest, lingered. Meanwhile, exciting developments had taken place, the most significant being the Continental Illinois crisis. The upheaval within Continental Illinois came as no surprise to Hefner. The accommodations that Continental bankers had seemed willing to make to avoid writing off loans to Hefner and his companies had led him to assume, correctly, that there was a critical muddle of sick loans on the bank's books, beyond the oil-and-gas portfolio. A comforting thought this was not. A Continental Illinois Bank in government receivership would place Hefner at the mercy of collectors whose main motive would be to clean up a vast mess as expeditiously as possible. So far, Hefner had had the luxury of working with lenders whose motives were survival and profit. A four-and-a-half-billion-dollar federally insured bailout, however, altered the context in a way that made Hefner's debt look paltry. He owed the bank only a hundred sixty-three million. The magnitude of Continental Illinois's problems placed him in danger of losing his debtor's leverage. At last, Hefner could appreciate the pitiable circumstances of those short-hitters who had gone to the Penn Square Bank during the boom and had borrowed only a million or so. Come the bust, they had been hauled off to debtors' prison. What if it turned out that Hefner, heaven forbid, had not borrowed enough? Only a super-resilient mortal could withstand the burden of that much irony.

There would be no conceding defeat, however. Robert A. Hefner III continued in every visible respect to subsist in majestic fashion. His eight-passenger Westwind jet had been sold, but there were still wings—a trusty Sabreliner eight-seater—in the hangar. The yacht *Anadarko* no longer belonged to Hefner, but quotidian creature comforts remained. The good show remained. The financial affairs of GHK Companies had stagnated in what seemed an intractable workout. Almost as soon as the terms of a workout got papered up, reality would indicate that the numbers did not fit. The GHK's leases were expiring, and that meant that the company's assets were diminishing every day. Fewer than seventy-five employees were left on the payroll, down from a hundred eighty. Several of the senior technical and management people had departed; Hefner and his son, Robert IV, had jointly assumed the role of chief explorationist. Every few months, there would be a new deadline, another round of squeezing the big zeros, a new quest for major long-term financing. On and on and on.

Hefner continued to try to make it work, continued to invoke "methane" and "salvation" in the same breath. He was still available to testify before Congress. Addressing a Senate subcommittee on energy regulation, he spoke of a new "emerging methane industry"—of a national transition from an oil-based to a methane-based industrial economy. He compared the present to the oil-glutted chaos of the Depression years, which had contributed directly to the birth of the vertically integrated major oil companies. And the truth was that as Hefner and his creditors tried to imagine how he could ever repay his debts the major oil companies were putting their many dollars to work, buying minerals cheap, turning the Anadarko into a bargain basin.

It was an evening in the earliest autumn, only days since the beastly summer heat had broken. The jury in the trial of Bill Patterson had begun its deliberations that afternoon. The day had been cloudy and blustery. Now the wind had died and the dark felt soft and cool and quiet. Bob Hefner had more than a casual interest in the outcome of the Patterson trial. His testimony had been one of the highlights, and the issue addressed by that testimony—the "sale" to Hefner, for thirty-one million three hundred thousand dollars, of seven drilling rigs that Hefner did not care to possess—was still much alive. In suit and countersuit, Chase Manhattan and Hefner were pursuing claims against each other that totaled two hundred fifty million dollars. One document described during the trial was a Penn Square Bank memorandum which stated that Hefner had a net worth of four hundred forty-six million dollars. Hmm. Well, at least Hefner still had his homestead, and it was a fine one. He sat in his living room. An almost life-size portrait of him hung in the entrance hall. A tall and broad doorway led into the living room, which had a high ceiling decorated with a fresco of blue sky and clouds. At eye level there were fresh flowers, crystal, silver, gilt, and a wall of glass, with a door that led to an atrium. A stereo piped in a Mozart concerto. It was not a modest room. The bounty was eclectic: overstuffed sofas; leather armchairs and side tables, antiques and reproductions; wooden floorboards from the French provinces; high-tech brass floor lamps; a zebra hide in repose next to an ebony grand piano; dense art books (Rodin, Renoir, Picasso, Bonnard, Velázquez)

planted here and there; a small Rodin on a table; on the walls a
Picasso, a Redon, an Utrillo; a pair of paintings of huge tortoises
flanking a doorway; skylights; horses all around, in oil and watercolor, cast in bronze, sculptured in stone, liberated from a French
carousel and charging from the wall, galloping out of *trompe l'oeil*
sconces; more *trompe l'oeil* above the fireplace mantel; in the
fireplace, methane jets to ignite real logs—a room dedicated to
comfort, style, and artifice.

As a witness for the prosecution, Hefner had proposed an
interesting domino theory, a variation of the parable of the kingdom that was lost for want of a nail in a horse's shoe. Because
Patterson had banked Frank Mahan and Billy Rowsey, the theory
went, a thirty-one-million-three-hundred-thousand-dollar loan to
Hefner was entered in Penn Square Bank's books and then sold to
Chase Manhattan. If that note had never been funded, Penn
Square at its moment of insolvency would not have carried a
thirty-one-million-three-hundred-thousand-dollar contingent lia-
bility. If no such liability had existed, Hefner and Continental
Illinois would have agreed to buy the bank jointly . . . and thus
Penn Square would have avoided a scorched-earth liquidation and
Continental Illinois would have been able to avoid being dragged
into the soup. On the witness stand, Hefner stopped short of
projecting this scenario to an implicit, apocalyptic conclusion:
What if Continental had been permitted to fail? What if it had
taken along, say, a hundred banks, as the FDIC and the Comptroller had insisted that it would? What if, in the panic that would
surely ensue, the American economy had imploded? And then? If
all that had happened, how much responsibility would have belonged to Bill Patterson? And if one were to project back over the
shoulder—scanning the chain of causation that preceded the QOL
transaction—what of Bob Hefner's contribution to all that? Was
the rubble of the bust disconnected from the grand designs, the
visions of Bob Hefner, that precipitated the boom?

Not every Hefner scenario had unfolded exactly as he had said
it would.

I had several conversations with Hefner in this house. As I sat in
his living room that September evening, I recalled one from a late
afternoon in the previous autumn. We were sitting in the atrium,

where there was a long narrow swimming pool; a terrace of red brick; dappling fountains; spouting statuary; a fireplace; lavender petunias and scarlet rhododendrons; potted magnolias. An electronic zapper delivered flying insects to their resting place. Slender vertical columns—square metal beams painted white—supported the open roof surrounding the atrium. There was no froufrou on the columns; deliberate classicism mingled with the contemporary. It was a relaxing place to visit. The nearer-my-Greek-god-to-thee ambiance encouraged the illusion that Hefner could go on like this forever. That day I mentioned the Robinson No. 1, the last of the ultra-deep wells that Mobil had bankrolled in Hefner's Elk City project. Of the wells drilled by Mobil and GHK, 75 percent were economical producers—if only someone would buy the gas, and at the right price. I had just returned from Elk City, where I had spent a chilly, misting afternoon watching an engineer and a crew of roughnecks try to fish a piece of severed drill string out of a twenty-nine-thousand-foot hole. That was the Robinson. For the time being, the Robinson was Hefner's last shot in Elk City. Parker Drilling's biggest land-based rig, the No. 201— a hook load capacity of two million pounds; sufficient to drill to forty thousand feet; custom-fashioned for GHK—was on the job. The Robinson would turn out to be a dry hole. Not quite realizing that, I announced that I intended to go back to Elk City when the Robinson was perforated. Hefner had a better idea. He held out his left hand, palm down, and talked about the Arco Lucille.

"Bobby dreams structures. He bends his data," Hefner's detractors said, meaning that wherever Hefner owned acreage he was inclined to envision geological features that a more objective technician might not see. The Lucille, in Cement, Oklahoma, was due to be perforated and tested the next day. At eye level, Hefner used his right index finger to point at the middle knuckle of his other hand. In Hefner's mind, the left hand represented a huge geological structure, and the knuckle was its crown. Atlantic Richfield, the operator of the Lucille, had confidence only in the knuckle, according to Hefner. Indications thus far were that the knuckle would produce a fine well—which GHK and Arco certainly hoped, considering that this well was expected to cost twenty-five million dollars. Hefner, however, could extrapolate from the knuckle back down the slope of his wrist and out beyond the manicured tips of his broad fingers.

The Arco Lucille would be the first significant test of the Arbuckle sediments in the Cyril Basin. What lay beneath the hand? One problem was that seismic pictures from below the Hunton formation, which began at nineteen thousand feet, were very difficult to read; the Arbuckle, into which this well was headed, was virtually opaque. That fact had presented a significant obstacle when GHK went looking for partners in the Cyril Basin. My own limitations as a geophysicist, however, made Hefner's theory sound dandy to me. If the Lucille turned out to be a great well, acreage costs in the Cyril Basin would rebound to the two- to three-thousand-dollar range. The enthusiasm would evoke Anadarko Basin in its heyday. If salvation was headed Hefner's way, he intended to renew his own leases and to lease as much of the left hand as possible. "If the Lucille is as good as I think it is, it could turn things around for this company," he said. "Isn't that something? How a single well could do that to a company our size overnight?"

Less than overnight—ten hours later, at high speed, half awake in the 5 a.m. darkness—I was driving to Cement, because Atlantic Richfield intended to perforate the Lucille at dawn. The tests that would follow the perf job would reveal whether GHK owned a quarter of a twenty-five-million-dollar dry hole or whether destiny had taken a more pleasant turn. The well had been drilled to a total depth of twenty-five thousand feet, into the Arbuckle, but the bottom seven hundred feet of the hole were obstructed by a length of ruptured drill string. The explosive charge of the perforating gun would detonate just above that.

I arrived at the well site before six o'clock, which turned out to be extra early. The well did not get perfed and tested that morning. Before the decision was made to postpone, however, I got a chance to stand around for a few hours with my hands in my pockets. At one point, I stood near a frac trailer with bald tires—maypops, those are called ("That tahr may pop any second")—and near a tawny, taciturn drilling foreman, a paragon of Okiesmo, who wore a gold hard hat with an Arco emblem and green khaki work clothes soiled with a substance that transcended grime. We kicked some rocks for a couple of minutes, in silence. Then I said, "You been here all night?"

"I've been here five hundred and ninety-five days."

"Oh, well, uh, how many people have been here that long?"

"Me."

A week later, I drove back to Cement, back to the Lucille, and watched another sunrise, again hoping to witness the perforation. At seven-thirty a technician from Schlumberger, the well-service company, squeezed the trigger on the perforating gun. Several Schlumberger employees had crowded inside a truck that was equipped with an excess of gauges and digital monitors. Nothing happened. Hours passed. The gauges beeped and blipped inconclusively. Perhaps brine in the well bore was creating a problem. Perhaps brine could be swabbed out of the well bore and then, perhaps, gas would bubble to the surface, lifting the brine out of the hole and permitting the perforated zone to flow. Or perhaps none of the above. Eventually, the perforating gun was raised from the well. Something in the well bore, it seemed, had short-circuited the electronic trigger and the gun had never fired. The well casing, in other words, had never been perforated. The lives of gas wells did not always go according to plan.

That certainly proved true of the Arco Lucille. Some weeks later, the perforating gun did at last go off. Bob Hefner would later refer to the Lucille as having "produced in some shallower zones," but for all practical purposes it was a dry twenty-five-thousand-foot hole, a twenty-five-million-dollar duster. It was not going to turn GHK around. And, since that was the case, Arco did not mind suing GHK to collect three million in billed but unreimbursed drilling costs. And GHK did not mind countersuing for more than a hundred million, alleging that Arco had ruined an infinitely promising well.

Now, a year later, I thought of other schemes, grand and less grand, that were not going to unfold. Bob Hefner was not going to pursue his notion of persuading the Ford Motor Company to mass-produce a methane-powered automobile. GHK would therefore not be buying a fleet of methane-powered company cars, and it would not be necessary to construct a methane-compression station at the PennBank Tower. Nor, for that matter, would The GHK Companies be occupying eight floors of the PennBank Tower, which now had a different name. The price of natural gas was going back to nine dollars no time soon. Oklahoma City was not going to become the Athens that Hefner had promised Beep

Jennings it would. It was going to be more like an exurb of Dallas. The long-term financing that Hefner had tried to arrange with Japanese bankers in the spring and fall of 1983—the attempt to take advantage of the Bank of Tokyo's desire to invest a billion dollars in American industry—that had not quite come together either.

Fortunately, Asia was a large place. If the Japanese lacked foresight, perhaps . . . *China*. Hefner had been doing some thinking and talking about China. He had been asking himself where GHK should go next. He had asked, "Where are the developing countries, and what are their natural resources?" Tang Ke, the Chinese minister of petroleum, had been a guest in Hefner's home the previous weekend. Tang Ke had come to the United States and had talked to Amoco, Exxon, Sohio, Manufacturers Hanover, Chase Manhattan, Phillips Petroleum, Pennzoil, Dresser Industries, Halliburton, and the chairman of The GHK Companies, Robert A. Hefner III. China intended to develop its energy. Hefner intended to persuade China to build its industry around methane, "to develop a systematic way of exploiting that natural resource."

"How are they going to measure their natural gas reserves?" I asked, then cringed at my simple-minded question.

"GHK's going to do it."

He believed it. He believed in it. GHK's technological expertise was unmistakably state-of-the-art; any day now, that fact would dawn upon the Chinese government.

Hefner said he had been interested in China since way back when—"always in the back of my mind, sort of like the Anadarko Basin." Now, when he thought of China, he thought about methane and about infrastructure and about how it fit into a vision he had of something called "a century of peace." In Mandarin, he knew how to say "hello," "welcome," "thank you," "natural gas," "hot sauce," "beer," and "to our future cooperation."

A few months earlier, Hefner had disappeared for a couple of weeks. The word went around that he had gone to Europe, where a secret billionaire waited in the wings. It sounded right. And that was that. Nothing more. Just a rumor. Standard Bobby Hefner. "Bobby Hefner is a survivor," even Hefner's critics would always maintain. Another rumor floated—that Hefner was about to launch a takeover of ONEOK Inc., the billion-dollar parent company of Oklahoma's largest natural gas utility. If Hefner could not get the pipelines to buy his gas and help his cash flow, then he would buy his own distribution network. Rumors would help for the time being, until something a bit more real came along.

Would it offend the People's Republic of China that Hefner's exploration companies had a negative net worth of two hundred and ten million dollars? Bob Hefner was not thinking about that at the moment. He was thinking about the past and about the future but not, apparently, about the vicissitudes of the present. "If I've contributed anything to life on this planet," he said, "it has been to heighten our understanding of the value of methane and of the crucial role that it will play in the survival and evolution of our economic system." A fond remembrance drifted into his consciousness—his biggest of all deals, the Mobil Oil Corporation promote that had ignited the Anadarko Basin. "I always wanted to be a private company but to do deals like the majors do," he said in his shadowy living room, leaning forward in his armchair. "If I had gone public right after the Mobil deal I could have put two hundred million into Treasury bills. If I had done that then I'd have done some deals with Boone Pickens and the Bass brothers. And I would have had the time to go on the board of Penn Square. And I would have enjoyed that because I've always wanted to be a merchant banker." He punched the fast-forward button in his imagination. "Then I would have done more deals with Boone and the Basses. Then I could be out buying the Anadarko Basin again, right now."

"But . . ." He paused, clasped his hands behind his head, leaned back, and smiled a tight smile. "But I'm not going to do it that way."

A NOTE ABOUT THE AUTHOR

Mark Singer was born in Tulsa, Oklahoma, and graduated from Yale University. He now lives in New York City with his wife and their three children. Since 1974 he has been a staff writer for *The New Yorker*.